DATE DUE			

Shocking! The Art and Fashion of Elsa Schiaparelli

Shocking! The Art and Fashion of Elsa Schiaparelli

Dilys E. Blum

Philadelphia Museum of Art
in association with

Yale University Press
New Haven and London

This book is published on the occasion of the exhibition
Shocking! The Art and Fashion of Elsa Schiaparelli

Philadelphia Museum of Art
September 28, 2003–January 4, 2004

Musée de la Mode et du Textile,
Union Centrale des Arts Décoratifs, Paris
March–August 2004

Shocking! The Art and Fashion of Elsa Schiaparelli has been
supported by Carefree and by an endowment from The Annenberg
Foundation for major exhibitions at the Philadelphia Museum of Art,
The Pew Charitable Trusts, the National Endowment for the Arts,
the Robert Montgomery Scott Endowment for Exhibitions, The
Women's Committee of the Philadelphia Museum of Art, and the
generous donors to Schiaparelli's List. Promotional support was
provided by NBC 10 WCAU and the Greater Philadelphia Tourism
Marketing Corporation.

Produced by the Department of Publishing
Philadelphia Museum of Art
2525 Pennsylvania Avenue
Philadelphia, PA 19130 U.S.A.
www.philamuseum.org

Edited by Kathleen Krattenmaker
Production by Richard Bonk
Color photography of Schiaparelli accessories and
    dressed mannequins by Lynn Rosenthal
Designed by Takaaki Matsumoto, Matsumoto Incorporated, New York
Printed in Germany by Cantz

Front cover/jacket: George Hoyningen-Huene (American, 1900–1968),
Elsa Schiaparelli in a white gown and coq-feather boa for summer
1932, published in *Vogue*, September 1, 1932 © *Vogue*, Condé
Nast Publications Inc.

Back cover/jacket: Elsa Schiaparelli, gloves for summer 1939,
green doeskin and gold kid. Philadelphia Museum of Art. Gift of
Mme Elsa Schiaparelli, 1969-232-69a, b

Library of Congress Cataloging-in-Publication Data

Blum, Dilys, 1947–
    Shocking!: the art and fashion of Elsa Schiaparelli/Dilys E. Blum.
        p. cm.
    "This book is published on the occasion of the exhibition . . .
Philadelphia Museum of Art, September 28, 2003–January 4,
2004."—T.p. verso.
        ISBN 0-87633-171-1 (alk. paper)
        ISBN 0-87633-172-X (pbk.: alk paper)
        ISBN 0-300-10066-3 (Yale distributing: alk. paper)
    1. Schiaparelli, Elsa, 1890–1973. 2. Schiaparelli, Elsa,
1890–1973—Exhibitions. 3. Women fashion designers—France—
Biography. 4. Women fashion designers—France—Exhibitions. 5.
Fashion designers—France—Biography. 6. Fashion designers—France—
Exhibitions. 7. Costume design—France—Paris—History—20th Century.
I. Philadelphia Museum of Art. II. Title.
TT505.S3 B58 2003
746.9'2'092—dc21   2003012593

Contents

6   Lenders to the Exhibition

7   Foreword

8   Preface

10   The Beginning

12   Pour le Sport

32   Architect of Fashion, Carpenter of Clothes

70   In the Shadow of Napoleon

100   After Dark

120   Art into Fashion, Fashion into Art

150   Metamorphosis

168   Six Collections
           The Circus Comes to Town
           A Pagan Collection
           Lucky Stars
           A Modern Comedy
           Return to the Bustle
           Music in the Air

220   A Matter of Prestige

248   Themes and Variations

288   Dressing for Film and Stage

292   Stylistic and Historical Chronology

302   Sources Consulted

306   List of Illustrations

315   Selected Bibliography

316   Acknowledgments

319   Index of Names

Lenders to the Exhibition

Azzadine Alaïa

Allentown Art Museum, Pennsylvania

Brooklyn Museum of Art, New York

Leslie Chin

Drexel University, Philadelphia. Historic Costume Collection

Filmmuseum Berlin. Marlene Dietrich Collection

The Goldstein Museum of Design, University of Minnesota, Saint Paul

Sidney Kimmel

The Kyoto Costume Institute, Japan

Library of Congress, Washington, D.C. Prints and Photographs Division

Gene London

The Metropolitan Museum of Art, New York. The Costume Institute

Musée Galliera, Musée de la Mode de la Ville de Paris

The Museum at the Fashion Institute of Technology, New York

Museum für Kunst und Gewerbe Hamburg

Museum of Costume at the Bath Assembly Rooms, England

The Museum of the City of New York

Peggy Guggenheim Collection, Venice

Andrea Pfister

Royal Ontario Museum, Toronto

Salvador Dalí Museum, Saint Petersburg, Florida

Schiaparelli France, Paris

Sandy Schreier

Lucien Treillard

Union Centrale des Arts Décoratifs, Musée de la Mode et du Textile, Paris

Mark Walsh

Foreword

In October of 1942, when World War II was at its height and artists fleeing from Europe sought refuge in the United States, the brilliant Paris fashion designer Elsa Schiaparelli lent her name and support to an exhibition in New York titled *First Papers of Surrealism*, organized for the benefit of the Coordinating Council of French Relief Societies. Writing to his close friend Walter Arensberg, Marcel Duchamp referred to Schiaparelli and the great Surrealist poet André Breton as his partners in this enterprise, for which Duchamp was to invent a maddening and yet striking installation using a mile of string that crisscrossed the gallery, effectively preventing the viewers from coming close to any work of art. By 1950, Duchamp had helped Arensberg and his wife, Louise, to reach the momentous decision to bequeath their superb collection of early modern art to the Philadelphia Museum of Art. Almost twenty years later Schiaparelli followed suit, making the spectacular gift of seventy-one of her own designs, which has in turn engendered this book and the exhibition it accompanies.

Schiaparelli's gift was prompted in part by the Museum's involvement with the Philadelphia branch of Fashion Group International, which through Libby Haynes Hyman, regional director, and Rubye Graham, fashion editor of the *Philadelphia Inquirer* and chairman of the Fashion Group's Museum Committee, took part beginning in 1947 in an initiative to encourage major gifts of designer clothing to American museums. The Philadelphia Museum of Art was a particularly fitting recipient of such support, for it has one of the country's oldest textile and costume departments, founded in 1893 as the Department of Textiles, Lace, and Embroidery. The Museum's involvement with the Fashion Group through the years, ranging from exhibitions to biannual "Crystal Balls" to honor such celebrities as Marlene Dietrich and Princess Grace of Monaco, drew Schiaparelli's attention and convinced her that this was a fitting place to house favorites from her own wardrobe, garments she felt distinguished her career and demonstrated her individual approach to fashion design.

Shocking! represents the first time so much of Schiaparelli's gift has been exhibited together—and the first time that selections from the Museum's collection have been joined by some of the eighty-eight models and 5,800 original sketches donated by the designer to the Musée de la Mode et du Textile, Paris, in 1973. The outstanding collections at the Musée de la Mode and the Philadelphia Museum of Art complement one another, with Philadelphia representing Schiaparelli's most significant prewar designs and the Musée de la Mode especially strong for the postwar years. Bringing together these two collections, supplemented by generous loans from public and private collections in the United States, Europe, and Japan, provides an unprecedented overview of Schiaparelli's extraordinary career and an exciting sense of just how far she was able to push the boundaries of fashion into the realm of art.

Dilys Blum, the Museum's inspired and indefatigable Curator of Costume and Textiles, has devoted the better part of five years to research into Schiaparelli's life and art, and the intricate interweaving of images and text in this publication bears witness to her profound understanding of Schiaparelli's achievement. Doing justice to that achievement would not have been possible without the enthusiastic participation of many colleagues, and we especially thank Béatrice Salmon, Director, Pamela Golbin, Curator of Twentieth-Century Collections, and the rest of the staff at the Musée de la Mode. This important international project has also relied greatly on the financial support of an impressive partnership of donors. The National Endowment for the Arts, The Pew Charitable Trusts, the Robert Montgomery Scott Endowment for Exhibitions, The Women's Committee of the Philadelphia Museum of Art, Carefree, NBC 10 WCAU, the Greater Philadelphia Tourism Marketing Corporation, and an endowment for major exhibitions at the Museum created by a grant from the Annenberg Foundation were joined by generous individual donors to Schiaparelli's List.

Schiaparelli has ardent admirers around the world, including many distinguished and celebrated designers. We are delighted that so many of them have joined the Honorary Committee, which helps the Museum to extend the reach of the exhibition and communicate its excitement to a new audience. We owe warm thanks to Count Guido Sassoli de Bianchi, President of Schiaparelli France, for his efforts on behalf of this project and for invaluable access to the designer's archives. It is a special pleasure to have the blessing of Schiaparelli's accomplished granddaughter, Marisa Berenson, who has given gracious support on so many fronts.

In a city teeming with young designers and noted for its outstanding schools, colleges, and universities devoted to training students for careers in the arts, the Philadelphia Museum of Art rejoices in the opportunity to present the work of a great artist who we hope will inspire others to let their imaginations soar.

Anne d'Harnoncourt, *The George D. Widener Director*

Selections from Elsa Schiaparelli's gift to the Philadelphia Museum of Art of seventy-one items from her personal wardrobe were first shown in the landmark exhibition *The 10s, the 20s, the 30s: Inventive Clothes, 1909–1939*, organized by Diana Vreeland at the Costume Institute of the Metropolitan Museum of Art in 1974, and traveled the following year to the National Museum of Modern Art, Kyoto. Some of the thirty Schiaparelli designs that were lent to these two exhibitions were photographed by Irving Penn for *Inventive Paris Clothes, 1909–1939: A Photographic Essay*, published in 1977. In 1984 the Musée Galliera (Musée de la Mode de la Ville de Paris) organized the first Schiaparelli retrospective, drawing primarily from their own small collection and from items held privately by the collector BillyBoy. None of the Schiaparelli designs in Philadelphia were included in the exhibition, however, nor were any of the Schiaparelli models and original sketches in the collection of the Musée de la Mode et du Textile, Paris, which is especially strong in the post-war years. This book accompanies the exhibition *Shocking! The Art and Fashion of Elsa Schiaparelli*, in which selections from the collections of the Philadelphia Museum of Art and the Musée de la Mode are united for the first time, supplemented by additional Schiaparelli designs and documentary photographs from public and private collections in the United States, Europe, and Japan.

I have intended this book to be an overview of Schiaparelli's design career—from 1927, when she presented her first collection, to 1954, when she closed her couture salon. One of the objectives has been to clarify the chronology of Schiaparelli's career. Her autobiography, written in 1954, moves between the first- and third-person voices and sometimes conflates events, resulting in a confused timeline. Information about the designer is relatively scarce, with the exception of two publications that paved the way for this book: the catalogue from the 1984 Musée Galliera exhibition and Palmer White's *Elsa Schiaparelli: Empress of Fashion*, from 1986. Although Schiaparelli's relationships with family, friends, and colleagues could be awkward and at times contentious, she rarely featured as a subject of gossip and is profiled only briefly, if at all, in the biographies and memoirs of others (usually those involved in the fashion and textile industries). The same stories, taken for the most part from public-relations material and from Schiaparelli's own mythmaking in her autobiography and in the many interviews she granted, are repeated over and over and have become a part of fashion lore. Schiaparelli fiercely guarded her privacy, and diaries and letters have not been found from which to draw conclusions about her most intimate thoughts and feelings. The business records of her couture salon are not accessible (and may not even survive), apart from books of press clippings. Quite a bit can be gleaned, however, from contemporary articles in fashion magazines and newspapers, such as *Vogue*, *Women's Wear Daily*, and the *New York Times*, which provided much of the information presented here. Most important, there are the clothes themselves, which if studied carefully provide insight into the social, political, economic, and artistic events of Schiaparelli's time and also reveal much about her quixotic personality. The couturière, especially during the late 1920s and 1930s, was quick to respond in very individual ways to the prevailing cultural winds and, through her friendships with many in Paris's avant-garde, was able to meld art and fashion in unprecedented ways.

Although Schiaparelli's couture house produced thousands of designs, only a small percentage of the actual garments survive. This is not surprising, since many of the women most famous for wearing her clothes "borrowed" from the salon and did not actually own the clothes, while the model gowns that were purchased by wholesalers and store buyers to be copied were returned to Europe or sent to Canada and South America to avoid customs duties before the three-month time limit expired. These garments often ended up in the secondhand clothing market, to be resold through "model" shops like Anna Lowe. What survives is happenstance. Accessories like hats date more quickly and thus disappear, and many of Schiaparelli's exquisitely tailored suits very likely were recycled for their cloth during World War II. Garments for special occasions, however, such as evening gowns and evening coats, often made their way into public or private collections. Although much has been lost, we are lucky that so much remains, for Schiaparelli's individual models offer an interesting and often surprising commentary on her approach to design and views on fashion.

This book is intended to place Schiaparelli's work in context by juxtaposing new color photography of many of her garments with documentary and fashion photographs from her lifetime. The material has been organized both chronologically and thematically and concentrates on Schiaparelli's production of haute couture clothing and accessories rather than on her perfume business, which was organized as a separate entity, or her many licensing arrangements, for which she sold the use of her name but did not supply the designs. Throughout the book, I have used the term "presentation" to designate the date a collection was shown, which was six months in advance of the "season" for which it was intended. Thus, for example, the garments Schiaparelli showed at the end of January or the beginning of February were labeled *été*, or summer. The choice to differentiate between presentation and seasonal dates was made so that the interlocking themes and events of Schiaparelli's career could be followed more closely, focusing on the elements that distinguished her designs. For this reason, I have included a stylistic and historical chronology.

Each chapter of the book is introduced by a short, highly focused essay followed by captioned illustrations showing Schiaparelli's clothing and accessories, original sketches from the house of Schiaparelli and such stores as Bergdorf Goodman, fashion illustrations, and contemporary works by some of the twentieth century's greatest artists, craftspeople, and photographers. The process of designing for the couture relies on teamwork and collaboration. Schiaparelli was a master at directing the many highly skilled people with whom she worked, and credit must be given for their contributions in helping her realize her vision. The juxtaposition here provides a fairer representation of the collaborative nature of fashion design, without in any way lessening Schiaparelli's accomplishment. In fact, it was Schiaparelli's very skill and creativity in drawing out the best in people, as well as her often uncanny ability to anticipate the "next wave," that secured her unparalleled status in the history of fashion.

Fashion is visual, and no words can adequately describe the impact of seeing the real thing. The intention here is to provide material for further study and discussion and to open up new avenues of research. I have thus refrained from making sweeping generalizations and have allowed the facts and the images to speak for themselves.

The Beginning

The period between the world wars was dominated by two of the twentieth century's greatest couturières, Gabrielle (Coco) Chanel and Elsa Schiaparelli. Their rivalry was legendary. Although they traveled in the same social circles and had many of the same friends, their approaches to fashion design and their backgrounds could not have been more different. Chanel viewed dressmaking as a profession while Schiaparelli regarded it as an art. Chanel, seven years older than Schiaparelli, came to designing by a route that was very different from that which the younger designer pursued. An illegitimate child born into poverty, Chanel lost her mother at age twelve and, soon after, was left by her father in an orphanage and was later sent to a convent boarding school. With the help of a lover, she left the convent and moved to Paris. There she occupied the demimonde, rising from shop girl to concert-hall singer to mistress of a number of important personages, including the Duke of Westminster. By 1912 she had opened her own millinery shop, again with help from a lover, and later opened a couture salon at 21 rue Cambon, where the simple, sporty styles she invented would become synonymous with her name.

Schiaparelli's entry into the world of fashion was even more circuitous. Elsa Luisa Maria Schiaparelli was born on September 10, 1890, at the Palazzo Corsini in Rome, where her father, Celestino, was a scholar of Oriental languages and literature (Arabic and Islamic) and head of the Lincei Library. Her father's brother, Giovanni, was an astronomer and the discoverer of the canals on the planet Mars, and a cousin, Ernesto, was a famous Egyptologist. From her earliest years Schiaparelli was rebellious, always questioning and pushing the boundaries of acceptable behavior in her conservative upper-middle-class Italian household. Her father was strict but loving, her mother perhaps too critical, and her Aunt Lily, whom she greatly admired, passionate. Elsa's natural shyness and insecurity were traits that she frequently camouflaged with brusqueness.

The adult Schiaparelli recalled the ups and downs of her early childhood with great fondness, and her memories of that time had a profound impact on her designs. She remembered dressing up in bustled gowns stored in a trunk in the attic and the long hours she spent in her father's library pouring over illustrated books and illuminated manuscripts. And she distinctly recollected being introduced to vivid pink—a color that, under the designation "Shocking," would become associated with her name—as an infant, while parked in a carriage among the begonias. Like Chanel, she was convent educated, but she also attended a Protestant school, which seems to have been even less suited to her temperament, causing her to rebel against its strictness. Her rising passions were subsumed in poetry, and when she was twenty-one, a slim volume of her poems, titled *Arethusa*, was published at the suggestion of her cousin Attilio by the Roman publisher Quintieri. Two years later she left Rome for London in order to help care for the twins of a married friend of her older sister, Beatrice. A brief stopover in Paris left her enamored of the city, and she resolved to return someday.

In London, Schiaparelli's tremendous need for what she liked to describe as physical and spiritual privacy drew her one day early in 1914 to a lecture given by a young spiritualist and theosophist, Wilhelm Wendt de Kerlor, a follower of Madame Blavatsky. She was enthralled. Her meeting with de Kerlor after the lecture and their soul-searching discussions led to their engagement within twenty-four hours and marriage at a London registry office. After residing briefly in London, the couple left for Nice, where de Kerlor had family. In 1916, looking for more opportunities for de Kerlor to lecture and spread his philosophy, they set off for the United States from Bordeaux, arriving in New York on April 20 aboard the S.S. *Chicago*. Among the other passengers was Gabrielle Picabia, wife of the Dadaist painter Francis Picabia. Both Gabrielle and Schiaparelli would separate from their husbands while in the United States, and Gabrielle would prove to be extremely influential in Schiaparelli's life.

Once in New York, de Kerlor began to have doubts about his calling, and the couple drifted from city to city, moving first to Boston, then to Washington, D.C., and back to New York, where they resided at the Brevoort Hotel, a favorite among French expatriates. In 1917 Schiaparelli was asked to accompany the aspiring opera singer Ganna Walska to Cuba, where Walska made a disastrous début in *Fedora* and was booed off the stage. Schiaparelli's connection with her husband was by now intermittent, on account of his frequent womanizing, and the fatal blow to their relationship appears to have been his affair with the dancer Isadora Duncan. The Surrealist painter and photographer Man Ray, in his autobiography, *Self Portrait*, describes an incident involving de Kerlor at the Pepper Pot, the cafe below the Greenwich Village chess club frequented by Marcel Duchamp and other avant-garde artists. De Kerlor apparently came to blows with the chess master Soldatenkov after making a flippant remark to Soldatenkov's beautiful American wife.

Schiaparelli and her husband had been living on her dowry, which was rapidly dwindling, and after their separation she took a series of part-time jobs to make ends meet. She did translations, worked for importing houses, watched the ticker tape for a Wall Street broker, and worked as a stand-in for a film being shot in New Jersey, a job that she got through the photographer Edward Steichen, a member of the community of artists centered in Greenwich Village. Her friendship with Gabrielle Picabia brought her into contact with a number of these artists, among them Man Ray and Duchamp. She was one of several young women who responded to Man Ray's invitation to be photographed in his Greenwich Village studio.

Soon after the birth of her daughter, Maria Luisa Yvonne Radha (Gogo), around 1920, Schiaparelli separated from her husband for the last time. Her daughter was sent to live with a nurse in Connecticut, while Schiaparelli found lodgings in Patchin Place in the West Village. During the summer of 1921 she traveled to Woodstock, New York, which was popular with artists and writers. There she spent time with Blanche Hays, who was soon to be divorced from the renowned lawyer Arthur Garfield Hays. In June 1922, Blanche, sympathetic with Schiaparelli's marriage problems and reduced circumstances, persuaded her friend to accompany her to Paris.

Having returned at last to the city she had so admired, Schiaparelli and her daughter stayed briefly with Gabrielle Picabia, who was also now residing in Paris, and then later shared an apartment with Blanche Hays and her daughter, Lora. It was through Mrs. Hays that Schiaparelli had her first exposure to the world of haute couture, while accompanying a friend of Blanche's on a shopping expedition to meet the couturier Paul Poiret. Recognizing her flair with clothes, Poiret soon took Schiaparelli under his wing. He often supplied her with coats and gowns, and he invited her to attend his famous midnight party held on December 24, 1924, to celebrate his move from the rue Saint-Honoré to an ultramodern house at the Rond-point des Champs Elysées. Schiaparelli had been making simple but striking clothes for herself as well as for Gabrielle Picabia and Blanche Hays. With their encouragement and that of Poiret, she began working as a freelance designer for small fashion houses. An American friend of Blanche's, a Mrs. Hartley, took over one of these businesses, Maison Lambal, in late 1925 and employed Schiaparelli as the designer. The venture lasted just over a year, but the experience gave Schiaparelli the confidence to strike out on her own.

Pour le Sport

In January 1927, at 20 rue de l'Université, Elsa Schiaparelli launched her first collection under her own name, with what Thérèse and Louise Bonney described in their 1929 shopping guide to Paris as "strikingly original sweaters." These sweaters—some knitted in two or three shades of wool in bold blocks of color and others in which wool was combined with accents done in metal thread—featured modern geometric designs that were then the height of fashion. Worn with crêpe de chine skirts with front pleats, they were accessorized with matching scarves and sport socks that had the sweater's pattern repeated on the sock's cuff. For her May 1927 collection Schiaparelli favored gray and added hand-knitted wool jackets edged in grosgrain ribbon that fastened with a double button at the waist, matching pullovers, and wool skirts—clothing ideal for resort wear, walking in town, or shopping. The designer's name quickly became synonymous with the hand-knitted sweater, so that by August 1928 *New Yorker* magazine could confidently state that "Schiaparelli, after all, belongs to knitted sweaters, or they to her."

Although her first sweaters were certainly well received, it was a black-and-white pullover sweater with a large trompe l'oeil bowknot in her November 1927 collection that was to change Schiaparelli's fortune and become one of her most copied designs (pp. 18–19). The December issue of *Vogue* heralded this sweater as "an artistic masterpiece" and "a triumph of colour blending." In Schiaparelli's hands the sweater had become much more than a purely utilitarian piece of clothing worn to keep out the damp chill of French winters. It had achieved the status of chic. In her 1954 autobiography, *Shocking Life*, Schiaparelli recalls wearing the new sweater to a smart luncheon and creating a sensation: "All the women wanted one, immediately."

The bowknot sweater's success can be attributed not only to its distinctive trompe l'oeil design but also to the way it was knitted. Schiaparelli had her sweaters made up by an Armenian woman, Aroosiag Mikaëlian, known as Mike, who with her brother produced knitted goods for the wholesale trade. She had found Mike after seeing a woman wearing a sweater knitted by her in an unusual stitch that gave it, in Schiaparelli's words, "a *steady* look." Mike's technique resulted in sweaters that held their shape better than other hand knits of the period and, when two colors of yarn were combined, produced a tweedlike effect. White flecks on black, for example, were achieved by carrying the white Shetland-

wool yarn across the back of the black stockinette ground and catching it behind every third or fourth stitch as it was knit.

The bowknot sweater met with a particularly enthusiastic response in the United States. Schiaparelli gives an account in her autobiography of the sale of the sweater to an American buyer who, according to an unpublished manuscript by the *New York Times* and *Christian Science Monitor* fashion columnist Kathleen Cannell, was introduced to Schiaparelli by Hazel and Peggy Guggenheim. Totally unprepared for the buyer's order of forty sweaters with matching skirts, Schiaparelli had Mike recruit other Armenian knitters, and they managed to complete the order in two weeks. Schiaparelli herself, together with an assistant, made up the skirts from yardage purchased from the bargain counter at the Galeries Lafayette department store.

Immediately after her November 1927 collection was presented, New York sportswear wholesaler Wm. H. Davidow Sons Co., whose imports included original designs and adaptations by many artists associated with the modernist movement, including Sonia Delaunay and Erté, announced that they had been named the exclusive American distributor of Schiaparelli sweaters. A sketch of the bowknot sweater was featured in the firm's advertisement in *Women's Wear Daily*, where it was touted as "the latest word from Paris." The sweater was eagerly copied by other American wholesalers and was offered in myriad colors, including shades of blue, purple, and green as well as the original black and white, a color combination *New Yorker* writer Janet Flanner referred to as "chic melancholy." By the end of 1928 Schiaparelli's signature design had become so ubiquitous that instructions for knitting the "Chic Bowknot Sweater" appeared in the November issue of America's most widely read women's magazine, *Ladies' Home Journal*, where the designer's name is not even mentioned.

In the late 1920s the copying of French hand-knitted sweaters by foreign manufacturers became a major concern to the French fashion industry, which was increasingly agitated by American newspaper advertisements featuring inexpensive Viennese copies of French knits. The problem arose because foreign buyers were permitted to purchase single models from the French couturiers, which they could then have copied. French buyers, on the other hand, were not allowed to make copies but could only purchase original models in the quantities they needed. Schiaparelli's designs were among those copied most extensively. Her first private customer, the American writer Anita Loos, discovered her character Lorelei Lee from the 1925 hit novel *Gentlemen Prefer Blondes* appropriated by the American department store Stewart & Company for its advertising campaign of summer 1928. The ads in *Women's Wear Daily* were written in Lorelei Lee–style lingo and featured a young woman wearing a copy of one of Schiaparelli's sweaters, which was selling for a mere $4.95. By comparison, in late September 1927 Macy's had offered an original Schiaparelli model with a modernistic skyscraper pattern for $34.75. The American designer Elizabeth Hawes recalled her own involvement with copying a Schiaparelli design for Macy's in her 1938 book *Fashion Is Spinach*. While working as a stylist for the department store, Hawes purchased an original Schiaparelli sweater in Paris and arranged to have it copied in Vienna for $3.25, which would allow the store to retail the reproductions for $12. In this case, however, the appropriation was all for naught. Macy's apparently decided that its customers of 1927 were not ready for such avant-garde fashions. But by May 1928 times had changed, and soon after the landmark *Exposition of Modern French Decorative Art* held at Lord & Taylor earlier that year, Macy's organized an *International Exposition of Art in Industry* featuring the work of modern American and European designers, although fashion was not represented.

Furthering Paris's dispute with American department stores, *Les Echos*, the Paris trade weekly, devoted a full page in mid-June 1929 to criticizing a Macy's advertisement in the *New York Times* that featured hand-knitted copies of sweaters by Jane Règny, Lucien Lelong, and Schiaparelli selling for $17.74; the originals would have retailed for between $35 and $50. According to *Les Echos*, Macy's made only one purchase of an original sweater directly from a designer (the Règny); the other models were acquired indirectly and then copied in Vienna. French designers resented what they saw as commercial dishonesty and the exploitation of French creativity, but it was not until the mid-1930s that Paris couture was able to place restrictions, albeit limited, on the purchase of original models and the copying of designs.

On December 5, 1927, Schiaparelli registered her company in equal partnership with Charles Kahn, a businessman associated with the Galeries Lafayette department store. Schiaparelli's apartment at 20 rue de l'Université, where she both lived and worked, had become too small, and the infusion of capital through her partnership with Kahn provided her with the opportunity to move to larger premises at 4 rue de la Paix, which included a salesroom, workroom, sitting room, and bedroom (p. 16). A black-and-white sign reading "Schiaparelli Pour Le Sport" was hung on the front door. On January 31, 1928, the designer presented her first collection in the new salon, expanding her offering of hand-knitted sweaters, coats, and skirts to include bathing suits, beach pajamas to wear over the suits, and crocheted berets. Sweater patterns that season included designs with knitted insets suggesting belts or knitted-in scarves positioned as sashes with detached ends that knotted at one hip (p. 13). There was also a sweater with a knitted-in collar and tie, a variation of the bowknot design. The prominence of clothing for seaside and beach in the collection was echoed in knitwear that featured nautical designs, such as a sweater fashioned in the style of a French sailor's middy blouse (pp. 22–23). Bathing suits included one-piece designs and two-piece suits with short sweater tops or knitted tunics worn over flannel shorts (pp. 24–26). In later collections sweaters would feature stripes and plaids, large abstract turtlelike patterns across the front, and trompe l'oeil skeletons and sailors' tattoos, as well as African designs inspired by the exhibits at the *Exposition coloniale internationale de Paris*, held in 1931. Sweaters remained an essential part of Schiaparelli's collections until the early 1930s, when they were replaced by the couturière's distinctive blouses.

Beach pajamas, which the exiled Russian fashion designer Mary Nowitzky is credited with introducing during the late 1920s, continued as fashionable seaside or poolside attire and were an essential part of most couture sportswear collections. Schiaparelli's first beach pajamas were made up in shantung silk and included a two-piece design with a tailored jacket and a one-piece version buttoning up the front, with an inset belt and a tailored collar (p. 29). For her December 1928 collection, designed for spring 1929, there was an ensemble in black cotton printed with a large white floral pattern. Its long, straight trousers were worn with a black jersey sweater and a straight sleeveless coat lined with *éponge*, a soft, porous fabric.

In September 1929 Schiaparelli was invited by the American silk manufacturer Cheney Brothers to create a group of eight pajama costumes using the company's boldly printed silks to promote its fabrics for 1929–30 Southern resort wear in their New York showroom. According to the company's advertisement

Elsa Schiaparelli was photographed by Thérèse Bonney (p. 12) wearing a hand-knitted sweater from the first collection presented at her new salon at 4 rue de la Paix, in January 1928. The model had a knitted-in bow and yoke and was imported to the United States by New York wholesaler Wm. H. Davidow Sons Co. in a mixture of brown, white, and orange. A smart detail is the triangular pocket on the left cuff. The hat is by Suzanne Talbot.

The fashion for wearing a sports frock with the hipline draped with a kerchief tied at the side was interpreted by Schiaparelli in the V-necked wool sweater in the fashion sketch on page 13—model "No. 115" from the designer's first rue de la Paix collection, presented in January 1928. The scarf has been knitted into the sweater, and the separate knitted ends tie loosely on one hip like a real kerchief. The perfect golfing sweater, it was seen on the links at North Berwick, Scotland, where it was worn by Miss Oonagh Guinness, daughter of Irish brewer Ernest Guinness and the youngest of the "golden Guinness girls." Syrie Maugham, wife of the writer Somerset Maugham, also wore the sweater, at her home in Le Touquet, France. A sweater with a knitted-in collar and tie and an inset belt was included in the designer's midseason collection, presented in April 1928. These two ensembles were among a number of designs purchased by the New York wholesaler Wm. H. Davidow Sons Co. in 1928.

in *Women's Wear Daily*, the "Staccato Prints" were a "vivid, dynamic, rhythmic series" created to portray "the zing and abruptness of modern life." This collaboration is one of the first examples of Schiaparelli's aggressive marketing strategy and endorsement of American manufacturers, who in turn were eager to ally themselves with a designer viewed as the most modern and innovative in Paris couture. U.S. manufacturers did much to establish name recognition for Schiaparelli, thus helping her gain a foothold in the American market. In November 1929 she made a three-week business trip to the United States, her first time back since leaving New York in 1922, in order to oversee the presentation of her latest collection at Stewart & Company in New York. The collection included clothes for the active sportswoman, be she aviatrix, tennis player, skier, swimmer, or just a sunbather on the beach. Many of the outfits were designed specifically for her good friend Comtesse Gabrielle di Robilant, who accompanied Schiaparelli on the trip and also acted as her model. Elements destined to become synonymous with the Schiaparelli style were already much in evidence. The designer's creative employment of unusual materials included a rubberized wool and silk mixture used for a raincoat and patent-leather trim on a coarse natural linen aviation costume. Striking color contrasts, another hallmark of the Schiaparelli style, ranged from the starkness of black and white to black with brown and orange with green. Ski outfits had metal "slide closings," or zippers (in later years Schiaparelli would use colorful plastics), rather than the usual buttons or hooks and eyes. The designer used the zippers as front closings and also on sleeves and pockets—and daringly left them visible, so that they served a decorative as well as functional purpose. Comfort and ease of movement were emphasized. A cotton tennis costume, for example, had a divided skirt and a separate top cleverly held in place with a tab between the legs, a forerunner of the bodysuit.

The divided skirt, or *jupe culotte*, had been growing in importance since the mid-1920s and was especially favored by active women engaged in motoring, traveling, or recreational walking. The division between the legs was always handled discreetly, with the line disguised by pleats, overlapping panels, or a wraparound skirt. Although the designer Paul Poiret had been advocating the trouser skirt for several years, even predicting that by 1958 women would be wearing trousers, most manufacturers still considered it a novelty and too extreme for most customers. By 1928, however, it was seen more frequently—worn by a spectator at the Professional Golf Tournament at Stoke Poges, England, for example, and by American actress Anna May Wong for traveling. But the undisguised divided skirt that Schiaparelli wore in London during spring 1931 provoked a strong outcry in the British press, where it was denounced as unfeminine (p. 30). Spanish tennis champion Lili de Alvarez's decision to wear Schiaparelli's divided skirt dress with detachable tunic at the North London Tennis Tournament was also strongly criticized (p. 31). The British reaction may have been a result of timing, since it followed on the heels of the infamous 1929 trial of British writer Radclyffe Hall and the banning of her book *The Well of Loneliness* (1928), which sympathetically depicted the tragic life of a "sexual invert." Up to this time, the eccentric dress of trousered women had been viewed as an artistic affectation, but after the trial any form of dress deemed to be masculine, such as the divided skirt, was decried as anti-feminine and was associated with lesbianism. Fortunately, the negative reaction that greeted Schiaparelli's culottes did not last. The divided skirt quickly became a sportswear staple in the wardrobes of American and British women and would soon be adopted for evening wear in the form of casual pajamas for at-home entertaining.

By 1930, with sports clothes becoming more standardized in design, the major couturiers began to leave their production to specialty houses such as Jane Règny, concentrating instead on more "feminine" collections of day and evening wear, which they viewed as requiring more creativity and skill in execution. Schiaparelli, too, began to diversify her collections and in 1930 added her first evening dress, a wraparound design that tied at the side and had a low V-neckline in front and in back (p. 100). But while she switched her focus to clothing for day and evening in the 1930s, sportswear would continue to play an important role in her designs and would become an essential part of the ready-to-wear collections sold in the "Schiap" boutique of the salon she would open in 1935 on the Place Vendôme.

In 1929 the American sisters Thérèse and Louise Bonney collaborated on a delightful guide to Paris that was designed to reveal the secrets of shopping for antiques, contemporary design, and the latest fashions to the thousands of Americans who visited the city each year. Thérèse Bonney, who is remembered today as an outstanding World War II photojournalist, had established a press and photographic service in Paris by 1927 under the slogan "Pictures with Ideas." These images of the interior of Schiaparelli's salon at 4 rue de la Paix were taken shortly after the designer's move from 20 rue de l'Université and were included in Thérèse's photographic documentation of Paris fashion salons and interior design studios, produced at about the same time as the shopping guide. In a note on the back of one of the photographs, Thérèse describes Schiaparelli's black-and-white salon as an "ultra modern sports shop." In the top photograph, at left, a portrait of Schiaparelli, most likely the work of Pavel Tchelitchew, hangs on the wall over a banquette draped with scarves and a table holding several sketchbooks. On the back of the middle photograph, Thérèse comments on the "odd Parchment lamp on work table"—possibly an early design by Jean-Michel Frank. The ceramic figures seen on the fireplace mantel in the same photograph are the work of Vally Wieselthier of the Wiener Werkstätte. In the bottom image, framed photographs of Schiaparelli's young daughter, Gogo, sit on the mantel together with an adjustable iron lamp. The cushions on the sofa (another possible Frank design) are printed velvet with a design reminiscent of the fabrics Paul Poiret used during the early 1920s for his extravagant wraps.

The Bonney sisters' *Shopping Guide to Paris* recommended Schiaparelli as the newest house for sports clothes and commented: "A free-lance designer for other houses, Schiaparelli felt the pulse of the style world, sprang into the market overnight, and made an instantaneous success. She designs her models herself, and has them made under her direction. This combination of individual design and direction is worth money, and she values her products accordingly. But if you have followed her contributions you will know that you get 'value received.' She is apt to launch jewelry to go with sweater suits, one of her successful originations being shell jewelry in twisted ropes with bracelets to match. She has just begun to present some smart models in coats."

By August 1927 modernist sweater designs, primarily block and cube patterns in shaded tones, were being included in Paris couture collections. The first collection Schiaparelli presented at her new salon on the rue de la Paix, in January 1928, included these two hand-knitted sweaters with asymmetric geometric patterns in black and white, which were shown with circular crêpe or wool skirts. American buyers were enthusiastic about the designs but, because they were hand knit, had reservations about being able to market the originals at a reasonable price.

Schiaparelli's signature bowknot sweater (previous page), from her November 1927 collection, was her first big success and became one of her most copied designs. Before achieving the final version, Schiaparelli experimented with several renditions of the design. Archival photographs support her statement that most of these attempts were less than successful.

In 1928 Gimbel Brothers department store of New York sold copies of Schiaparelli's new geometric and knitted bowknot designs for $7.99, showing them with matching or contrasting silk skirts. The window display above stressed the appropriateness of the Schiaparelli sweater for golf. Although knitted skirts were in most respects ideal, since they stretched to fit a woman golfer's widest stance, they became a liability in the rain, lengthening and clinging to the legs. The perfect garments, as American golfer Glenna Collett noted in her 1929 book *Ladies in the Rough*, were probably the plus fours, or knickers, worn by male golfers, but as she observed: "Their undoubted utility can never outweigh their obvious futility as a means of adornment."

Glenna Collett, the pioneering U.S. women's golf champion who set the record for winning the most amateur championships, received a trophy in 1929 at the Oakland Hills Country Club in Birmingham, Michigan, wearing a version of Schiaparelli's famous bowknot sweater (right). In *Ladies in the Rough*, Collett offered these observations on the dress of the woman golfer of the late 1920s and its significance in helping to popularize the sport: "She has come a long way in realizing the freedom of modern dress. None can deny that the absence of cumbersome skirts, swelling grandly about the legs and hampering milady's game, has been a contributing factor in stimulating interest among women in all branches of outdoor sports. Modified dress for golf has had the same effect on the game as the one-piece bathing-suit, introduced by the audacious innovator, Annette Kellerman, has had in making swimming one of the most popular sports for women."

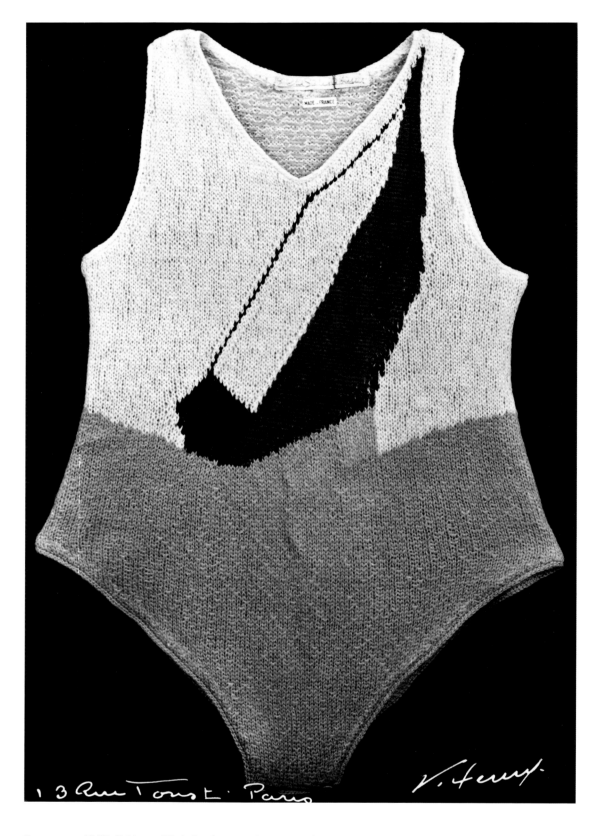

The increased interest of the couture in sports fashions designed specifically for the beach and seaside was reflected in the popularity of nautical themes in clothing, such as anchor and star embroideries, sailor collars, and flannel jackets decorated with brass buttons for summer and resort wear. The concepts were easily adapted to knitwear, and for summer 1928 Schiaparelli included the trompe l'oeil pullover on the previous page, based on a French sailor's middy, with its collar extending across the back of the sweater.

For summer 1928, Schiaparelli's knitted one- and two-piece bathing suits in striking color combinations were imported to the United States exclusively by Saks Fifth Avenue. Among the styles available was the one-piece suit shown above, with a stylized silhouette of a sailboat across the front. The sleeveless sweater with its fish motif (right) originally

formed the top of a two-piece suit that would have included flannel trunks with a snugly fitting knitted band around the hips and buttons up the sides. To complete the ensemble Schiaparelli included matching thick-soled knitted bootees with tops that could be turned down and a knitted helmet to wear over a rubber bathing cap.

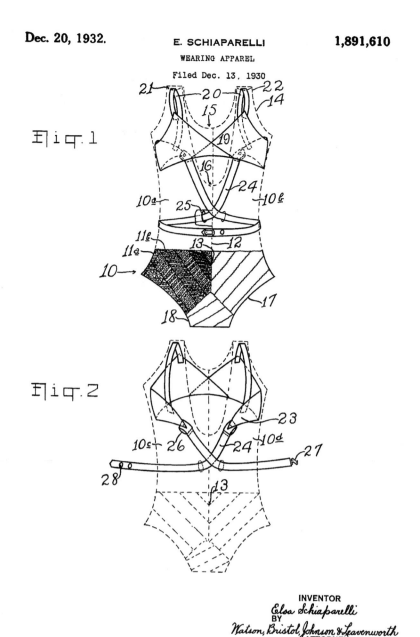

Dec. 20, 1932.   E. SCHIAPARELLI   1,891,610
WEARING APPAREL
Filed Dec. 13, 1930

Fig.1

Fig.2

INVENTOR
Elsa Schiaparelli
BY
Watson, Bristol, Johnson & Leavenworth
ATTORNEY

George Hoyningen-Huene's photograph of a bathing suit from Schiaparelli's first rue de la Paix collection has become one of the most celebrated images in twentieth-century fashion photography (left). Published in a July 1928 issue of *Vogue*, "No. 1" was modeled by Bettina Jones, who later married the French politican Gaston Bergery. (Jones was to become Schiaparelli's assistant and right hand, taking responsibility for the salon's imaginative window displays.) Jones wears a one-piece hand-knitted black-and-white-striped wool bathing suit under black flannel shorts that have a yoke of crocheted wool and button up both sides with pearl buttons; on her feet are matching black-and-white-striped bathing socks. The original ensemble, recorded in archival photographs, also included a long-sleeved wool pullover sweater with a sailor's collar and a knitted helmet designed to be worn over a rubber bathing cap.

Schiaparelli registered a number of innovative patents during her career. The first was for a novel backless bathing suit that incorporated a brassiere constructed to be invisible through the open back (above). The brassiere was adjustable, with straps that crossed low on the back and wrapped around the waist to fasten in the front. Filed simultaneously in France and the United States in November and December 1930, respectively, the patent received final American approval in December 1932. Best & Company department store in New York sold the patented design, made in a thick herringbone striped knit, during the summer of 1930.

During the late 1920s and early 1930s beach pajamas were a staple of the fashionable resort wardrobe. They were worn for lounging on the beach or for lunching at the casino, with or without a bathing suit underneath. Schiaparelli's first designs, shown in the 1928 photographs by Thérèse Bonney on the right, included practical one-piece knitted pajamas with ribbing around the waist, often with a matching jacket. In the Man Ray photograph above, from 1930, Schiaparelli wears a dramatic black-and-white printed silk beach ensemble of her own design. The pattern of large leaves is very much in the spirit of the textiles used by her mentor, Paul Poiret. The one-piece design had full trousers and was worn with a long, loose coat and knitted hat. By 1932 women were substituting the wraparound apron dress for general beachwear, but Schiaparelli continued to regard beach pajamas as less formal and more comfortable, since the wearer could dispense with such foundation garments as girdles and garters.

French designers had been playing with the idea of the divided, or culotte, skirt for several seasons, and by spring 1927 it had found its place in the wardrobe of active, fashion-conscious women. In May 1931 Schiaparelli wore her true divided skirt, undisguised by panels or a wraparound skirt, in London during a trip to buy tweeds (left). The garment caused much controversy and was loudly condemned by the British press.

In 1931 Schiaparelli also designed a silk tennis outfit with a divided skirt and detachable tunic for the Spanish tennis player Lili de Alvarez, seen above at the North London Tennis Tournament at Highbury in April. The English press vehemently criticized de Alvarez's choice of a divided skirt. The question in everyone's mind was whether she would be allowed to wear it at Wimbledon. She did—and lost.

Schiaparelli's cleverly designed resort outfit for summer 1930, based on the idea of the apron, is seen above in a fashion sketch from New York wholesaler Wm. H. Davidow Sons Co. The original model was made up in four shades of tussore silk and constructed as two half-dresses, each with one armhole. The ties of one dress half passed through slits on the other half, to tie on the same side. A coordinating silk cardigan completed the ensemble. The concept of the wraparound dress, previously reserved for sportswear, was extended by Schiaparelli to include designs for town and evening wear. Buyers and manufacturers greeted the idea with enthusiasm, since it helped solve the problem of producing clothes to an exact fit.

Architect of Fashion, Carpenter of Clothes

In 1929 the attic rooms Schiaparelli occupied on the top floor of 4 rue de la Paix were exchanged for salons and workrooms two floors down. By 1932 her space had further expanded to include the second floor. Four hundred employees were now turning out from seven to eight thousand garments in eight ateliers. To "Pour le Sport" she added "Pour la Ville" and "Pour le Soir." The new salon, designed by Jean-Michel Frank to look like the interior of a boat, had white walls dramatized with touches of black and bright colors. Ropes draped along the walls were hung with scarves, sweaters, and hanks of colorful wool yarns. There were shiny black patent-leather curtains, black wooden furniture, and carpets made from strips of every conceivable color. A map of the Basque coast (described by *Vogue* in 1930 as the one corner of Europe that had retained an untouched and unspoiled chic), vividly painted in greens and blues on white, completed the décor. Some of the salon's furnishings may have been purchased at designer Eileen Gray's 1929 closing sale at her company Jean Désert, whose sales registers indicate that Schiaparelli bought a white-painted armchair, a mattress covered in shiny black cotton, and a metal-framed mirror.

At about the same time Schiaparelli's salon was being redesigned, Frank also updated her new apartment on the boulevard Saint-Germain, and its modern dining room was featured in *The Studio Yearbook* for 1931 (pp. 36–37). Coco Chanel, a guest at the first formal dinner party held there, was appalled by the apartment's stark modern décor, as Schiaparelli reported in her autobiography: "At the sight of this modern furniture and black plates she shuddered as if she were passing a cemetery." The evening was unseasonably warm, and bits of the white rubberized fabric covering the chairs transferred to her visitors' clothing, an unfortunate effect that Schiaparelli wryly observed was reminiscent of the trompe l'oeil sweaters that had paid for the meal. Frank's first important clients were the Vicomte Charles and Vicomtesse Marie-Laure de Noailles (also one of Schiaparelli's first clients), for whom he designed the interiors of their Robert Mallet-Stevens villa at Hyères in southern France and their house in Paris. Frank's later interior designs for Schiaparelli's apartment on the rue Barbet-de-Jouy and her new salon on the Place Vendôme, opened in 1935, would reflect his move away from pure modernist interiors to more personal spaces, echoing the prevailing changes in architectural design in the 1930s and the couturière's own changing aesthetic.

Schiaparelli's modernist salons and apartments were fitting backdrops for her clothing designs. Her special appeal to Americans had its origin in the relationship of her designs to American modernism, with its emphasis on simplicity, continuity of line, color contrasts, and "sharp *contrasts in light and shadow* created through definite and angular mouldings and by broken planes," as defined by the furniture designer Paul Frankl in his 1928 book *New Dimensions. Harper's Bazaar* for April 1932 summed up Schiaparelli's attraction: "She gives her clothes the essence of modern architecture, modern thought, and modern movement." Her fashions were especially appropriate to the American machine age, for in the words of *New Yorker* writer Janet Flanner, they had "special applicability to a background of square-shouldered skyscrapers, of mechanics in private life and pastimes devoted to gadgetry." Schiaparelli's affinity with modernism was reflected in her own wardrobe, which was invariably black, white, or black and white. British *Vogue* for January 1930 described the designer as "one of the most ardent supporters of black and white, and her enthusiasm is shared by many women who find this combination distinguished and becoming." In 1931 she was seen lunching at the Ritz dressed in the inevitable black and white, accompanied by a white Pekingese clad in a black velvet coat she had designed.

Schiaparelli's designs played off contrasts: black and white, dull and shiny surfaces, thick and thin fabrics, unexpected color combinations. The couturière defined elegance as a sense of the fitness of things. The modern woman, she believed, required simple, practical clothing that had multiple uses, thereby cutting down on the need for a large wardrobe, a concept especially appealing during the economic crisis of the Depression. Thus one little plaid silk jacket, for example, could serve several purposes: covering a low-cut evening gown, brightening up a sleeveless dress, or adding a bit of glamour to an evening pajama for casual entertaining. Her approach to design was defined in the tenth of her "Twelve Commandments for Women"—"Never fit a dress to the body, but train the body to fit the dress." Schiaparelli's silhouettes were frequently described as having a strict neatness, with angles replacing feminine curves. Barely five feet tall, she designed with herself in mind. Shoulders were broadened to give the illusion of a narrow waist and small hips. The effect was first achieved with padded shoulders, introduced in August

1931 with her "wooden soldier" silhouette. In October *Vogue* remarked: "Clothes carpenter that she is, Schiaparelli builds up the shoulders, planes them off, and carves a decisive line from under the arms to the hip-bone, gouging in the waist." Next, she added fur "macaroons" to the tops of sleeves, followed by skillfully constructed "shoulder trays" that, for May 1933, developed into Siamese-dancer-style "angel wings." By August 1933 the shoulder fantasies had disappeared, to be replaced by a stylish rounded but still padded look that gave way the following season to box shoulders. Schiaparelli kept her silhouette slim, with a slightly raised waistline and longer skirt to help lengthen the figure. Clothing, she believed, should be closely connected to the frame of the body, just as in architecture a building's form is drawn from its structural skeleton. Thus many of her early designs, such as surplice bodices and apron dresses, wrapped around the figure.

The simplicity of Schiaparelli's designs, especially the surplice bodices with their winding sashes and wraparound dresses that buttoned in back or tied at the side (p. 40), made her designs easy to wear and easy to copy. For American manufacturers of ready-to-wear they were the perfect answer to the problem of mass-producing a fitted silhouette. It also gave the home dressmaker an opportunity to re-create high-priced couture garments using her own sewing machine. Beginning in 1929, Schiaparelli was one of at least sixteen Paris couturiers whose designs were made available from leading American department stores and also from the *Ladies' Home Journal* through the magazine's exclusive contract with the Paris Pattern Company.

Aerodynamic forms were introduced into Schiaparelli's silhouette the same year that the all-metal Boeing 247 aircraft, the first modern passenger plane, made its début. Her October 1933 showing for spring 1934 included coats swept forward in "stormy weather" and "windblown" silhouettes, while imaginative "aeroplane" evening dresses had winged hip flounces at the back (p. 33). The following season the movement had become a "typhoon," with windblown drapes at front and back and bold "fish" and "bird" outlines for evening. An inveterate traveler, Schiaparelli designed practical clothes for the woman on the move. Although at the time she had never flown, in 1930 she was asked to write an article for the *Ladies' Home Journal* on aviation clothes. Titled "Smartness Aloft," it appeared in March and was illustrated with a photograph of her friend the Comtesse Gabrielle di Robilant wearing a pilot's costume Schiaparelli had designed for her, and which she had shown the previous November at a Stewart & Company fashion show in New York. The natural-colored linen crash overall had long trousers that fitted snugly at the ankles and was trimmed with patent-leather winglike inserts and cuffs, which Schiaparelli used because of the visual relationship of patent leather to the shiny wings of an airplane. Zipper fastenings were located on the wrists, on the pockets, and at the neck. The overall was worn with a black knit hat and collarette, both made by milliner Madame Agnès, and comfortable low-heeled shoes. The outfit was designed to be worn over a simple jersey suit, so that upon arriving at one's flying club, the overall and cap could quickly be whisked off, leaving the wearer smartly attired. Schiaparelli's aviatrix clients included Amelia Earhart, and in 1936 she provided British airwoman Amy Mollison (née Johnson) with the wardrobe for her solo flight to Cape Town, South Africa (p. 75).

The simple, slim silhouette Schiaparelli favored demanded that a greater emphasis be placed on interesting fabrics, especially textures—from rustic Scottish wools to novelty fabrics such as Meyer's wool woven with white ostrich, which she used in 1928 for a skirt and coat ensemble. She enthusiastically endorsed the latest technological developments in fabrics and often initiated design ideas for them, working closely with fabric manufacturers such as Bianchini, Colcombet, and Ducharne. A number of times she found inspiration in a mill's discards and experimental pieces, which gave her the reputation of making successes out of other people's mistakes. In Schiaparelli's hands synthetic fabrics became chic, and she was credited with making rayon fashionable by using unique weaves that took on the appearance of wools, linens, or silks but still retained the distinctive draping quality that was one of the fabric's greatest assets. She made a success of rayon crêpes in bold, rough textures and relief patterns, and she was the first to use rayon woven with Lastex, which made the fabric stretchable, eliminating the need for buttons when it was used for bands, cuffs, and inserts. She was also the first to use deep-pile velvets, water-repellant transparent velvets, and slit cellulose film. Some of the textured rayon fabrics she launched in May 1933, including ciragril, a lacquered gauze or fine mesh used for evening gowns, were exclusive to her house and often carried her name in various forms: ray*esca*, a dull crêpe with groups of alternating ridges; *elsa*cloc, with a dull cloqué bead pattern; and jer*esca*, a new jersey.

The use of Schiaparelli's name during the early 1930s to endorse American-made fabrics attests to her success in setting the latest trends in textile materials and design. The relationship was mutually beneficial.

In the portrait by artist-decorator Jean Dunand on page 32, Schiaparelli wears model "No. 102," one of the great successes of her April 1933 collection for fall, which was available in New York at the store Jay Thorpe, located on West 57th Street. Made in one of Schiaparelli's exclusive fabrics, rayesca, a matte crêpe with a V-ridged pattern, in the new color "Pansy" blue, the evening dress had one of the season's distinctive shoulder treatments—padded puffs. Dunand's lacquer portraits were widely acclaimed, and among his other sitters were the milliner Madame Agnès and the couturière Madeleine Vionnet.

The blue-green satin evening gown in the house sketch on page 33, with its winglike flares at the back, illustrates one of Schiaparelli's aerodynamic silhouettes for spring 1934. French actress Arlette Marchal was among those attracted to the new outline, and she wore this version in André Berthomieu's 1933 film *La Femme idéale* (p. 61).

American manufacturers and retailers were eager to expand sales at home and abroad, while Schiaparelli sought to increase her name recognition and gain a foothold in the American market. Textiles were among the first products made in the United States to receive the designer's imprimatur, followed shortly afterward by hosiery and shoes. In 1929 she created beach pajamas for Cheney Silks to use in the promotion of their fabrics for resort wear, and for the Cotton-Textile Institute's promotion of American cotton she designed a cotton terry-cloth beach wrap and gingham beach pajamas. Other endorsements included Westcott colored hosiery and Selby Arch Preserver Shoes in 1930, DuPont rayon Kaskade velvets and Walther Woolens in 1932, and Ameritex-Sudanette cottons in 1933, among others. Schiaparelli was so successful in the United States that she made the cover of *Time* magazine on August 13, 1934, and was noted in the accompanying article as one of the "arbiters of the ultra-modern *haute couture*." She made connections with textile manufacturers closer to home as well. Her interest in British fabrics led her to use undyed Scottish wools and unusually colored tweeds, and she helped to make humble Viyella, a combination of cotton and wool, into a fashionable fabric.

Looking to expand, and at the suggestion of her English beau, Peter, Schiaparelli opened a London branch in November 1933 at 6 Upper Grosvenor Street. Having a salon in London meant that British trade buyers would no longer be admitted to her Paris openings, a practice introduced by the couturier Edward Molyneux, who had himself opened a London branch in 1932. In addition, Schiaparelli's clothes would not be available in exclusive London shops, such as Fortnum and Mason, as they had previously but would have to be purchased from her salon. Her London branch was under the direction of a Mrs. Harrison who had previously worked with Molyneux, and the first showing held there was a glittering affair. Schiaparelli exhibited thirty-eight models, some of them created especially for her London clients and highlighting British woolen fabrics and hand knits. The "stormy weather" silhouette so successful at the mid-season Paris showing was greeted with equal enthusiasm in London. Schiaparelli's British clients included Princess Marina, Duchess of Kent; the Duchess of Westminster; and Wallis Simpson, the future Duchess of Windsor. A controversy erupted over another royal client in 1935, when Schiaparelli entered into litigation against her former French cutter and fitter, Albert Cezard. Cezard had left her London salon on September 1 of that year to join couturier Norman Hartnell, who was making dresses for the royal wedding of Lady Alice Scott to the Duke of Gloucester. Schiaparelli attempted to restrain Cezard from working for her competitor, based on an agreement he had signed when entering into her employment that specified he was not to work for any competitor for six months after leaving her. The court, perhaps diplomatically, reserved judgment until after the royal wedding, which allowed Cezard to cut the bride's wedding gown. Schiaparelli may have found some consolation in the fact that several of the bride's relatives wore gowns that she had made. In the end the ceremony was a private affair held in the chapel of Buckingham Palace, for the bride's father had died a few weeks before the wedding. Schiaparelli ultimately lost her suit.

Having spent time in Great Britain in her youth, Schiaparelli always considered it a second home, and she particularly loved her small mews house in London, which she decorated smartly and inexpensively with unpainted wooden furniture from the department store John Lewis, upholstery in pale blue quilted glazed chintz, and white sailcloth window curtains. Her love of Britain, in particular her warm feelings for Scotland and the surrounding area, made itself felt in her Paris collections. Scottish wool yarns were used for sweaters, colorful wool tweeds from Linton of Carlisle showed up in jackets and skirts, and in 1934 she introduced her "Loch Ness" bonnets and tartan tams. During the life of her London salon, between fall 1933 and summer 1939, clothing by Schiaparelli appeared in more than thirty British film and stage productions, far more than the total of twenty-eight French and American plays and films traced so far, suggesting that locating a branch of her salon in London had done much to raise the profile of her clothes there. Schiaparelli closed down her London business just weeks before Europe's entry into World War II. With war on the horizon there were ample reasons for the decision, but the London press speculated that it was the fault of copyists.

The Studio Yearbook for 1931 featured this photograph of the dining room of Schiaparelli's apartment on the boulevard Saint-Germain. Jean-Michel Frank updated the original interior by pulling out everything except the arched bookshelves and based his design on the colors white, yellow, orange, green, and black. Walls were painted white, and white rubberized fabric was used for the curtains and chairs. The two divans were upholstered in the same fabric, but in brilliant green. Two small dining tables were lacquered black with gray streaks, and white Tunisian rugs were spread on the floors. The ethereal painting over the fireplace is by Russian painter Pavel Tchelitchew, one of a small band of "Neo-Humanist" artists working in Paris at that time. In 1934 Frank used the same color scheme to decorate Schiaparelli's new apartment on the rue Barbet-de-Jouy.

The Surrealist artist Man Ray photographed Schiaparelli (above) wearing the dress she described in her autobiography as the most successful of her career. From her fall 1930 collection (presented in May 1930), the ensemble—the only evening dress she showed that season—included a plain black crêpe de chine gown with shaped sections at the waist to give it a slightly bloused effect; this was worn under a short white chiffon jacket with a long sash that wrapped around the front and back to tie at one side. Caresse Crosby, who with her husband, Harry Crosby, founded Black Sun Press in 1927, cut a striking figure when she wore the same design to a New York party given in her honor by William Averell Harriman, heir to the Union Pacific Railway fortune, and his wife, Marie. As Crosby described in her autobiography, *The Passionate Years*: "After dinner, drinking coffee with the ladies, I chose a green mint from the tray while I stood before the fireplace. My low-cut black crêpe (Schiaparelli said it was the best dress she ever designed) was supplemented by a little white chiffon bolero, long tight sleeves attached to a great trailing sash. I wore Harry's last present, my beautiful diamond necklace . . . and my jade and diamond earrings, green mint was the perfect accessory to that toilette." Madame Agnès's appearance in the same ensemble at a performance of Johann Strauss's *Die Fledermaus* at the Théâtre Pigalle in Paris was equally memorable. According to *Harper's Bazaar* for June 1930, Agnès accessorized it with plain black crêpe sandals and long white gloves with heavy outside seams, "which perfectly harmonized with her black and white hair, and she looked like a modern mantelpiece ornament in black and white china."

Edward Steichen took this photograph of the Comtesse
di Zoppola (above) for *Vogue*, June 1, 1931. The
countess is wearing what was then the latest trend in
formal evening wear, dinner pajamas. Schiaparelli's
chic wide-legged pajamas were made up in orange
crêpe de chine and were worn with a short cloth-of-gold
jacket that wrapped at the front. From her February
collection for summer 1931, the ensemble reflected
the influence of the forthcoming *Exposition coloniale
internationale*, which was to open in Paris in May.
Inspired by the exhibition, the collection included

fabrics suggesting the rustic hand weaves and metallic
textiles of Morocco, as well as such jewelry as the
heavy wood and silver necklace worn by the countess.
Schiaparelli appeared in the same ensemble, but
wearing a heavy necklace and ring of amber beads,
at Madame Agnès's evening opening of her colonial-
inspired millinery collection. From Agnès's collection
Schiaparelli selected a cone-shaped hat based on
Cambodian headwear, done in braided strips of black
and white suede.

Schiaparelli's collection for winter 1930–31 featured afternoon ensembles such as this dress and coat. The outfit was originally owned by the artist Vera White, who with her husband Samuel S. White 3rd formed a significant collection of early modern art that included the iconic Man Ray photograph *Marcel Duchamp as Rrose Sélavy*, now in the Philadelphia Museum of Art. The seven-eighths-length herringbone wool coat was worn over a dress that combined the same rough-textured wool with fine silk crêpe. This dull black color attracted great interest among American buyers, as did the wraparound effect of the dress bodice. The bulkiness that would have been created by an all-wool dress was offset by having the yoke, hip band, and sleeves in silk. Vera White's wardrobe also included Schiaparelli's sweater with the sailor collar (pp. 22–23) and the brown wool jacket with brass curtain-ring clips (p. 53).

In the Man Ray photograph at right, Schiaparelli wears an evening gown from her April collection for fall 1931 that carried a trompe l'oeil design painted by the decorative artist Jean Dunand, who was famous for his metal and lacquer work. White or champagne-colored rayon evening gowns were hand decorated with black or brown banding suggesting the folds of classical Greek garments. The painting formed an integral part of each gown, supplementing the cut. In this example, shades of black and gray on white were applied to the front and back to simulate pleats of black chiffon. Dunand's technique of painting dress fabrics with dilute sepia and colored lacquer applied through a stencil had been used by the artist for the gowns he created for Madame Agnès, which she exhibited at the 1925 *Exposition des arts décoratifs et industriels modernes* in Paris.

Marie-Laure, Vicomtesse de Noailles, was photographed by Man Ray (above) wearing "No. 861" from Schiaparelli's summer 1931 collection, a black wool coatdress with a white piqué top ending in a peplum over the hips. During the 1920s and 1930s, Marie-Laure de Noailles and her husband, Charles, were the foremost patrons of modern art in France, from painting to film, and their Cubist-style villa at Hyères in southern France, designed by Robert Mallet-Stevens, became a meeting place for artists, many of whom made contributions to the villa's interior and gardens. Schiaparelli's use of contrasts in Marie-Laure's dress—stark black and white and two different textures of fabric, in this case wool and cotton—was characteristic of her designs during the early 1930s.

In the Man Ray photograph at left, Schiaparelli wears
her Dunand-painted dress (p. 43) with a dramatic,
short, coq-feather cape—a combination she wore to the
gala opening of the smart restaurant Ambassadeurs in
May 1931. Schiaparelli may have designed the cape as
an homage to the great Russian ballerina Anna Pavlova,
who had died in January of that year and whose
signature solo piece was "The Dying Swan" (above).
During her trip to Cuba in 1917 with the opera singer
Ganna Walska, Schiaparelli was often mistaken for
Pavlova, who was performing there at the same time.

In this photograph by George Hoyningen-Huene for the September 1932 issue of *Vogue*, Schiaparelli has on the gown she wore in June to *Le Bal blanc* (The White Ball), where it caused a sensation. The ankle-length gown was of white ciré peu d'ange jersey cut in the style of a garden apron, with narrow straps crossing at the back and little pockets at the front, over which the designer wore a lei of white coq feathers. 1932 was the year for feathers. Marlene Dietrich started the craze with the costume she wore as Shanghai Lily in the movie *Shanghai Express*, and soon they could be seen everywhere. Schiaparelli used them as boas and on evening wraps to emphasize her wide shoulder line. Daisy Fellowes, soon to become the Paris editor of *Harper's Bazaar*, wore the designer's brilliant blue coq-feather collar with a clinging black crepon gown to a gala evening at the Ambassadeurs restaurant and again with a white "mourning crêpe" dress to *Le Bal blanc* (also called *Le Bal des gigolos* because it was hosted by young bachelors). The feather craze culminated in 1933 with the Schiaparelli collar worn by Daisy Fellowes to Lady Mendl's June ball—shiny black heron feathers that jutted out and curved up like the shoulders of a Cambodian dancer's costume.

Architect of Fashion, Carpenter of Clothes

This black evening gown by Schiaparelli for winter
1931–32, with its sweeping train and high waist, was
in keeping with the prevailing Directoire (1795–99)
spirit of design that season, which emphasized the
long, slender, molded silhouette. The gown's train could
be looped up to fasten with a clip under the band at
the waist for dancing. The fabric, an extremely crinkly
rayon crêpe called Riboulding that Schiaparelli also
used for day dresses, was the sensation of the season.

Schiaparelli's low-necked evening dress in heavily crinkled gray rayon crêpe was worn with a plum-colored velvet evening jacket. The straight silhouette, the high waist, and the slightly padded shoulders were distinctively Directoire in feeling. In the photograph at left, the romantic mood of an early-nineteenth-century-painting-come-to-life was captured by Edward Steichen for the November 1931 issue of *Vogue*. Schiaparelli was photographed at the winter ski resort Saint-Moritz (above) sporting the identical gown and hairdresser Antoine's silver lacquered wig. She wore a blond version of the wig for skiing instead of a hat.

The low-backed dark red crêpe evening dress from Schiaparelli's summer 1932 collection, at right, features one of the designer's new wide, asymmetrically draped necklines, a variation of the knitted trompe l'oeil scarves used earlier on her sweaters (pp. 18–23). The bright coral scarf, made from wide crinkly silk ribbon, begins at the lower right of the back, drapes over the left shoulder, and ends in an oversize bow on the front just at the right armpit. Schiaparelli used the same crinkly silk ribbon for short capelet scarves that served as evening jackets.

The padded shoulder first made its appearance in Schiaparelli's collection in August 1931 for winter 1931–32. Although the designer had experimented with padded shoulders in previous seasons, it was her famous "Hotchacha" coat in navy corduroy that was greeted so enthusiastically by American buyers. It started a trend that Hollywood embraced with a vengeance, particularly fashion and costume designer Adrian. British *Vogue* for September 16, 1931, described it as Schiaparelli's "wooden soldier silhouette" and noted that "it transforms you completely: wide, padded epaulette shoulders, high, double-breasted closing, very chesty chest, lines carved sharply under the arms to the waist, and a straight column from there down." The thick fur pelt that forms the collar and lines the front closing of the rough wool jacket at right is what gives it the distinctive chesty look. Brass curtain-ring clips substitute for buttons, and when unclipped the front opens into fur revers. The jacket was worn with gauntlet gloves.

Schiaparelli's ensemble "No. 1045" for spring 1932 (above) included a deep sunset-rose coat with squared shoulders and sharp, wide revers (lapels), worn with a pale banana-beige wool dress and a scarf made of three different colored scarves braided together—beetroot, yellow, and tangerine or rusty rose-pink. The designer's entire collection for this season was presented in the "Chez Josette" salon of Saks 34th Street in New York.

It included fifteen original models, of which twelve were copies that could be bought off the rack. The remaining three, because of their unusual fabrics, were a special order available within a week. The originals sold for $150 and up, while the copies ranged in price from $29.50 to $125. "No. 1045" was one of the designs that was copied, with the coat selling for $29.50. Lord & Taylor offered the dress and scarf for $28.

Cathleen Mann, Marchioness of Queensbury and daughter of the Scottish painter Harrington Mann, was photographed by Madame Yevonde in 1932 (left) wearing one of Schiaparelli's successes of the spring 1932 season. The ashy pink, slightly fitted hip-length jacket was combined with a violet-brown skirt and a dotted blouse that tied at the neckline. The model was purchased by the New York wholesaler Wm. H. Davidow Sons Co. Miss Mann was a painter and designed costumes for several films during the mid-1930s, including the 1934 film *The Iron Duke*, for which Schiaparelli dressed the actress Lesley Wareing.

Schiaparelli designed clothes with a very high waistline, right under the bust, for the actress Ina Claire, photographed here by George Hoyningen-Huene in March 1932 (above). Miss Claire also wears the designer's famous "Mad Cap"—a knitted tube of fabric that took on practically any shape. The actress's adoption of the hat started a craze, and it was seen everywhere. An American manufacturer copied the design and began his own business, calling it Madcaps. The hat was reproduced so much that Schiaparelli

eventually wished she had never thought of it. As she recalled in her autobiography, in which she idiosyncratically switches between the first- and third-person voices: "From all the shop windows, including the five- and ten-cent stores, at the corner of every street, from every bus, in town and in the country, the naughty hat obsessed her, until one day it winked at her from the bald head of a baby in a pram." She refused to sell the hats anymore and had her salesgirls destroy all those in stock.

The three-piece ensemble from Schiaparelli's February 1933 collection seen in the fashion photograph above was worn by the designer (above, right) for her arrival on the ocean liner *Conte di Savoia* for a two-week visit to the United States. The wide-shouldered jacket, made up in a diagonal knit fabric in dark navy and white, wrapped over at the front and was belted at the waist. A shell-pink, waffle-knit scarf was looped around the neck and tucked into the front of the jacket. Schiaparelli wore a boxy mink coat with slightly puffed shoulders over the suit and accessorized it with a navy blue knitted hat with a tuck to give height, mesh hose, and low-cut brown cordovan oxfords. According to the press release issued by her American representative,

Chanderhall, this was her first visit to the United States since fall 1929: "The steady growth of her house has prevented her from taking vacations for many years and her forthcoming visit is in the nature of a holiday which she has chosen to spend in America." The only public engagement she accepted was an invitation to speak at a Fashion Group luncheon in New York, where she voiced her disapproval of trouser fashions for the street.

For her August 1932 collection Schiaparelli launched a new silhouette, a new fabric, and a new color, all of them enthusiastically received by the fashion press. The long slim silhouette of "No. 445," shown in a photograph by Edward Steichen for *Vogue*, October 15 (right), was broken only by the moderate square bustle at the end of the deep, open back. The design was made up in Jersela, a satin rayon jersey exclusive to the house, in "cabbage rose," a shade described as close to the color of Russian borscht. In sympathy with her American clients and the ongoing battle to repeal Prohibition, Schiaparelli christened this the "speakeasy" silhouette, since the small shelf created by the gathers at the back of some of the gowns was an ideal place to conceal a flask.

"Why should Madam be afraid? Schiaparelli isn't."

It was Schiaparelli's pioneering shoulder treatments that distinguished much of her work during the first half of the 1930s. The molded silhouette, emphasizing the width of the shoulders to give the illusion of a narrow waist and small hips, was an antidote to the straight up-and-down lines of the 1920s. The French film *Je te confie ma femme*, released in 1933, included two of the designer's most recognizable shoulder treatments. The film still at left (top) illustrates Schiaparelli's new shoulder detailing, which through the use of circular fagot-stitched bands set at the top of the sleeves made a woman appear to have wide shoulders. The still at lower left, from the same movie, features the actress Arletty (Léonie Bathiat) wearing a dress with "shoulder trays"—fluted bands of fabric mounted at the top of the shoulder line to give a squared look to the silhouette.

New Yorker magazine for January 21, 1939, included this cartoon by Mary Petty (above, left). Extremes in fashion were a Schiaparelli trademark, and she herself was fearless when it came to wearing them. As she recalled in her autobiography: "I have never been shy of appearing in public in the most fantastic and personal getup."

The "architectural" fashions Schiaparelli showed in spring 1933 included designs with broad, high shoulders reminiscent of a football player. The house sketch above (top) illustrates the couturière's signature design that season: a short, navy blue cartridge-pleated cape worn over a crêpe dress with a solid navy skirt and a navy-and-white printed bodice with ruffles at the shoulder. In the second sketch (above, bottom), a brown tweed three-quarter-length coat with sharply pointed shoulders is worn with a matching skirt and a blue plaid blouse.

Schiaparelli was known for her use of interesting and unusual materials, and fabrics with a crinkle effect had been included in her collections since 1932. The boldly crinkled rayon crêpe fabric called "treebark," introduced in August 1933, foreshadowed the use of similarly textured natural and synthetic fabrics during the late twentieth century by the Japanese designer Issey Miyake. The slim-fitting dinner dress at left, from Schiaparelli's February 1934 collection, included a dramatic wing-collared taffeta jacket in the new windswept, or "typhoon," silhouette.

Schiaparelli's October 1933 showing for spring 1934 included several versions of her exciting new aerodynamic silhouette. The unadorned gowns were made in both matte velvets and shiny, stiff satins and featured "wings" formed from flat flounces at the front that were brought up from the knee and over the hips to stand out in a flare at the back just below the waistline. The dramatic line, akin to a ship in full sail, and the satin fabric that reflected light in flashes caught the attention of the French actress Arlette Marchal, who wore the gown in André Berthomieu's 1933 film *La Femme idéale*. She and the gown illustrated the cover of the magazine *Le Film complet*, shown here at right.

13e Année. N° 1523.   16 pages. — **30** centimes   - n° 279 - 18-8-34.

LE FILM COMPLET
DU SAMEDI

LA FEMME IDÉALE

avec
René Lefèvre   et   *Arlette Marchal*

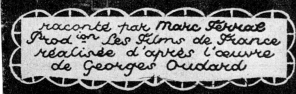

raconté par *Marc Ferral*
Prod ion *Les Films de France*
réalisée d'après l'œuvre
de *Georges Oudard*

Voir, page 16, notre page illustrée: CINÉ=REVUE

In the bedroom of her Paris apartment on the rue Barbet-de-Jouy, shown above, Schiaparelli used the same blistered rayon fabric that she used for dresses for a bedcover, chair covering, and curtains. White walls set off the lavender-blue fabric. The oak-and-black-mirrored dressing table, the bureau, and the lamps were designed by Jean-Michel Frank. A white bear rug covered the floor.

Schiaparelli moved into a new apartment on the rue Barbet-de-Jouy in 1934 and, once again, had it decorated by Jean-Michel Frank. The color scheme was the same one the interior designer had used for Schiaparelli's apartment on the boulevard Saint-Germain (pp. 36–37). The living room, seen here at right, was furnished with an orange leather sofa and informal small chairs slip-covered in canary yellow and milk-white quilted chintz. These were set against walls of white and almond green. The parquet floors were covered with leopard skins and white wool Tunisian

rugs. The unusual lamps, with block bases and parchment shades, were a Frank design used in her previous apartment. Above the fireplace is the painting *Bazar de l'Ocean* (1920), by the Surrealist artist Pierre Roy. Schiaparelli possibly purchased it sometime before 1930, when it was shown at New York's Brummer Gallery in Roy's first American exhibition. The sailboat in the painting may have been the inspiration for Schiaparelli's knitted one-piece bathing suit for 1928 (p. 24), which incorporates a similar image.

Schiaparelli's blue *robe d'interieur* for spring 1934 (left), made up in the designer's signature "treebark" crêpe and trimmed with chestnut fur, was ideal for at-home entertaining. In this version the pattern of the "bark" is about a quarter inch thick. The length, weight, and crêpiness of the fabric necessitated a straight, albeit clinging, silhouette.

Schiaparelli was photographed by George Hoyningen-Huene (above) for the November 1933 issue of *Vogue*, wearing a dinner suit and cape from her winter 1933–34 collection. The ensemble was made up in a new quilted taffeta fabric created especially for her by the silk manufacturer Bianchini. According to the story, she went to Mr. Bianchini's Paris office one day and

told him she wanted a fabric pattern with thick raised lines. He took a piece of taffeta, pinned some string underneath it in a lattice pattern, and "Armada" was born. The hip-length flared cape was lined with crêpe de chine, had a small standing collar, and closed with buttons rather than clips. The ostrich-feather hat is by Suzanne Talbot.

Architect of Fashion, Carpenter of Clothes

One of the most dramatic designs in Schiaparelli's April 1934 showing was the model illustrated in the fashion sketch above (perfect for the races at Longchamp), made up in one of her newest materials, "pavé," a matte cloqué crêpe. The dull-black Spanish ensemble included a dress and a short cape that substituted for a jacket that season. The dress was worn with a Spanish-influenced stiffly starched white linen collar that *Women's Wear Daily* for June 8, 1934, reported was shaped "like a giant squat spool." A black hand-knitted "sombrero" completed the ensemble.

For the April showings for fall 1934, Schiaparelli and other designers responded to the Holy Week celebrations in Seville, which for years had been suppressed but had just made an impressive comeback. *Harper's Bazaar* for June 1934 reported that within ten days of the event Spanish fashions began appearing in Paris. Coincidently, an exhibition of the work of the Spanish artist Francisco de Goya opened that May in London. Inspired by the clothes in Goya's paintings, Schiaparelli featured an evening

dress of gray "chichi," a matte crêpe with a ruffled, tucked edge. The hem of its slightly belled skirt curved up to reveal cherry-red chiffon ruffles, and it was worn with a feathery red plush capelet in the fabric called "King Kong." In the evening dress shown above, also made up in chichi, Schiaparelli called attention to the bosom by veiling the décolletage with a fanlike spread of black lace. Other Spanish touches in the collection included severe black town clothes and Goya-inspired headwear fashioned as wide-brimmed toreador hats.

The photograph at right, by Surrealist photographer Dora Maar, captures the drama of the frothy tulle cape Schiaparelli showed in April 1934. In deep currant red, it was held in at the waist in front and fell loosely at the back. It was worn over a white dress with a train, made of one of the designer's newest fabrics, Fildifer, a metallic rayon.

The most dramatic new fabric development during the mid-1930s was the "glass" fabric Rhodophane, first used by Schiaparelli in August 1934 for a dress in the winter 1934–35 collection. The following season she expanded her use of Rhodophane to jackets, capes, and belts, as well as dresses. Because of its fragility and brittleness, textile manufacturer Colcombet's transparent fabric was often interwoven in flat, ribbonlike strips with silk, rayon, or metal threads to give it stability. Socialite Madame Vittorio Crespi was photographed by George Hoyningen-Huene (left) for the January 1935 issue of *Vogue* wearing a stiff, pale blue satin evening dress with a shimmering Rhodophane apron from Schiaparelli's October 1934 showing for spring 1935.

Shoulders continued to inflate during winter 1934–35, and Schiaparelli's collection for that season included bottleneck sleeves that were long and tight toward the wrist and ballooned slightly at the shoulders, peasant sleeves with armholes cut high and full on top, and parachute sleeves that had their counterpart in her capelet-collared wool coats with parachute folds, such as the one shown above, worn with a high-crowned hat squared off at the top.

In the Shadow of Napoleon

In 1935 Schiaparelli moved from smaller premises at 4 rue de la Paix to ninety-eight rooms at the more imposing 21 Place Vendôme, formerly the location of Chéruit, a couture house founded in 1906. The other tenants of this vast seventeenth-century square dominated by a bronze column supporting a statue of Napoleon included the famous Ritz Hôtel and the great jewelers Chaumet and Boucheron. Schiaparelli had been offered Paul Poiret's former salon at 1 Rond-point des Champs-Elysées, but despite the location and elegant space, she preferred to remain true to her roots and stay within the area where her business first started. Her good friend Jean-Michel Frank, who had decorated her salon on the rue de la Paix in 1931 and her two Paris apartments, was asked to update the beautifully proportioned interiors of the new salon, which was classified as a historical monument and was thus protected from major alterations. The designs for both her home on the rue Barbet-de-Jouy and the new salon on the Place Vendôme echoed the changing aesthetics in architectural design during the 1930s from pure modernist interiors to more personalized spaces. Frank's stark interiors were replaced by designs that were more traditional in style yet still suited to contemporary taste. He had recently redecorated the salons of two other couturiers. For the Chicago-born Mainbocher, the first American to open a couture house in Paris, on the avenue George V, he painted the walls white, outlined the woodwork in pale gold, and slipcovered the furniture in pale floral tints. For the Parisian Lucien Lelong he installed plaster drapery. For Schiaparelli, Frank painted the entire interior of her salon white, including the intricately carved moldings, and used lights concealed in abstract plaster columns he designed in collaboration with the artist Alberto Giacometti to flood the rooms with soft light. Alison Settle, editor of British *Vogue*, observed that in Frank's designs "light was the point of the decoration, . . . light flooding the stairs, light flooding from fixtures holding perfumes and accessories, light shining in windows, so that the whole place seemed bathed in light."

On the second floor of 21 Place Vendôme, one large and two smaller salons were used as showrooms, with the rest of the space divided into offices and workrooms. Cotton dress fabrics were used in the interior decoration rather than traditional heavy furnishing fabrics. The salon's floor-to-ceiling windows were hung with white wide-wale piqué draperies edged with bias ruffles and tied back with blue-and-

white-striped woven piqué that was also used for the bias-cut flounced slipcovers on the furniture. White bias piqué cording, dark blue cotton pompoms, and decorative tassels were used as trim. The dressing rooms were curtained off with white wide-wale piqué that was also used, pinch-pleated, to cover the walls. Tall screens were covered in blue chintz, with the three separate panels of each screen outlined in white cotton braid. Navy and white pin-checked gingham and navy denim trimmed with white ball fringe were used as slipcovers on the dressing-room chairs. Ashtrays with spiraling bases, designed by Giacometti, were scattered throughout the space. The lower floor was transformed into a boutique, the first of its kind, called the "Schiap Shop," where simple little dresses, knitted clothes, bathing suits, shorts, lingerie, dressing gowns, knitted hats, jewelry, and bags were sold, "ready to be taken away immediately." In one corner of the ground floor, Frank designed the perfume shop to look like a birdcage of gold-painted bamboo (p. 158).

The salons were filled to capacity for the February 5, 1935, presentation of Schiaparelli's first collection in the new space, called "Stop, Look and Listen." The day before the opening, Columbia Broadcasting System (CBS) conducted a radio interview with the designer, relaying her thoughts on the latest spring and summer trends to its American audience. To celebrate her success and the opening of her new salon, Schiaparelli had designed cotton and silk fabrics printed with her own press clippings (p. 76). These she had made into dresses, blouses, and beach hats inspired by the folded-paper hats of Danish fishwives, observed during a recent trip to Scandinavia (p. 77). The fabric was designed in the spirit of Picasso's and Braque's papiers collés, of which Dadaist Tristan Tzara had said: "A shape cut out of newspaper and incorporated in a design or a picture unites the commonplace, a piece of everyday reality, with another reality constructed by the mind. The difference between various kinds of matter, that the eye is able to translate into tactile sensation, gives a new depth to the picture, in which weight is inscribed with mathematical precision on the symbol of volume, and its density, its taste, its consistency, place us before an unique reality created by the forces of the mind and of dream." For the rest of the decade, many of Schiaparelli's designs would be linked with the work of contemporary artists.

Never publicity shy, Schiaparelli persuaded Johan Colcombet, whose company had printed the press-clippings fabric, and the artist-decorator

Jean Dunand, who had decorated the smoking room on the *Normandie*, to each wear a lounging ensemble of robe, slippers, and nightcap made up in the material during that ship's maiden voyage to New York in May 1935. The textile design was particularly popular for cruise and resort wear. Jane Clark, wife of the art historian Kenneth Clark, purchased a silk day dress in the same print, along with its matching cotton "folded-paper" hat, at the designer's London salon and wore it on an Orient Line cruise in 1935. The fabric continued to be used for boutique items—including scarves, men's ties, and tobacco pouches—until 1954, when Schiaparelli's salon finally closed.

While other couturiers presented full skirts in their February 1935 showings, Schiaparelli and the couturière Alix introduced evening gowns of draped fabric that spiraled around the body, an homage to the beautiful fourteen-year-old Indian princess Karam of Kapurthala, who had enthralled Paris during the summer of 1934 with her exquisite wardrobe of woven and embroidered saris (p. 79). (During her 1936 visit to Paris she exchanged these for European clothes.) Paris had long been a playground for visiting maharajas, several of whom had American or European wives. Schiaparelli's Indian clients included the Ranee of Pudukota (the former Molly Sorrett of Australia, one of her first clients) and the Maharanee of Indore, whose husband was an enthusiast of avant-garde art and a patron of the sculptor Constantin Brancusi. The Indores' palace in India, Manik Bagh (Jewel Gardens), had been designed and furnished by the modernist German architect Eckart Muthesius in 1930 and was decorated with avant-garde furniture designs by Le Corbusier, Charlotte Perriand, and Eileen Gray and carpets by Ivan Da Silva Bruhns. The Maharanee usually ordered her wardrobe from Schiaparelli by mail. For each new collection she was sent sketches and swatches, and her selections were then made to her measurements in the Paris workrooms. During a visit to Paris in 1935 the Maharanee ordered twelve ensembles for herself and a complete Schiaparelli wardrobe for her three-year-old daughter. Schiaparelli often designed clothing for her own daughter and for the daughters of her clients, such as Rosamund Fellowes, daughter of Daisy Fellowes, and "Little Sixte," a daughter of the Princess Bourbon de Parme. Among her first designs for children were those she made in 1934 for the child star Nova Pilbeam to wear in the British film *Little Friend* (p. 290). Copies of these simple coats and dresses were sold through Bonwit Teller in a joint promotion with the motion picture.

One of the most anticipated social events of the 1935 summer season was the Honorable Reginald Fellowes's Oriental Ball, *Une Soirée chez le gouverneur*, which was attended by all the visiting maharajas and their wives. The event was conceived as an evening at the residence of a mythical colonial governor and took place in the Felloweses' garden—transformed for the evening into an Oriental paradise, with palm trees, window boxes piled high with orchids, perfumed fountains, colored lights, and a statue of Buddha set up at one end of the garden. Many of the guests dressed in Schiaparelli, including the hostess, Daisy Fellowes, who wore Antoine's black-lacquered wig with a white satin gown, Chinese in cut, that fastened with heavy white soutache frogs and had real orchids caught up in the train (p. 82). Schiaparelli came dressed as a Venetian "blackamoor" in a gold doublet with black hose, a costume that she had designed for herself (p. 83). Lady Mendl, the former Elsie de Wolfe, so-called originator of interior design, wore a dress from Schiaparelli's spring collection, a carbon-blue Ranee crêpe gown with an "Italian primitive" head veil falling from a jeweled crown of gold, coral, and turquoise (p. 85). The actress Myrna Loy appeared in Schiaparelli's yellow-and-white muslin gown with the skirt shirred up the front. The Indian and Italian themes were to meet up again at a gala several weeks later at the Interallied Club on the night of the Grand Prix, when Lady Mendl, Daisy Fellowes, and the Comtesse di Robilant appeared in the same long crinkled-taffeta Venetian capes in rose and green (p. 84), while Schiaparelli wrapped herself in another of her own designs, an Indian-inspired flame-silk sari coat striped with black and gold (p. 80). The Comtesse Colloredo-Mansfield and at least two other women wore the designer's metal-striped Indian gauze dresses with divided skirts.

Schiaparelli was to write in her autobiography, *Shocking Life*, that "fashion is born by small facts, trends, or even politics, never by trying to make little pleats and furbelows, by trinkets, by clothes easy to copy, or by the shortening or lengthening of a skirt." This was never more true than in 1935. The failure of the Stresa Front, the threat of the Italian-Ethiopian War, and Mussolini's loan exhibition of Italian masterpieces at the Petit Palais in Paris all left their mark on fashion. Hindu-style draped scarves shown by Schiaparelli in February evolved into April's "Fra Angelico" veils and Venetian capes, and in August politics

Around 1935 François Kollar captured Schiaparelli in a photograph for *Harper's Bazaar* that shows the designer seated in her salon at 21 Place Vendôme reviewing the sketches of her recent collection (p. 70). She is positioned next to the window, through which the plaza's famous column topped by a statue of Napoleon can be seen.

and fashion were interwoven, with Schiaparelli designing both Royalist and Republican clothes so that women could "meet the uncertain political temper of the times" in attire appropriate for either thrones or democracies, with a few modernist touches added for the Left. *Le coq gaulois* (the Gallic rooster), the national symbol of France "crowing lustily for tomorrow," provided the leitmotif for a collection with rooster-red coats (p. 104) and coxcomb hats. In the event that monarchies returned, there were toque hats reminiscent of those worn by Napoleon's Imperial Guards, gold franc buttons, and evening clothes of rich satins, velvets, and brocades in royal blue and imperial purple. For Republicans, practically designed clothes reflected the simplicity of modern life. Colored plastic zippers replaced buttons in some models (pp. 88–89), while hooks and eyes were not only functional but also decorative. For the Left, there was a radical change in the evening silhouette, with long skirts draped up to reveal narrow-legged pants in contrasting colors.

In November 1935 Schiaparelli was invited to participate in the first French trade fair in Moscow along with producers of French luxury goods, including the textile manufacturers Bianchini and Colcombet. The Soviet interest in fashion had been growing steadily, and in 1934 the Moscow House of Clothing Design had been established as their first "design house." The country's first fashion show had been held two years earlier, but the emphasis then had been on practicality rather than on style. In January 1934 the *New York Herald Tribune* reported that the communist youth paper had declared that the state clothing trust was ignoring the pleas of Soviet women for stylish dress. This was after several of the clothing models enthusiastically received by the audience of forty thousand at a Moscow fashion show were rejected for mass production in favor of older, "uglier" models that were easier to make. Schiaparelli was not the first foreign fashion designer to be invited to Moscow. The American designer Elizabeth Hawes had visited Soviet Russia earlier that year, in June, when she presented a showing of her personal wardrobe modeled by herself and an American girl she had met in Russia. At a meeting of the Fashion Group in New York in November, Hawes observed that despite having to wait six months for an appointment with a dressmaker, Russian women still tried to dress fashionably.

The organizers of the trade fair had difficulty persuading fashion designers to participate, but the trip to the Soviet Union appealed to Schiaparelli's sense of adventure, and she ended up as the sole representative of Paris couture. She traveled with her publicity assistant, Mrs. Hortense MacDonald, and with the English photographer Cecil Beaton, who unfortunately had visa problems and was forced to leave the train in Warsaw and follow them the next day. Schiaparelli lined her booth at the trade fair with her press-clippings-printed silk and covered the floor with another of her exclusives, Colcombet's black "treebark" crêpe, over which was laid a fan-shaped display of colorful international fashion magazines. On December 1 the Soviet government, intent on modernizing its textile and clothing industries, invited her to review a fashion show of Soviet-made garments. She was asked to critique the presentation and exhibit the ensemble she had shown at the trade fair, which she had designed especially for the Russian working woman and was presenting to the Soviet Sewing Trust as a gift. The design was based on the outfit that Schiaparelli and her saleswomen wore every day, a simple black wool dress. The Soviet version zipped up one side and was worn with a white linen collar (detachable so that it could be cleaned or replaced) and a tasseled leather belt (p. 92, center). The ensemble included a "turncoat" wool felt jacket—black for day, reversing to vivid scarlet at night. In place of a handbag, a black crocheted hat concealed a pocket at the top that closed with a zipper trimmed with a red tassel. Although the audience liked the dress, the hat was unanimously rejected as too great a temptation to pickpockets, especially on crowded public transport. For the occasion Schiaparelli wore a simple tweed suit and a sky-blue scarf printed with the latest French hit songs, both her own designs. Following her visit the Moscow Technical Institute opened a branch in 1936 devoted to artistic clothing design and construction.

Schiaparelli returned from the Soviet Union with a pair of Russian white felt boots amid speculation that her next collection would be inspired by her visit. The trip had no apparent influence on her designs, however, with the exception of the silhouette she presented in February for summer 1936, which was inspired by Russian parachute jumpers, with small-shouldered bodices and skirts that swelled from the waist to the hem and drifted as one walked (p. 92, left). Even that inspiration was not entirely new, though, for several of the designer's earlier collections had explored the parachute theme in tiered capes, collars, and sleeves. Schiaparelli's summer 1936 collection also included many early- and mid-nineteenth-century references—a return to empires gained and lost—including extremely high waistlines, Victorian bouquets, dust-ruffle hems, and bowler hats.

Controversy over Schiaparelli's Soviet trip and negative allusions to her political sympathies were fueled by the marriage of her sales assistant Bettina Jones to Gaston Bergery, a former communist party deputy, leader of the *Front Social*, and creator of the *Front Commun*. Paris's conservative right-wing newspaper, *Je suis partout*, which was to become notorious for its anti-Semitic rhetoric during the Occupation, accused Schiaparelli of communist sympathies and directly attributed the visit to the urging of Bettina, continuing further with the assertion that Schiaparelli was closing her recently opened London salon for one in Moscow. In response, Hortense MacDonald fired off several letters demanding a retraction. The event turned out to be a foreshadowing of the unsubstantiated rumor and innuendo concerning Schiaparelli's politics and loyalties that were to follow her for years to come. Favorable comments on the couturière's visit to the Soviet Union were generally limited to the "Red" press in France and Great Britain, while the reaction in the United States was more neutral: the wire services simply described the clothes, and *Vogue* printed one of caricaturist Miguel Covarrubias's "Impossible Interviews," in which Schiaparelli and Stalin engage in an imaginary dialogue centering on women's natural desire to be fashionably dressed (p. 93).

Schiaparelli designed a special wardrobe for pioneering airwoman Amy Mollison (née Johnson) to wear on her solo flight in May 1936 from Gravesend, England, to Cape Town, South Africa, during which she established a new flight record. The extremes in climate she encountered required changes in clothing. For the first leg of the journey, Miss Mollison wore the outfit seen in this portrait—Schiaparelli's signature press-clippings blouse and a mist-proof blue woolen suit with a divided skirt; the ensemble also included a matching wool three-quarter-length topcoat. During a refueling stop on the northern edge of the Sahara she changed into a lighter cream silk toile suit, again with a divided skirt, and a blouse printed with a pattern of postage stamps. One of Schiaparelli's famous coarse mesh chenille snoods covered her hair during the journey. For evening, Miss Mollison brought along a high-waisted straight gown in heavy white crêpe embroidered with black sequins and a full-length black moiré cape with squared shoulders.

To celebrate the January 1, 1935, opening of her new salon at 21 Place Vendôme, Schiaparelli, inspired by the papiers collés of Pablo Picasso and Georges Braque, commissioned the textile manufacturer Colcombet to print fabric designed as a collage of her press clippings from American, English, Swedish, German, and French newspapers (above). Printed in both cotton and silk, the fabrics were made up into clothing and accessories, such as beach hats, small handbags, and men's neckties, one of which textile manufacturer Johan Colcombet wore onboard the ocean liner *Normandie* during her maiden voyage to the United States in May 1935, when he and artist-decorator Jean Dunand also wore lounging ensembles made up in the fabric. Fashion shows were presented *en voyage* and again in New York's harbor and included sixty special costumes designed by milliners and couturiers from the Association PAIS (Protection des industries artistiques saisonnières), including Schiaparelli.

Cecil Beaton, best known in the 1930s for his fashion photography and illustrations, was a frequent contributor to *Vogue*. He provided the magazine with this illustration titled *Fun at the Openings* (right), a sketch of a number of Schiaparelli's "fantasies," for its April 1935 issue. The editor gave instructions that Beaton's original sketch be blurred for engraving because, rather than reproducing the original words of Schiaparelli's press-clippings fabric, he had faked several of the notices. "Vogue wins Bérard, Loses Huene to enemy" is a reference to Christian Bérard having joined *Vogue* as an illustrator and the defection of *Vogue*'s photographer George Hoyningen-Huene to *Harper's Bazaar*. Even more controversial was Beaton's transformation of Schiaparelli's portrait in the original

printed textile to one of Hitler in his illustration, and his substitution of the original text with an anti-Semitic reference, the words "Dirty Jews" linked to "Mrs. Bloomingdale," who was Jewish. In January 1938 Beaton was fired from *Vogue* for inserting anti-Semitic words into his illustrations for Frank Crowinshield's article on New York society in the forthcoming February issue of the magazine (although he stated that his actions were misunderstood, his previous conduct casts doubt on these claims). Beaton was not the only one to appropriate Schiaparelli's press-notice print for his own means. The design was copied by an Italian manufacturer in 1936, with fascist propaganda substituted for the fashion commentary.

Victorian parasol of taffeta and ribbon; Altman

Schiaparelli thought up all the fantasies on this page

Big beads on a crêpe kerchief

A Tyrolian belt, bag, and short gloves; Bonwit Teller

An Easter-egg metal vanity and glass fan; Altman

Another fan of crumpled glass fabric on glass sticks; Altman

Beach hat of chintz printed like newspaper; Altman

Brevity-in gloves alternating strips of calf and Irish crochet

Tyrolian flowers on a box-calf belt

A newspaper chintz beach hat boosting Schiaparelli; Altman

Schiaparelli's black rayon draped gown for summer 1935 (left), with pink and yellow bead-embroidered borders, spirals around the body like an Indian sari. It was available in the United States at Bergdorf Goodman.

The legendary beauty of the Indian princess Karam of Kapurthala was captured by Cecil Beaton (above) for *Vogue*'s July 1935 issue, a year after her first visit to Paris in the summer of 1934, when at age fourteen she had entranced the city with her grace and charm. Schiaparelli drew on the memories of the young princess's exquisite saris to create an Indian-inspired collection in February 1935, in which slender evening gowns spiraling around the body were worn with scarves called *ihrams* that either draped over the head or were worn as loose shoulder panels.

In the photograph above, Nusch Eluard, wife of the Surrealist poet Paul Eluard, wears a Schiaparelli sari dress from the February 1935 showing of her "Stop, Look and Listen" collection. Man Ray took the photograph and radioed it to *Harper's Bazaar* just in time for it to appear in the March issue. The Indian-inspired gown was available in vivid blue or desert pink Ranee rayon crêpe and had a loose shoulder panel, or *ihram*, that could be worn over the head as

a veil. An enormous gold embossed clip held the fabric in place at the back of the waist. In the photograph Nusch holds one of Schiaparelli's frosted "glass" fans, made of the cellophane fabric Rhodophane; a gold egg-shaped vanity case on a gold leather thong dangles from her wrist. The same model was worn by José Laval, daughter of the French premier, and by actress Helen Vinson in the British Gaumont film *King of the Damned* (1936).

Schiaparelli was photographed by Roger Schall in one of her own designs, an Indian-influenced wrap of flame-colored faille striped in black and gold (above), also seen in the Bergdorf Goodman sketch on the right. She wore the "sari" coat to Madame Jacques Balsan's summer soirée, where three of Paris's best-dressed women appeared in identical Schiaparelli evening capes (p. 84).

7 c. 1937

One of the major social events of the 1935 Paris summer season was the Honorable Mrs. Reginald (Daisy) Fellowes's Oriental Ball, *Une Soirée chez le gouverneur*, which was attended by all the visiting maharajas and their wives, resplendent in turbans, saris, and magnificent jewels. Schiaparelli's designs were seen on many of the guests and combined the Indian theme of her February collection for summer 1935 with the Italian-primitive influences of the April showing for fall 1935. The hostess, photographed by Horst P. Horst for *Vogue*, August 1, 1935 (left), wore a blue-and-black lacquered wig by hairdresser Antoine with Schiaparelli's high-necked Chinese-style white satin gown that fastened down the front with heavy white silk soutache braid frogs. Real orchids caught up the back and sides of the gown, which opened to reveal harem-style satin trousers gathered at the ankle. Schiaparelli, photographed by Horst for the same issue (above), came dressed as an eighteenth-century Venetian page, wearing a turban extravagantly trimmed with brilliant blue-green, blue, and pink feathers, a cloth-of-gold coat, black silk stockings with a bright blue ribbon garter over her left knee, and red kid gloves. She carried a "blackamoor" mask mounted on a fan.

Such was the popularity of Schiaparelli's designs that in July 1935 three of Paris's best-dressed women wore her voluminous hooded "Venetian" evening cape (above) to a soirée given at the Interallied Club by Madame Jacques Balsan (the former Consuelo Vanderbilt) on the night of the Grand Prix. The cape, inspired by the *Exposition de l'art italien de Cimabue à Tiepolo* at the Petit Palais, which opened in May 1935, was made in a fabric exclusive to Schiaparelli, Bianchini's Simoun, a crumpled silk taffeta. Lady Mendl wore the green taffeta version over a pale rose evening dress, Daisy Fellowes appeared in vivid rose with a white gown, and Comtesse Gabrielle di Robilant wore the same rose cape but with a blue gown. Reflecting in 1974 on Schiaparelli's significance as a designer, the fashion writer Kathleen Cannell wryly observed in the *Christian Science Monitor* for February 25: "Schiaparelli . . . inaugurated the reign of what might be called democratic fashion. Hitherto, if two women met wearing identical costumes, hysterics, husbandly duels, and changes of couturiers ensued. But as many as four young women might foregather in the same Schiaparelli suit and they would good humouredly decide on which wearer displayed the greatest chic."

For Daisy Fellowes's Oriental Ball, Lady Mendl wore an evening gown of carbon-blue Ranee rayon crêpe (the Indian influence) with a matching "Italian primitive" scarf. Worn over the head and falling past the shoulders at the back and sides, the scarf was held in place by a cap of gold, coral, and turquoise beads. Alternatively, it could be worn as a cape, with the jeweled "cap" on one shoulder and the scarf draped over the arm. In the photograph by François Kollar at right, the ensemble is worn by an unidentified model.

In 1934 Schiaparelli launched three perfumes: Soucis, Salut, and Schiap. Soucis was described as subtle and discreet—ideal for bridge and cocktail parties. Schiap, tangy and bittersweet, was for sports; and Salut, clinging and suggestive of the Madonna lily, was for evening. Ilse Bing's early fashion photographs included work for French *Vogue* and *Harper's Bazaar.* In March 1934 she photographed five of Schiaparelli's latest designs for the Paris edition of the *New York Herald Tribune.* Her study at left, for the newly launched Salut perfume, was taken that same year but apparently never used for the advertising campaign. The trapezoidal Salut bottle and its cork box, both designed by Jean-Michel Frank, were photographed by Lusha Nelson (above) for the September issue of *Vogue.*

Schiaparelli's April 1935 showing for fall combined the previous season's Indian-inspired silhouettes with a new influence that drew on the early Italian paintings that were to be included in the enormous exhibition of Italian art at the Petit Palais, scheduled to open in May. The collection featured many new textured fabrics, from the deeply crinkled taffeta used for the long Venetian evening capes seemingly worn by all of Paris (p. 84) to the rustic hemplike weave of the evening gown at right, printed with Madonna lilies, the leitmotif of the designer's recently launched Salut perfume.

Schiaparelli shocked the buyers attending the August opening of her collection for winter 1935–36 by using colorful plastic zippers in the most unexpected places. They zipped pockets, necklines, side seams, sleeves, and shoulder seams and even served double duty on an evening gown that could be worn with the back zipped up for dinner or unzipped for a more formal occasion. In the black, white, and royal blue taffeta evening gown at left, a very visible black plastic zipper is used on the diagonal across the front of the draped skirt, emphasizing both the asymmetry of the neckline and the curves of the body. The dress was worn with the new hip-length, Victorian-inspired blouselike basque jacket with short vents in the front that fastened asymmetrically with a gilt fish for a button. The plastic zipper on the gown was made by the Japanese company YKK, founded early in 1934. Plastic zippers were a direct result of the expiration of the zipper patent. The Lightening Fastener Company of Great Britain began experimenting with plastic in place of metal in zippers in 1932. In 1933 Harry Houghton of their Canadian division offered Schiaparelli $10,000 to use their zippers in her clothing. Schiaparelli used Lightening plastic zippers for the collections shown in her London salon, Éclair plastic zippers for her Paris collections, and Hookless Fastener Company (Talon) zippers from Meadville, Pennsylvania, for models made in or exported to the United States. According to Schiaparelli, the shipment of the winter collection to the United States was held up by an agreement between France and the United States on the importation of foreign-made zippers. Although the situation was resolved and the collection allowed into the United States, the Tariff Commission in July 1936 announced a significant increase in the duty on zipper imports, from forty-five percent *ad valorem* to sixty-six percent. As a result, garments destined for the American market often incorporated American-made zippers.

In this film still from the British motion picture *I'd Give My Life* (1936), the new plastic Lightening Fastener zipper closes the front of a wool jersey dress by Schiaparelli, worn by actress Frances Drake, seen here with Guy Standing. The couturiers Charles Creed, Jeanne Lanvin, Edward Molyneux, and Victor Stiebel also contributed to the star's film wardrobe, which was copied and marketed in the "Frances Drake Fashion Campaign" at the cinema shops and Hollywood fashion shops of the London branch of the Modern Merchandising Bureau.

The heavy, dark purple, ottoman silk evening dress with deep back décolleté at left has rose and navy moiré taffeta dramatically swooping into long drapes down the back of the skirt. A label inside the dress reads "hiver 1935–36," but the design was actually included in the October 1935 presentation for spring 1936, when it was shown in black draped with rose and black. It is likely that the private client for whom the dress was made purchased it before the new collection was officially presented to trade buyers, and so it was given the current season's designation— winter 1935–36. The dress's back panels are a further elaboration of the aerodynamic silhouettes that Schiaparelli had been showing in 1934, although by now the form had become more restrained. The dark purple color is in keeping with the Royalist and Republican themes of her winter collection.

For the Maurice Chevalier film *Le Vagabond bien-aimé*, or *The Beloved Vagabond* (1936), Schiaparelli designed five ensembles for Joanna Rushworth, played by Betty Stockfeld, and two for Blanquette, played by Hélène Robert in the French version of the film and Margaret Lockwood in the English version. The costumes were made in London at Schiaparelli's Upper Grosvenor Street ateliers. In the film still above (left), Betty Stockfeld wears a pink organdy skirt and a matching jacket with short, full, leg-of-mutton-style sleeves. Miss Stockfeld's outfit is accessorized with blue suede elbow-length gloves and a straw leghorn hat trimmed

with cornflowers, poppies, and daisies. She carries a pink organdy ruffled parasol similar in design to the Victorian-inspired parasols Schiaparelli included in her summer 1935 collection. One of the evening gowns worn in the film, made up in green satin, was adapted for the summer 1936 collection in pink satin with can-can net ruffles at the hem. It is seen above in a multiply exposed Man Ray photograph for *Harper's Bazaar*. Curiously, Betty Stockfeld was immortalized by Salvador Dalí in his 1939 gouache, *Actress Betty Stockfeld Is Metamorphosed into a Nurse,* on the cover of the magazine *Pour vous.*

Schiaparelli's new silhouette for her summer 1936 collection was a salute to the Russian parachute jumpers she had watched during her visit to the Soviet Union several months earlier. She had found inspiration in the parachute before, in her August 1934 collection, when it influenced the broadly layered shoulders of her coats. This time she adapted it to the entire silhouette, which swelled from waist to hem, the godet seams in the skirt giving it the effect of an opening parachute. In the house sketch above, the black rayon sleeveless dinner dress is worn with a sheer black blouse and a blue linen jacket decorated with fronds of black braid and three large black buttons. The ensemble was also available with a white linen jacket, a combination worn by the French film star Annabella, who had been a client of Schiaparelli's since 1933 (she would marry Tyrone Power in 1939).

At the first French trade fair to be held in the Soviet Union, in November 1935, Schiaparelli was the sole representative of the French couture. She had been asked to design a chic but practical outfit for the Russian working woman that could be worn from morning till night. The result, which she brought with her on the trip, was a variation of the dress she and her saleswomen wore; it can be seen on the head *vendeuse* of her hat salon in the photograph at upper right. Schiaparelli's Soviet design, shown directly above, consisted of a plain, black, lightweight wool dress with a simple detachable linen collar and a leather belt. It was worn with a three-quarter-length wool "turncoat" that reversed from black for day to vivid red for evening; the screw-on buttons could be attached to either side. The crocheted cap contained a concealed pocket in the crown that closed with a tassel-trimmed zipper.

The celebrated caricatures of the Mexican artist Miguel Covarrubias included the "Impossible Interview" between Stalin and Schiaparelli at right, published in *Vogue* on June 15, 1936, after Schiaparelli's controversial trip to Russia in November 1935 as part of a French trade delegation. The caption under the cartoon read: "Stalin: Can't you leave our women alone? Schiaparelli: They don't want to be left alone. They want to look like the other women of the world. Stalin: What! Like those hip-less, bust-less scarecrows of your dying civilizations? . . . You underestimate the serious goals of Soviet women. Schiaparelli: You underestimate their natural vanity. Stalin: Perhaps I had better cut your parachute down! Schiaparelli: A hundred other couturiers would replace me. Stalin: In that case, cut my ropes!"

COVARRUBIAS

Schiaparelli's shirttail coat for 1936 was the most talked-about model of her midseason collection. Made up in white flannel, the short, youthfully casual coat swung out from the shoulders and was cut exactly like a man's shirt, with the same type of tailored small collar and front closing but with slightly fuller sleeves above a fitted cuff. Buyers predicted that, like Chanel's little black dress, it would become the "Ford" for spring. The model in the photograph by Cecil Beaton at left wears it with a straw hat with mica visor and a white silk dress. Beaton relates the circumstances under which he took this picture, a milestone in the history of fashion photography, in his 1951 *Photobiography* (where he incorrectly dates the series of photographs of which it forms part to 1937; the series appeared in the January 1936 issue of *Vogue*): "I discovered in the Champs Elysées an office building under construction. The workmen had unconsciously created a fantastic décor of cement sacks, mountains of mortar, bricks, and half-finished walls. Mannequins nonchalantly reading newspapers or idling elegantly in this incongruous debris created an extraordinary effect. The results were received with much hesitation by the magazine editors, and instead of being published, as had originally been planned, on six pages, they appeared, somewhat shamefacedly, squashed together on two pages with a trick layout. Nevertheless, even today New York fashion photographers are still searching for corners of desolation and decay, for peeling walls, scabrous billboardings, and rubble to serve as a background for the latest and most expensive dresses."

Schiaparelli's bowler hats, said to have been inspired by the trademark brown derby worn by the legendary Irish-American politician Al Smith, were the sensation of her spring 1936 showing. They were eagerly snapped up by American buyers, a number of whom returned to New York wearing the black version tied with a colored veil. In this photograph by Man Ray for the March 1936 issue of *Harper's Bazaar* (above), the hat is worn with Schiaparelli's pink plaid wool jacket and straight black wool skirt. Macy's sold a copy of the original hat, available in eight exciting colors, in their lower-priced millinery department for just $2.77 (the original model having cost the store $50.77); the department stores Franklin Simon's and Arnold Constable & Co. offered their own version for $5.75. The hat was originally designed for the Duchess of Kent, who, still in mourning for the late King George, wore the designer's black felt bowler with one of her three-piece suits and a silver fox scarf while traveling to Belgrade to spend a holiday with Prince Paul and Princess Olga of Yugoslavia.

Schiaparelli's winter 1936–37 collection featured her youthful Surrealist suits, including those with bureau-drawer pockets designed in collaboration with Salvador Dalí. The novel buttons and pockets of this suit from the same collection (right), vaguely lip shaped, foreshadow the Surrealist suit with similar pockets embroidered in the shape of actual lips that Schiaparelli included in her winter collection the following year. The suit has a dark brown velvet skirt and a purple tweed jacket with brown velvet collar and insets at the top of the pockets. Two large brown leather buttons close the front of the jacket. The suit was available from both Bergdorf Goodman and Lord & Taylor, whose label is affixed to this example, next to the original "Schiaparelli Paris" label. New York wholesaler Wm. H. Davidow Sons Co. also purchased the design. Davidow, the first American company to offer Schiaparelli's sweaters wholesale, continued to buy the couturière's day and sports clothes until she closed her salon, selling them to retailers as direct copies of the original models and as adaptations.

Schiaparelli was photographed arriving in New York on the S.S. *Europa* en route to the West Indies (above). She wore an unclipped beaver coat and Cossack hat over a suit of carbon-blue tweed with a tan over-check, a ribbed blue sweater (which matched her brilliant blue mascara), and an orange taffeta scarf. A huge hexagonal topaz pin set in a gold frame was pinned to the lapel of the suit, and she wore a matching topaz ring. In an interview she gave to the *New York Times* on December 4, 1936, she declared that during her brief stay in the city she planned "to spend four weeks indulging herself in a shopping spree in American stores," especially the five-and-tens, which she said gave her thrills. She advised every woman to have as few clothes as possible, concentrating on quality rather than quantity. According to her, the ideal wardrobe should include one fur coat, one tweed suit, a dark tailored suit, a silk dress for afternoon wear, at least four hats or as many as one could afford, six pairs of shoes, and as many accessories as were necessary. Her one word of advice to the American woman was always to take a man along when she shopped, "because men love simplicity, and that type is always the smartest."

Many of Schiaparelli's hats were distinguished by their dramatic sculpted shapes, as can be seen in the models shown on these two pages. The creativity of French milliners and other hat designers was underscored in a decision by the Cour d'Appel de Paris (Paris Court of Appeals) in 1934, which declared a woman's hat a work of art and therefore protected by copyright. As reported in *Women's Wear Daily* on July 31, 1934, the decision included this statement: "It cannot be denied that hats designed by fashion houses are inspired by the same science of form, volume, line and color which is the basis of painting and sculpture. Such hats are unquestionably true creations of the artistic mind." Prior to setting up her own millinery salon in summer 1934 with Madame Marcelle as the *modéliste*, Schiaparelli had her hats

made by the same group of Armenian knitters that supplied the house with sweaters, as well as by two of Paris's leading milliners, Suzanne Talbot and Madame Agnès, whose designs were in the vanguard of modern fashion. Among the first hats shown in the newly formed department were velvet berets. Variations on this classic French form, a perennial favorite, included the narrow up-tilted felt beret on the right,

for winter 1937–38. The mahogany brown felt tricorn hat from the same collection, on the left, called "His Honor," was inspired by the hat worn by the Lord Mayor of London as he drove through Paris to the opening of the British Pavilion at the *Exposition internationale des arts et techniques dans la vie moderne* held in Paris in 1937.

After Dark

During the 1920s the social life of Paris was dominated by Americans and other members of the international set. Some kept suites all year round at the Ritz Hôtel, others at the Claridge, the Crillon, or the Majestic. They had cocktails at the Ritz or at Henry's, dined at Ciro's or Delmonico's, and frequented the nightclubs and jazz clubs in Montmartre and the Latin Quarter. They shopped on the rue de la Paix and attended the races at Longchamp. But with the stock market crash of 1929 and the ensuing Depression, Americans retrenched, and Paris was left once again to the Parisians. One result was that the city became quieter and more sedate. *Women's Wear Daily* observed in February 1931 that "the Paris of the lively can-can has become the Paris of the cloister." During the city's "Americanization," its French residents had entertained mostly at home. In the new, more subdued atmosphere they reemerged at little restaurants, galas, charity events, and fancy dress balls, a trend that was to continue throughout the 1930s. *Vogue* reported in February 1932 that the social routine now began late in the afternoon with a six o'clock cocktail party, continued with dinner at a small restaurant and then a visit to the cinema (which had replaced the theater as the entertainment of choice), and ended late in the evening at a nightclub in Montparnasse or Montmartre. The city's newspapers and magazines applauded the effort to restore Paris to the Parisians and supplied detailed accounts of who was wearing what (when and where), a subject that previously had been of little interest to the French press but that now helped to ensure that Paris would remain the supreme arbiter of taste and continue to set the styles despite the depressed economic climate. The smartly dressed French woman, rather than the model shown to the trade, would now introduce the latest trends.

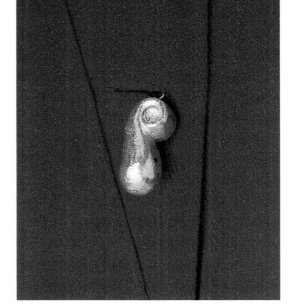

The changing social life was reflected in fashion, with the evening pajamas worn at home for entertaining replaced by more formal dinner and evening gowns. Early in 1932 *Vogue* noted that by June of the previous year Paris had "dropped elegance for chic . . . it is chic without being obviously elegant—a way of dressing life as it is being lived today." In contrast to the more casual approach to formal dressing in the United States, Parisians distinguished between dinner clothes and formal evening clothes. According to a radio interview in 1934 with Alice Perkins, the Paris fashion editor for *Women's Wear Daily*: "In Paris, a dinner means dinner clothes and a ball means ballroom ones. In Paris, at the less formal evening functions they carry over the tailored silhouette of their daytime clothes, but do it in exciting fabrics. The dresses are slim and slinky with low backs hidden under jackets, but they are made of metal cloths or shiny satins or embroidered with sequins. This sort of costume is worn with a hat, usually a tiny one that need not be taken off in the theatre, such as a cap of sequins or a turban of metal cloth."

Although Schiaparelli had made her name in sports and day clothes, she was quick to adapt to new trends and seemingly fearless when it came to trying new things. Her first foray into evening wear was a toga-like satin evening wrap included in her collections for 1928 (copied by Saks Fifth Avenue in fur), but it was not until 1930 that she added evening gowns to her models. Her first design was a long, black, ciré satin dress with a high waistline that wrapped around the figure and tied with a bow at the side (opposite). The second, shown in May for fall 1930 (p. 38), was a design that she described in her autobiography as her most copied: "It was the first evening dress with a jacket and created a turmoil in the fashion world—a plain black sheath of crêpe de Chine down to the ground, with a white crêpe de Chine jacket with long sashes that crossed in the back but tied in front. Stark simplicity. That was what was needed. This proved the most successful dress of my career. It was reproduced all over the world. I made another of the same type, but this time the sash did not cross but merely tied and ended with a bunch of cock feathers." Other designs for 1930 included an evening gown of black and white reversible satin and another of black sequins. In 1931 the bicolored gown emerged as the latest trend. Schiaparelli's version, in rayon, was painted by the decorative artist Jean Dunand in shades of black and gray to resemble pleats and was worn by the designer with a waist-length wrap of white coq feathers to the reopening of the new ultramodern restaurant Les Ambassadeurs in the Hôtel de Crillon (pp. 43–44). For winter 1931–32 she designed dresses with long trains that could be draped around the body and caught up at the waist for dancing, a silhouette that foreshadowed her sari dresses for 1935–36.

During the summer of 1932 Schiaparelli, an inveterate partygoer, attended the *Bal blanc*, or White Ball, held in the former quarters of the Sporting Club off the Champs Elysées. Attended by a thousand guests, it was organized by six of the elite young men of Paris society—a prince, a viscount, three counts, and a baron—earning it the alternate designation *Bal des gigolos*. Everyone and everything at the ball was white, from the guests' evening wear to the dress of the waiters and gypsy musicians to the floral decorations. Only champagne was served. For the event, Schiaparelli designed an ankle-length gown for herself in white ciré peu d'ange jersey, a matte fabric she had launched in her midseason collection and that had been praised by the fashion press as a refreshing change from the usual satin for evening (pp. 46–47). The gown was in the form of the type of apron used for gardening, with straps tying at the back and two pockets at the front. It was worn over an underdress and was accessorized with a necklace of white coq feathers, a chic departure from the standard ermine evening wrap. More innovations were apparent the following season, in her winter 1932–33 collection, shown in August 1932. The evening wear included her "speakeasy" silhouette, with the fullness at the back extending into a pleated shelf that ostensibly provided space for hiding a flask (p. 57), a form that would develop into the bustle dress in 1939. By September 1934 the *New Yorker* was praising Schiaparelli for "making some of the most adroitly cut and luxurious evening gowns in Paris." She had successfully managed the move from sports to full-fledged acceptance as one of the premier designers of evening wear.

Schiaparelli's success in the depressed couture market of the 1930s is notable and can be attributed not just to her innovative designs but also to her marketing savvy. The worldwide effect of the stock market crash hit the couture fairly hard. In 1931 exports of French apparel and lingerie to the United States were down fifty percent from the previous year. The haute couture adapted itself to the new conditions by showing fewer models and cutting prices. Some houses were forced to restructure their finances or went into bankruptcy while others amalgamated and combined enterprises. Mary Nowitzky, for example, who was credited with launching the vogue for sports and evening pajamas, found herself in financial difficulty and in early 1932 was granted a two-year extension on her indebtedness in order to pay back her creditors. Smaller establishments and lesser-known couturiers, such as Schiaparelli, whose designs were fresh and original, had an advantage over the houses with international reputations because they had lower overheads and fewer restrictions on their creativity, and they were also better able to meet deliveries to trade buyers because of their smaller orders. Schiaparelli's growth and financial stability during the Depression were also ensured, at least in part, by her willingness to work with American manufacturers in creating models from their fabrics for advertising purposes, and also by her endorsement of other American-made products, such as shoes and hosiery, which she used in her Paris collections. In this way the manufacturers were able to add a bit of luster and prestige to the marketing of their goods at home, thereby helping their own sales, while at the same time Schiaparelli was able to widen her markets.

The expansion of Schiaparelli's establishment and its relocation to the Place Vendôme in 1935 prompted many more design innovations for evening, in keeping with her move around this time toward thematic collections. Among her new designs were dramatic "Venetian" hooded capes of crinkled taffeta and simply cut woolen coats, some of which were starkly plain while others had brightly colored linings and lapels embroidered with sequins and beads. Schiaparelli's most significant contributions to evening gowns in the late 1930s were her waltz-length dresses—introduced in 1937 in response to the renewed popularity of the waltz, which was then replacing the rumba and swing—and her two-piece evening ensembles that emphasized an hourglass figure. The form of the latter owed much to the influence of the actress Mae West, who had enthralled Paris as Lady Lou in the 1933 movie *She Done Him Wrong*. The showing of the film coincided with the Louvre's exhibition *Décor de la vie 1870 à 1900* (or Design for Living, 1870 to 1900), leading *New Yorker* columnist Janet Flanner to refer to these as the "two period furniture hits in Paris." Miss West's influence on fashion was to culminate in the costumes Schiaparelli designed for her to wear in the film *Every Day's a Holiday* in 1937; in the bottle design by Léonor Fini for Schiaparelli's signature fragrance, Shocking, which took the form of a dressmaker's dummy with Mae West curves; and in the bustle dresses Schiaparelli designed for the ball marking the fiftieth anniversary of the Eiffel Tower in 1939. But the silhouettes that were to have the most significant impact on evening fashions were the ensembles Schiaparelli referred to as "Exposition dinner costumes," designed to be worn to the many restaurants at the 1937 *Exposition internationale des arts et techniques dans la vie moderne* held in Paris. The ensembles featured fitted embroidered jackets worn over long gowns with deep back décolletage and were accessorized with large, dramatic hats (p. 113). These were seen at every nightclub, restaurant, and party that season.

Bettina Jones (later Bergery), Schiaparelli's assistant and window dresser, was photographed wearing the designer's first evening dress to the fashionable Paris nightspot Florence's in January 1930 (p. 100). Taken by George Hoyningen-Huene, the photograph appeared in the March 1930 issue of *Vogue*. That same month Schiaparelli was pictured in the *Ladies' Home Journal* wearing the gown, in a photograph accompanying an article she wrote on aviation fashions, titled "Smartness Aloft." The lustrous black ciré satin floor-length draped gown wrapped around the body and tied with a bow at the side of its high waistline. Its deep V-shaped décolletage, dipping to the waist at the back, was to become a signature feature of Schiaparelli's evening dresses. The design derived from a black-and-white printed pinafore-style day dress and matching jacket that the couturière had shown in October 1929.

Schiaparelli's evening clothes were often embellished with elaborate embroidery or distinctive fastenings. The gold buttons on page 101, shaped like escargots, embellished an otherwise plain red wool coat for evening. Schiaparelli was known for her unique buttons, many of which were individually handcrafted by Jean Clement and Roger Jean-Pierre.

In her evening wear Schiaparelli found an outlet for yet another aspect of her creativity. Unlike her sports and day clothes, her evening fashions were often deliberately provocative, exhibiting a subtle or sometimes blatant sexuality. The designer clearly enjoyed being "shocking," as her choice of the word for her signature fragrance and her new color pink attest. But while her early sportswear designs like the trouser skirt challenged contemporary mores and conventions, her evening wear had an almost aggressive seductiveness that stood in sharp contrast to the somewhat masculine quality that characterized the "hard chic" of her daytime clothes. She played with notions of concealment and exposure. Her evening jackets typically covered deep back décolletage. A gown from her winter 1937–38 collection hugged the body so tightly that it required a slit up the front so the wearer could move, revealing the leg with every step (p. 118). Her bolero jackets and her evening gowns with padded brassieres built into bodices stressed the importance of the bust, just as her bustle dresses emphasized the buttocks. Her accentuations of the female body coincided with the "surreal" dresses that Salvador Dalí claimed, in *The Secret Life of Salvador Dalí*, to have invented, "with false insets and anatomical paddings calculatingly and strategically disposed in such a way as to create a type of feminine beauty corresponding to man's erotic imagination." Schiaparelli collaborated with Dalí and a number of other artists during the mid- and late 1930s and also created her own Dada- and Surrealist-inspired designs, challenging sensibilities in still other ways.

Wool evening coats and capes, particularly in bright reds, were featured by all the leading couturiers during August 1935, breaking with the tradition of employing wool for morning, silk for afternoon, and brocade or velvet for evening. The hit of the season, in keeping with the military theme of the collections, was Schiaparelli's impeccably tailored floor-length coat made up in Ducharne's vivid *rouge gaulois* (left), a thick wool twill similar to the cloth used for British Horse Guards' uniforms. The gold snail-shaped buttons give the regimentally correct silhouette a touch of whimsy.

The new silhouette for the winter 1937–38 couture collections continued the trend away from the exaggerated lines of previous seasons to clean lines that followed the curves of the body. The new emphasis on a simple silhouette demanded rich detailing in embroideries and fabrics. Schiaparelli's models were embellished with lavish gold embroideries and striking metallic fabrics. Among her more distinctive designs was a long, elegant, purple wool tunic-length jacket with a mandarin collar, shown here at right and in the house sketch above. The ensemble, characterized by *Vogue* as a "Persian Prince dinner-suit," is embroidered with thick gold metal strips à la Louis XV and closes with brightly colored engraved metal buttons that look like the gold-framed bases on the seals of Victorian watch chains.

Schiaparelli's collection for spring 1937 was heralded by *Women's Wear Daily* on October 28, 1936, as "brand new . . . brilliant and optimistic." Among the eighty-some models presented, the long evening capes, with their military style and attention to detail, reigned triumphant. On the dark navy wool sentry cape shown at left and in a photograph by Man Ray above, two gold ingots connect to fasten the neck, while a broad band of red taffeta is embroidered with strips and coils of gold plate to form a chevron across the front. Schiaparelli brought this cape on her trip to New York in December 1936 for a month-long vacation.

The wool evening coats presented in August 1936 for winter 1936–37 were enthusiastically received by the press, trade buyers, and private clients. One of the season's outstanding successes was the long nubby black Linton tweed design at right. It is lined in sapphire blue taffeta, and its revers are lavishly covered in matching blue oversize sequins. Beautifully cut, the coat is fitted to the waist, with the six gores at the back extending from the neck to the barely flared hem. The buttonless coat opened to reveal a slim, molded evening dress in lamé or satin. Daisy Fellowes wore the coat over a sapphire blue gown to the premiere of Edouard Bourdet's new play *Fric-Frac*, starring another Schiaparelli client, Arletty, at the Théâtre de La Michodiere on October 16, 1936.

In 1935 Persia changed its name to Iran, and Emperor
Reza Shah Pahlavi, in an effort to unify the country's
diverse populations, imposed European dress on his
subjects, including abolishing the wearing of the veil.
Schiaparelli responded by adding a few Persian-inspired
designs to her collections over the next few seasons.
The black wool evening cape seen on these two pages,
shown in October 1936 for spring 1937, is lined in
"Parlor" pink taffeta, which is also used to define
the large Persian *boteh* (paisley shape) on each
shoulder, densely embroidered with magenta crinkled-
glass flowers and leaves and strips of pink and gold
plate. The model was perfect for "a thousand and one
nights," especially for evenings at the Scheherazade
restaurant at the Paris exposition. The cape appeared
on the cover of *Jardin des Modes* for February 1937
and was photographed again in 1950 for another
fashion magazine, *L'Album du Figaro*, by Henry Clarke.
In Clarke's photograph (not illustrated) the model
Bettina Bergery stands in front of Salvador Dalí's
painting *Necrophiliac Springtime* from 1936, which was
owned by Schiaparelli (p. 139, top). Bettina is posed
with her head down, eyes closed, and hands crossed
over the front of the cape, reproducing the feeling of
a drawing Jean Cocteau made of the same cape for the
July 1937 issue of *Harper's Bazaar*.

One of the most talked-about fashions for summer 1937 was Schiaparelli's short, belled evening dress. Heralded as a brand new silhouette, it set a new fashion in skirt lengths, which were raised eight to ten inches from the floor. One model, also available in cotton, featured multicolored butterflies on sheer, pale pink silk organza (pp. 154–55). Another model was available in white silk crêpe de chine printed with a garland of pink roses laid over narrow stripes of blue and white in a manner reminiscent of bars of music (left), and was seen at society hostess Elsa Maxwell's Red, White, and Blue Ball. The flaring, circular, ballerina-length skirt was held out with starched petticoats, and the bodice had short, slightly puffed sleeves and an appliqué of pink roses at the neckline. The fuller skirt emphasized a narrow waist that was cinched with a "glass" belt painted blue. In the photograph at left, the gown is worn with high-heeled slippers made by André Perugia, who made many of Schiaparelli's boots and shoes. The dress was sold through Bonwit Teller's Salon de Couture and, as with all custom designs, could be altered according to the client's wishes (in one version, a longer skirt and no sleeves). Macy's presented three identical Schiaparelli waltz-length dresses at their "Importants of Paris" fashion show, in which the young models danced to the "Blue Danube Waltz" with three young men dressed in formal evening attire. The show's commentator noted that the waltz was resurfacing as the favorite dance in Europe, supplanting the rumba and swing in popularity.

In late 1936 Schiaparelli created cotton and silk novelty prints for the American market and sold them to manufacturers of fine fashions and to the fabric departments of better stores. The cotton prints were distributed exclusively by the manufacturer Everfast, while the fourteen silk crêpe novelty prints were exclusive to Drucker-Wolf, Inc. Among the designs were Schiaparelli's own initials, butterflies, and images of motion picture stars on strips of film. The example seen here, "Paris Exposition 1937," is printed with the stylized silhouettes of well-known Paris landmarks, including the Eiffel Tower and the Arc de Triomphe. The silk fabrics were immediately the subject of a suit by Drucker-Wolf against its printer, William Willheim Co., Inc., who at the height of the season, it was claimed, sold a quantity of defective silks to another company at a lower price. This company then offered the silks to Drucker-Wolf's customers at half the price, thereby destroying Drucker-Wolf's reputation and business relationships and rendering their exclusive contract worthless.

Glamorous evening clothes marked Schiaparelli's spring showing of her fall 1937 collection. Her long, narrow evening silhouettes, called "Paris 1937," were designed with the forthcoming Paris exposition in mind. The dresses featured floor-length skirts and low-cut bodices hidden under fitted jackets. These were worn with dramatic flaring "Merry Widow" hats with wide brims turned away from the face, a style originally made famous in 1907 by the actress Lily Elsie in Franz Lehár's opera *Merry Widow*. Schiaparelli's version was trimmed with metal ornaments resembling feathers rather than with real feathers as in the original. In this photograph by André Durst for the June 1937 issue of *Vogue* (right), a black rayon crêpe dress and jacket is worn with a large black straw hat, while a white rayon jersey dress draped across the front is worn with a long, glittering embroidered jacket and a white panama hat trimmed with golden wings. The oversize mesh bag was designed by Schiaparelli for the American firm Whiting Davis Co., which had been making similar metal mesh bags since the late 1800s. Several of these ensembles were seen at Longchamp in July 1937 during the night racing events.

The *Pavillon de l'Elégance* at the 1937 *Exposition internationale des arts et techniques dans la vie moderne* in Paris attracted considerable attention with its nearly seven-foot-tall pinkish beige plaster mannequins. Made by Siégel of Paris, the mannequins, designed by a noted sculptor with the apt name of Robert Couturier, provided a dramatic background for the works of French couture. This photograph by German photographer and artist Wolfgang Otto Schulze (known as Wols) of one of the displays shows Schiaparelli's controversial installation to the right. Displaying her genius for publicity, she defied the expectations of the display committee headed by couturière Jeanne Lanvin. Instead of harmonizing with the other displays in the pavilion, she iconoclastically

chose to leave her mannequin undressed, covering the single, bare reclining figure with a blanket of flowers much as one would drape a coffin (prompting someone on opening day to drop a condolence card on the display). The installation was modified after the opening, with the nude mannequin placed on top of the bed of flowers holding a pair of gloves in its exaggeratedly large hands. A floppy straw hat lay nearby, while a printed dress and a pair of beach sandals hung from a clothesline stretched between trees. Schiaparelli's recently launched perfume, Shocking, was also displayed. The perfume was presented as a large replica in synthetic glass lightly tinted pink, within which were real bottles of the designer's other perfumes.

The photograph at left shows the original window display in Schiaparelli's salon on the Place Vendôme for her best-known fragrance, Shocking, introduced in 1937 (almost all her perfumes began with the letter *S*). The bottle, designed by Surrealist artist Léonor Fini in 1936, was based on the form of a dressmaker's dummy. A "tape measure" around the neck crossed the bottle in the front and fastened at the "waist" with a button monogrammed with the initial *S*, and the stopper was surrounded with a bouquet of small pastel-colored porcelain flowers. The entire bottle was encased in a Victorian-style glass dome. Around the time she was creating the perfume, Schiaparelli was designing costumes for Mae West's film *Every Day's a Holiday*, and the shape of the bottle was inspired by the actress's hourglass figure.

The "Paris 1937" look was influenced by the costumes Schiaparelli had recently designed for Mae West's new movie, *Every Day's a Holiday*, and the costumes in the film were inspired in turn by the fashions of 1900 (the movie's opening scene takes place on the night of December 31, 1899). Miss West had requested that Schiaparelli make her costumes, but she never came to Paris for her fittings, instead sending a plaster form of her figure. Schiaparelli reports in her autobiography that the daytime costume seen in the publicity photograph above was originally designed in lilac broadcloth with the edges outlined in pink and mauve cording. The wardrobe department at Paramount Studios was forced to modify the designs because the star had gained weight. According to an article in the magazine *Photoplay* in

1941, "The Truth about Stars' Figures," neither a corset nor the design of the costumes could conceal Mae West's increased size. In response, the studio made sure that as often as possible she was seen sitting, reclining, or standing completely still while the other actors moved around her. The actress was filmed against dark backgrounds, and Schiaparelli's costumes were remade in darker colors for the black-and-white film so that West's silhouette would fade into the surroundings. The original pink and mauve color scheme was changed to this violet woolen street dress with gold and cream satin used for the epaulets at the shoulders, around the neckline, and down one side of the front from the neck to the hem. Gold and cream satins were also used to trim the handbag. The hat was violet satin with matching ostrich feathers.

The Edwardian-style cape that Schiaparelli designed for Mae West to wear in the movie *Every Day's a Holiday* (right) inspired the flounced tulle evening capes she included in her April 1937 showing. One of the season's outstanding successes, they were seen everywhere that summer. Mrs. Harrison Williams (later Countess Mona Bismarck) ordered hers in pale mauve, and another was spotted at the opening of the restaurant Les Ambassadeurs in the Hôtel de Crillon. In the photograph by John Phillips above, an artist from one of the fashion magazines sketches a mannequin in the ensemble at Schiaparelli's salon. In the background, to the left, is an ashtray with a spiral base and, on the mantel, a vase; both were designed by the artist Alberto Giacometti.

The new molded silhouette introduced by the Paris couture in August 1937 for winter 1937–38 was made possible by a long-line corset with a high bust. The form was echoed in dressmaking details that outlined the bust, a modern interpretation of the Directoire-inspired styles that dominated many of the fashions of the time. Schiaparelli's "brassiere" evening gown, seen in the fashion photograph at left, was a figure-hugging satin sheath in her new color "Sultry" rose (a cyclamen color lighter than Shocking pink). The gown is slit up the front to the knee, revealing a high-heeled open-toed pump with satin ties crisscrossing up the leg. Its long train also has a slit that allowed it to be held looped on the wrist to facilitate walking. In its review of the high points of the season's collections, the September issue of British *Vogue* commented that sex appeal was no longer a matter of subtle suggestion, particularly if one wore Schiaparelli's dress with its built-in "uplift" brassiere.

In Jean Cocteau's play *Les Monstres sacrés* (The Holy Terrors), which premiered at the Théâtre Michel on February 17, 1940, actress Jany Holt played a modern young woman. In the photograph above, taken by Man Ray for *Harper's Bazaar*, April 1940, she wears Schiaparelli's white crêpe full-skirted evening gown belted with shiny green leaves, with the same leaves adorning her hair. The sets for the play were designed by Christian Bérard in daring combinations of red that dramatically contrasted with both the white gown and the other costumes Schiaparelli supplied—black satin pajamas with an embroidered jacket and a dress printed with enormous roses on a black background.

Art into Fashion, Fashion into Art

Schiaparelli's famous collaborations with the artists Salvador Dalí and Jean Cocteau during the late 1930s changed the face of fashion. No longer was a dress merely a dress or a hat just a hat. Dalí's Surrealist painting *Anthropomorphic Cabinet* was revisited as the drawer-like pockets on a Schiaparelli suit (p. 133), while Cocteau's genius for expressing form with a single line revealed itself as a woman's face embroidered on one of her dinner jackets (p. 141). These garments became Surrealist objects themselves, a natural development given the innovations that regularly appeared in Schiaparelli's designs. With her daring originality and her understanding of the Surrealist ethos, Schiaparelli epitomized the artist-couturier. She was able to transform the ordinary and mundane into the strangely beautiful and contradictory. Her clothing and accessories were often outrageous and even shocking in their inventiveness, and the women who wore them became surreal apparitions, bringing to life one of the principles of the first Surrealist manifesto, written by André Breton in 1924: "The marvellous is always beautiful, anything marvellous is beautiful; indeed, nothing but the marvellous is beautiful." Dalí was one of the first to acknowledge Schiaparelli's influence. Writing in his book *The Secret Life of Salvador Dalí*, published in 1942, he describes Paris during the second half of the 1930s as represented "not by the surrealist polemics in the café on the Place Blanche, or by the suicide of my great friend René Crevel, but by the dressmaking establishment which Elsa Schiaparelli was about to open on the Place Vendôme. Here new morphological phenomena occurred; here the essence of things was to become transubstantiated; here the tongues of fire of the Holy Ghost of Dalí were going to descend." Dalí recognized the symbolic function of fashion in defining an era and understood the significance of Schiaparelli's position within the Paris avant-garde. While her collaborations with Dalí and Cocteau are well known, Schiaparelli's influence on the Surrealist community has yet to be fully acknowledged or documented. Her contributions have frequently been dismissed as derivative, and she has even been accused of stealing ideas. Rather, her fashions should be understood as another reflection of the zeitgeist of 1930s Paris, a time when a number of Surrealist artists were working in and interacting with the world of fashion and many couturiers were keenly aware of developments in the arts.

Schiaparelli's introduction to the artistic community of Paris actually began many years earlier in New York. In 1916 she accompanied her husband, Wilhelm Wendt de Kerlor, to New York City, sailing from Bordeaux aboard *The Chicago*. Among the other passengers was Gabrielle Picabia, wife of the Dada painter and poet Francis Picabia. During the voyage the three became friends, a connection that would later prove beneficial to Schiaparelli. By 1920 she had separated from her husband and reconnected with Gabrielle, who engaged her to assist with the sale of clothing designed by Nicole Groult, sister of the French couturier Paul Poiret (one of Schiaparelli's early inspirations). Although the business venture was a disaster, the two remained friends. It was Gabrielle who introduced Schiaparelli to the painter and photographer Man Ray and his circle, and Schiaparelli was among a small group of young women in New York who posed for him, his first photography models outside his own family. Sometime after she returned to Paris in June 1922, Schiaparelli reestablished her friendship with Man Ray, who had moved to the city in July 1921. In 1924 the photographer began working on a regular basis for the major fashion and style magazines—*Harper's Bazaar*, *Vanity Fair,* and the American, French, and British versions of *Vogue*. During the spring of 1930, when Schiaparelli was enjoying her first successes as a couturière, Man Ray photographed her in a number of her own designs, including beach pajamas (p. 28) and the evening gown with wraparound jacket that she later described as the most successful dress of her career (p. 38). Man Ray superimposed one of these images over the other in a striking "double" portrait now in the Musée National d'Art Moderne at the Centre Georges Pompidou in Paris.

Although Man Ray considered his early New York photographs of Schiaparelli unsuccessful, those he took of her in Paris he declared "a triumph." Several of the Paris photographs appeared in the Surrealist magazine *Minotaure*, launched by André Breton and published by Albert Skira for six years, from 1933 to 1938. Numbers 3–4 of the magazine (issued together on December 12, 1933) attest to Schiaparelli's presence within the Paris avant-garde and, even at this early date, to the impact of her clothing designs on the Surrealists. The Dada poet and writer Tristan Tzara illustrated his essay "D'un certain automatisme du goût" (Regarding a Certain Automatism of Taste) with three Man Ray photographs of knitted hats from Schiaparelli's winter

1933–34 collection, presented in early August 1933 (p. 127). The angle from which these were photographed plays up Tzara's thesis that contemporary women's hats resembled female genitalia—a subconscious transforming of women's desires into clearly readable symbols within the realm of fashion. In the same issue, Man Ray used a photograph of Schiaparelli to illustrate his classic essay on photography, "L'Âge de la lumière" (The Age of Light). Here he superimposed Schiaparelli's head, adorned with one of the waterproof lacquered wigs the renowned hairdresser Antoine had designed for her, on a plaster bust (p. 126), the photograph both deforming reality and transforming it into something altogether new, with its own integrity and meaning. Later, in 1953, the artist-illustrator Marcel Vertès incorporated this image into the surreal world he created in a collage for the interior of Schiaparelli's salon (p. 285). In the collage the Man Ray photograph is placed just below the statue of Napoleon (replaced by a ballet dancer) atop the column in the Place Vendôme, surrounded by butterflies, dinosaurs, and illustrations of some of the designer's most successful dresses, which Vertès had clipped from fashion magazines.

The importance of Schiaparelli's contacts within the Surrealist community is particularly evident in her accessory designs. During the Depression many artists and even writers, especially those at the beginning of their careers, freelanced as fashion illustrators or as designers of textiles and accessories. From 1928 to 1930, for example, the Russian-born writer Elsa Triolet designed and made necklaces that her companion Louis Aragon, cofounder of the Surrealist review *Littérature*, sold to Chanel, Jean Patou, and Schiaparelli. Man Ray photographed the most famous of these, the so-called aspirin necklace Triolet designed for Schiaparelli, which was made from white porcelain beads similar in shape to the French *pastilles* used as a headache remedy. Another artist who designed accessories for Schiaparelli was Alberto Giacometti, then still a member of the Surrealist group. He worked with her friend Jean-Michel Frank, assisting in the decoration of her apartments on the boulevard Saint-Germain and rue Barbet-de-Jouy, and the interiors of her salons on the rue de la Paix and later on the Place Vendôme. During the early 1930s he created for her a series of gilt metal brooches and buttons in the form of gorgons, sirens, birds, and angels.

Images of the hand, along with its double, the glove, featured prominently in Surrealist iconography and were developed by Schiaparelli into accessories that were themselves appropriated by artists and photographers as *objets trouvés* (found objects) in their work. Among the most significant were the miniature hands that Schiaparelli used as belt fastenings, buttons, and lapel clips. These first appeared in her fall 1934 collection in a variety of forms: a white plastic hand with red nails used as a belt buckle, a set of five hands fastening a coat and a cape, and a single hand closing the top of a box-shaped handbag. The designs bear a striking likeness to undated sketches made by the Swiss-German Surrealist artist Meret Oppenheim, including a belt fastening with two hands overlapping at the wrist and a porcelain hand grasping a buttonhole. Oppenheim had arrived in Paris in 1932 and was freelancing as an accessory designer, also posing for Man Ray from 1933 to 1936. She acknowledged selling only one design to Schiaparelli, in 1936, a fur-covered metal bracelet that Oppenheim happened to be wearing at the Café de Flore while seated with Pablo Picasso and Dora Maar, leading Picasso to observe that anything could be made of fur. The comment gave birth to what has become one of the most celebrated Surrealist objects, Oppenheim's *Déjeuner en fourrure* (Breakfast in Fur), a teacup and saucer completely covered in fur (p. 142).

The presentation of Schiaparelli's fall 1934 collection, with its hand motif, in late April of that year coincided with the May publication of Georges Hugnet's essay in issue number 5 of *Minotaure*, "Petite Rêverie du grand veneur" (Small Dream of the Great Huntsman). The article is illustrated by a series of photographs of hands in various poses that recall the tradition of carved hands worn as amulets, with the position of the fingers expressing different meanings. The poses struck by the hands in Hugnet's essay are similar to those of the hands Schiaparelli would incorporate in her later jewelry creations, particularly clips designed in 1936–37 by Jean Schlumberger (who would later become Tiffany's head designer), which were modeled after Victorian brooches in the shape of a hand (p. 128). Several varieties of these clips were made, and some may have been used in 1937 as *objets trouvés* in photographs and drawings by Man Ray and the writer-photographer Claude Cahun (born Lucy Schwob). One version was employed by Man Ray in his well-known portrait of Dora Maar (p. 129) and again in a self-portrait. A hand nearly identical to one designed by Schlumberger was incorporated by Cahun in photographs she used to illustrate Surrealist writer Lise

Pablo Picasso's *Portrait of Nusch Eluard* (p. 120), a painting of the wife of Surrealist poet Paul Eluard, was completed late in the summer of 1937 and appeared in *Cahiers d'Art* for 1939 illustrating a poem Eluard had dedicated to Nusch, "Je veux qu'elle soit reine!" (I wish she were queen). At least two elements of the ensemble worn by Nusch can be identified as coming from Schiaparelli's winter 1937–38 collection: the gilt cherub lapel clips, designed by Jean Schlumberger (p. 121), and the high, "windblown" hat with its sharply upturned silhouette. The lucky horseshoe trimming the brim of the hat was a motif used by Schiaparelli for fabric designs and jewelry (p. 294). Roland Penrose, describing Nusch's arrival at Picasso's studio in his book *Picasso: His Life and Work* (1958), commented on what she wore: "With her usual taste for originality and elegance, Nusch one day appeared at the rue de Grands Augustins in a new black dress and hat. On the lapels were two gilt cherubs and the top of the hat was ornamented by a horseshoe. The pale fragile face of Nusch, with her combination of ethereal charm and simple candid high spirits, looked all the more enchanting in the severity of these clothes. Picasso remarked that the hat was shaped like an anvil with the horseshoe in position to be hammered into shape. In the portrait he painted as soon as she had gone he traced the base of the anvil in transparent shadows vertically across the oval shape of the face. The gilt cherubs appeared on the lapels and her dark hair surrounded her head with the movement of clouds."

Deharme's 1937 book of poems *Le Coeur de pic* (The Woodpecker's Heart). For another book, Paul Eluard's collection of poems *Les Mains libres* (The Free Hands, 1937), Man Ray made a drawing titled *Hommage à Nusch* (Homage to Nusch) in which a hand holding a rose closely resembles a brooch from Schiaparelli's October 1937 collection (p. 131). *Les Mains libres* was dedicated to Nusch, Eluard's second wife, who was one of Schiaparelli's most loyal clients (Gala, his first wife, left him for Dalí). Nusch posed for her portrait by Picasso (p. 120) wearing Schiaparelli jewelry—two gilt lapel pins in the form of cherubs, designed by Schlumberger for the couturière's winter 1937–38 collection (p. 121).

Gloves played a significant role as accessories in Schiaparelli's ensembles, often adding a touch of whimsy or, at their most dramatic, a frisson of the unexpected. She embroidered rings on glove fingers, decorated them with butterflies, paired gloves in contrasting colors, and dramatized them with red fingernails or gold claws. The ideas for several glove designs again may have come from Oppenheim, whose sketches from 1935–36 closely resemble certain Schiaparelli designs, such as fur mitts shown in August 1935 and gloves painted with blue veins presented in August 1936. Another pair of gloves in the 1936 collection, black suede with red snakeskin fingernails (p. 130), were also made in white. The pairs together are uncannily reminiscent of hands painted by Picasso to look like gloves, which were photographed by Man Ray in 1935 (p. 131). The couturière and the artist were both playing with appearances but from opposite perspectives. Man Ray's focus on hands in various forms can also be seen in his use, beginning in 1932, of a mannequin hand to replace the sitter's in a number of portraits, including one of Schiaparelli wearing her lacquered wig, with her cheek resting against the wooden hand.

Schiaparelli's August 1936 collection for winter 1936–37 was significant in that it marked her first official collaboration with Salvador Dalí, although the artist was obviously familiar with her work by 1935. That year Dalí's impressions of New York City appeared in a series of illustrated articles in the tabloid-style magazine *American Weekly* from February through July. Titled "New York as Seen by the Super-Realist Artist," they contain several references to fashions associated with Schiaparelli, though she is not mentioned by name. Dalí's sketch in the March 31 issue features a hand wrapping around the waist of a woman, recalling Schiaparelli's white plastic hand used as a belt buckle, part of her fall collection shown in April 1934, and his drawing of aerodynamic fashions mirrors the couturière's "stormy weather" and "typhoon" silhouettes for 1934, with their emphatically bold backward-and-forward movements (the garments were available in New York at Bergdorf Goodman). In a gouache illustration titled "Night and Day Clothes," made during the winter of 1936, Dalí incorporated the zippers Schiaparelli had made famous the year before into his dress with sections that zipped open to reveal the body, which also featured the extremely pointed shoulders associated with the designer beginning in the early 1930s. For August 1936, Dalí and Schiaparelli collaborated on a group of "Surrealist" suits and coats with pockets that looked like miniature drawers, complete with dangling handles (pp. 132–33). The body fitted out with drawers was a recurring theme in Dalí's work as early as 1934. Both his 1936 ink drawing *City of Drawers* and the painting *The Anthropomorphic Cabinet* were purchased by the English art collector Edward James, who was Dalí's patron and whose arrangement with the artist entailed keeping Gala provided with designer dresses, including several by Schiaparelli.

The "chest" of drawers was not the only theme from Dalí's work to appear in Schiaparelli's collections. The lobster that appears on Gala's head in a 1934 painting and which he incorporated in 1936 into one of his most famous Surrealist objects, *Lobster Telephone* (p. 135), was still later translated into a textile design that Schiaparelli used for cotton beachwear and on a silk organdy evening gown for summer 1937 that was worn by Daisy Fellowes and by Wallis Simpson (soon to be Duchess of Windsor), who chose it for her trousseau of eighteen of the couturière's designs (pp. 134–35). For her winter 1937–38 collection, Schiaparelli and Dalí collaborated on a hat in the shape of a high-heeled shoe with a Shocking pink velvet heel, also produced in an all-black version (pp. 136–37). Gala was photographed wearing the shoe hat with its complementary black dress and a jacket with pockets embroidered with a pair of lips, a reference to Mae West's lips, which Dalí envisioned as a sumptuous sofa in his watercolor from around 1934–35 titled *Mae West's Face Which Can Be Used as a Surrealist Apartment*. In 1936–37 Dalí transformed his image of the lips into actual sofas, one of them owned by James and another, in Shocking pink satin, intended for Schiaparelli's London salon, which she apparently rejected. Schiaparelli, too, found inspiration in Mae West's voluptuous figure. The dressmaker's form sent to guide her designs for the actress to wear in the film *Every Day's a Holiday* inspired the shape of the bottle for the perfume Shocking, launched by Schiaparelli in April 1937. The design was by Léonor Fini, a young Surrealist artist who had recently moved to Paris from Argentina.

On January 17, 1938, the sensational *Exposition internationale du Surréalisme* opened in Paris, coinciding with the presentation of Schiaparelli's riotous Circus collection. This celebrated collection featured further collaborations between the couturière and Dalí—a dress printed with the illusion of torn animal flesh and accompanied by a veil with tears simulated by a layer of appliquéd fabric (p. 138), a dress with the padded silhouette of a skeleton (p. 175, top), and a hat in the shape of an inkpot. The tear dress mirrored the gown worn by the spectral female in Dalí's painting *Necrophiliac Springtime* (1936), then owned by Schiaparelli (p. 139, top). One of the most noteworthy elements in the Surrealist exposition was a "street" of sixteen mannequins, each "dressed" by an artist or writer, through which the spectators had to pass before reaching the exhibition hall. The combined effect of the various treatments—many of them quite bizarre—was so unexpected and visually stunning that it became the most photographed part of the exposition. This street of mannequins had a precursor in the quirky window displays of the Schiap boutique on the ground floor of the salon on the Place Vendôme. Bettina Bergery, Schiaparelli's assistant and one of Dalí's closest friends, was in charge of these, and they were well known for their outrageousness and wit. Bergery frequently dressed the two house mascots (life-size wooden mannequins), the golden-haired Pascal and his dowdy wife Pascaline, in the most outlandish garb or concocted figures made of anything from straw to small flags. She persuaded Dalí to assist with one of the displays, for which he dyed an enormous stuffed bear (a gift from Edward James) Shocking pink and cut a drawer in its stomach; Bergery dressed the bear in an orchid-colored satin coat and filled the drawer with jewels. For his installation at the exposition, Dalí appropriated Schiaparelli's Shocking pink knitted ski helmet from her August 1937 collection for his own mannequin to wear (p. 136). Mounted behind the figure were pages from several issues of his *American Weekly* articles featuring the Schiaparelli-inspired surreal fashions he had seen in New York. Later, for his *Dream of Venus* pavilion at the 1939 New York World's Fair, Dalí installed Schiaparelli's candy-colored astronomical necklace owned by Gala on one of the five live models (p. 145).

In 1938 Schiaparelli was asked by Dalí to design the costumes for a new ballet to be called *Tristan Fou*, based on Richard Wagner's opera *Tristan und Isolde*. Dalí's original sketches featured moving fantasy figures made up of dots and dashes to replicate what he described as "mobile jewels." This unrealized collaboration may have been the origin of the fabric design Schiaparelli featured a year later in her own installation at the New York World's Fair, in which a plaster slab with a figure carved into it had sequined fabric attached as a skirt, its design resembling Dalí's original drawings. The installation was possibly meant as a taunt to Chanel, a close friend of Dalí's who in the end provided the costume designs for *Tristan Fou*, which premiered at the World's Fair under the title *Bacchanal*. The final collaborations between Dalí and Schiaparelli were Dalí's designs for the label of her Shocking Radiance body oils in 1943 and the Baccarat bottle for her perfume Le Roy Soleil (The Sun King) in 1946.

Schiaparelli successfully applied Dalí's paranoiac-critical method—a "spontaneous method of irrational knowledge based upon the interpretive-critical association of delirious phenomena"—to her fashion designs, which could often carry alternate meanings. Thus a shoe was not a shoe but a hat. Although technically Cocteau was not a member of the Surrealist group, having been rejected for his idea of the *rappel à l'ordre* (call to order), he, too, employed the method in a classic double image he created for Schiaparelli, who used it on the back of a blue silk evening coat in her fall 1937 collection (p. 140). The linear design can be viewed either as two profile heads facing one another or as a rose-filled urn set atop a fluted column formed by a series of six parallel lines running from the waist of the coat to the hem. Another Cocteau design for the same collection again exhibits his extraordinary ability to express form by the use of a single line. On the gray linen jacket of a dinner ensemble the outline of a woman's head on the front extends into long golden hair flowing down the right sleeve, while at the waist a hand grasps a handkerchief (p. 141). Schiaparelli used a similar design by Cocteau on an evening dress, where the gown's shoulder strap serves as the upper arm of a hand that again holds a handkerchief. It is possible that the profile heads on the purple evening coat represent Tristan and Isolde, for an almost identical image of two heads in profile was used by Dalí in 1953 for a jewelry design on that theme and again in

1972 for a print of the same title. If the image has the same meaning in the Cocteau design and represents Tristan and Isolde, the golden-haired woman embroidered on the evening jacket may be a reference to the blond Norwegian soprano Kristen Flagstad, whose performances as Isolde in Wagner's opera *Tristan und Isolde* in 1936–37 were received with great enthusiasm. It is probably not coincidence that just a year later Dalí proposed that Schiaparelli design the costumes for *Tristan Fou*.

Schiaparelli was fortunate to have begun designing when she did, a time when so many artists—not just Man Ray, Dalí, and Cocteau but also Christian Bérard, Kees van Dongen, and Marcel Vertès, among others—were regularly providing magazines like *Vogue* and *Harper's Bazaar* with fashion illustrations, including interpretations of Schiaparelli's designs. She claimed in her autobiography, *Shocking Life*, that working with artists, fashion photographers, and artisans (including Roger Jean-Pierre and Jean Clement for buttons and François Lesage for embroideries) gave her "a sense of exhilaration." Her personal art collection was eclectic and included works by Victor Brauner, Cocteau, Dalí, Roberto Matta (whose brother Serge was a *modéliste* at her salon), Amedeo Modigliani, Picasso, Pierre Roy, Yves Tanguy, and Pavel Tchelitchew. Schiaparelli's interest in and study of art came through strongly in her work. Her rival, Coco Chanel, who disparagingly characterized her as "that Italian artist who's making clothes" was not the only one to note the connection. The Spanish couturier Cristóbal Balenciaga called her the only real artist in the couture, and Anaïs Nin, in a diary entry for October 1935, described Schiaparelli's salon presentation as a "magnificent work of art," writing that she could "well believe she was a painter and a sculptress before she designed dresses." Schiaparelli, too, saw her work as a step above the mechanics and minutiae of dress production—in fact as an art, though not always a particularly rewarding one. In her autobiography she described fashion design as "a most difficult and unsatisfying art, because as soon as a dress is born it has already become a thing of the past." She would have been pleased with Anaïs Nin's characterization, for she claimed she would have been happier as a sculptor. Sculpture was to her "one of the arts nearest creation. The feeling of molding between one's fingers a shape mirrored in one's mind is one of intense magnetism and divine sensuality." Schiaparelli's approach to "inventing" dresses, as she called it, was similar to sculpting in that she worked with the actual fabric, draping it on a live model and manipulating it into the desired effect. She did not work from sketches, nor did she use the plain white cotton fabric commonly employed when draping a garment in the design stage. Her contemporary, the couturière Augustabernard, who made use of a similar technique, described the process as "almost a living thing, moving, almost breathing, . . . the fabric to me often originates the idea." (Significantly, when Augustabernard closed her couture house in 1935, her two best fitters joined Schiaparelli.) For Schiaparelli, too, the material was very often the starting point of her design. She had close working relationships with fabric manufacturers, including Bianchini, Colcombet, and Ducharne, who willingly provided her with sample lengths of their most recent innovations, such as deeply crinkled crêpes that looked like tree bark, transparent materials that resembled glass, or shaggy metallic plush fabrics.

What appealed to Schiaparelli as a designer was the vision and act of creating. Her choice of a career provided her not only with a means of earning a living but also with the artistic outlet she craved. What she found "difficult and unsatisfying" about the profession was the reality of the finished garment, for she inevitably found the end result disappointing, as she would so eloquently remark in her autobiography: "The interpretation of a dress, the means of making it, and the surprising way in which some materials react—all these factors, no matter how good an interpreter you have, invariably reserve a slight if not bitter disappointment for you. In a way it is even worse if you are satisfied, because once you have created it the dress no longer belongs to you. A dress cannot just hang like a painting on the wall, or like a book remain intact and live a long and sheltered life. A dress has no life of its own unless it is worn, and as soon as this happens another personality takes over from you and animates it, or tries to, glorifies or destroys it, or makes it into a song of beauty. More often it becomes an indifferent object, or even a pitiful caricature of what you wanted it to be—a dream, an expression."

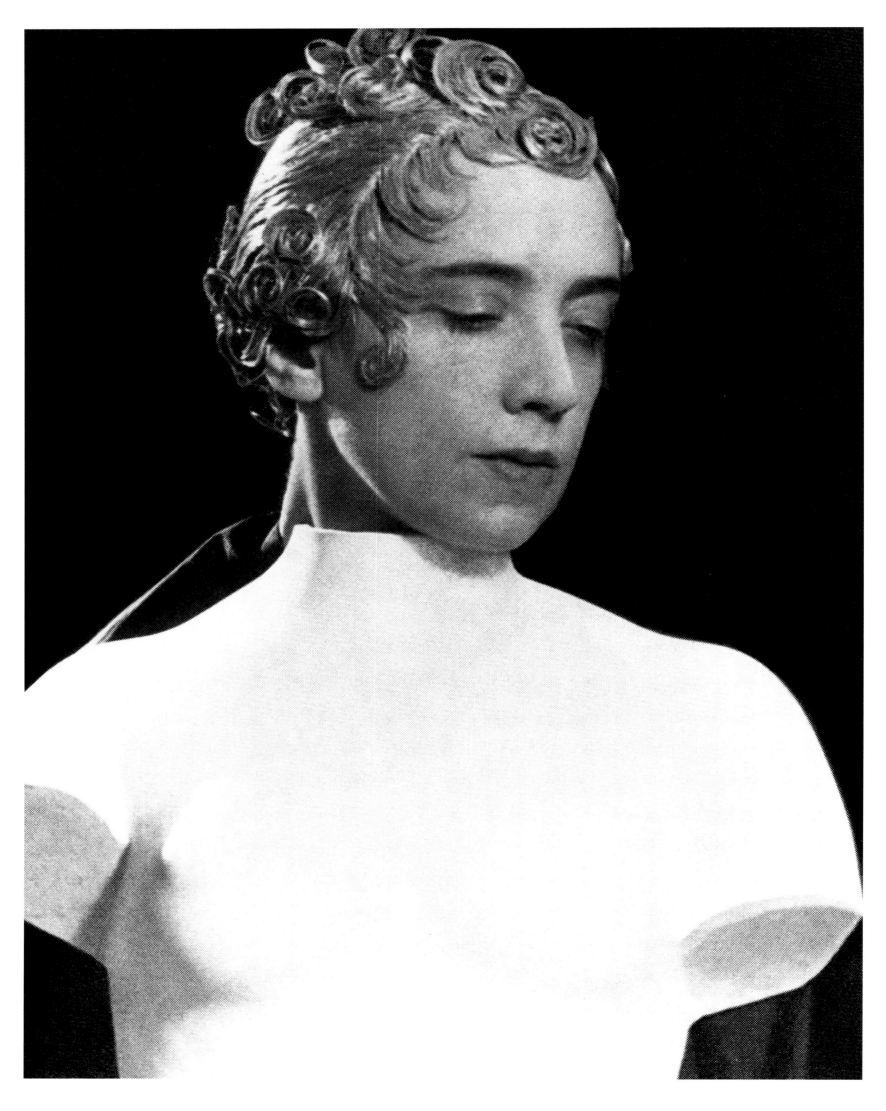

In the photograph by Man Ray at left, Schiaparelli's head has been superimposed on a plaster torso. The image was among those Man Ray used to illustrate his essay "L'Âge de la lumière" (The Age of Light) in numbers 3–4 of Albert Skira's art periodical *Minotaure* (December 12, 1933). The short, lacquered wig worn by Schiaparelli was created by the famous society hairdresser Antoine and caused a sensation during the winter of 1931 when the designer, vacationing at the ski resort at Saint-Moritz, wore a version in silver for evenings and a blond one for skiing.

Man Ray's photographs of three hats from Schiaparelli's winter 1933–34 collection (shown in August 1933) were used as illustrations for a theoretical text written by Tristan Tzara, founder of Dada. Titled "D'un certain automatisme du goût" (Regarding a Certain Automatism of Taste), the article was published in the same issue of *Minotaure* as Man Ray's photo essay "L'Âge de la lumière." Tzara put forth the idea that these hats, with their resemblance to female genitalia, were not merely fashionable accessories but had become sexual metaphors, reversing Freud's psychoanalytic interpretation of dreams in which a woman's hat is a symbol of the male sexual organ. Man Ray photographed the hats from an angle that emphasized Tzara's point. The design of one of the hats (top, left), based on a man's fedora, was called Savile Row after the London street noted for its fine tailoring establishments; a similar design appears in the upper right of the house sketch directly above. Schiaparelli's "Mad Cap," constructed with a single peak, also appeared in Tzara's *Minotaure* essay (top, right) and can be seen right of center in the sketch. Schiaparelli herself models the third hat in Tzara's essay, appropriately named "The Crazy Coxcomb."

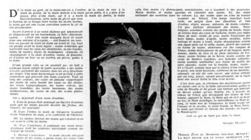

PETITE RÊVERIE DU GRAND VENEUR

par GEORGES HUGNET

The photographs of hands in various poses (above) illustrating Georges Hugnet's essay "Petite Rêverie du grand veneur" (Small Dream of the Great Huntsman), published in issue number 5 of *Minotaure* (May 12, 1934), are echoed in Jean Schlumberger's design for Schiaparelli's Victorian-style clip in the form of a hand (above, left), which is nearly identical to one incorporated by Claude Cahun in photographs she used to illustrate Lise Deharme's 1937 book *Le Coeur de pic* (The Woodpecker's Heart). Similar clips were used by Man Ray as Surrealist *objets trouvés* (found objects) in his works, including the 1936 portrait of the photographer Dora Maar (right), who was Picasso's muse, model, and mistress for many years.

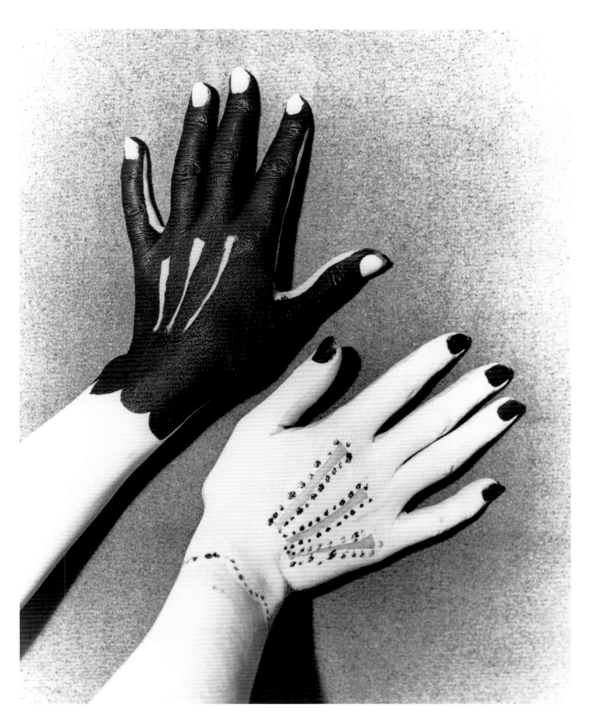

Man Ray photographed the hands above, painted by Picasso to look like gloves, in 1935. Schiaparelli reversed the equation in her August 1936 collection for winter 1936–37, producing suede gloves in both black and white, with red snakeskin fingernails to replicate human hands (left). The black gloves were worn with Surrealist suits with pockets that looked like miniature bureau drawers, designed in collaboration with Salvador Dalí (pp. 132–33).

The drawing by Man Ray illustrated above (top) appeared in Paul Eluard's book of poems *Les Mains libres* (The Free Hands, 1937). Titled *Hommage à Nusch* (Homage to Nusch), it is based on a photograph he took of Eluard's wife, Nusch, with Sonia Mosse. In the photograph the hands of the two women touch lovingly, recalling sentimental images in nineteenth-century paintings. That feeling is evoked in the drawing by the symbolism of a brooch in the form of a hand holding a rose, possibly a representation of one of the Victorian whimsies included in Schiaparelli's October 1937 presentation for spring 1938 (above). Nusch, always elegantly dressed, was painted by Picasso during the summer of 1937 wearing two cherub lapel clips from Schiaparelli's winter 1937–38 collection (p. 120).

The fashion sketch from Bergdorf Goodman above illustrates Schiaparelli's bureau-drawer suit, labeled number 435, and the glove with snakeskin nails, number 418. Although the suit was inspired by Surrealist themes, it was eminently wearable. Made up in a warm navy blue velour, the five "drawer" pockets had drop "handles" of black plastic. The suit was worn with a blouse of sky blue crinkled taffeta woven in shirred bands and a high-crowned navy felt hat with a rolled brim and a band of grosgrain ribbon. Bergdorf Goodman may have decided to modify the design, for the enlarged detail of the original drawer handles has been crossed out.

Salvador Dalí's 1936 sketch for clothing designed to look like a chest of drawers (above) was developed into a collection of bureau-drawer suits and coats that Schiaparelli presented for winter 1936–37, the first collaboration between the couturière and the artist. The sketch accompanied photographs by Cecil Beaton of two of these suits in the September 1936 issue of *Vogue*. Beaton created a surreal dream world for his photographs, which appeared in two separate issues of *Vogue*, the suits in September and a coat in October. One of the models in the photograph shown at right is holding up a copy of issue number 8 of the Surrealist magazine *Minotaure* (June 15, 1936), which featured a cover by Dalí of a minotaur with an open drawer in its chest, a lobster spilling from a hole in its stomach, and

clawlike red fingernails (above, right), all themes that would make an appearance in Schiaparelli's designs. Beaton described the technique he used to create the surreal landscapes for the bureau-drawer suits in his *Photobiography:* "Later we worked in the studio with large transparent screens of stretched white muslin, which enabled us to indulge in a great variety of shadow effects; and by placing strange objects, and even strange people, on the far side of the screen, we produced a background of fantastic silhouetted shapes." Schiaparelli's August 1936 showing was attended by a number of celebrities, including Dalí, the American novelist Louis Bromfield, and the art collector and patron of the Surrealists, Edward James.

Wallis Simpson was a frequent subject of Cecil Beaton's photographs during the 1930s. Shortly before Simpson's marriage to the Duke of Windsor in May 1937, Beaton was asked to take some official photographs of the bride-to-be at the Château de Candé, where she was staying as a guest of Charles Bedeaux. Since many of the past photographs of Simpson were unflattering, Beaton suggested more romantic-looking pictures, including this image of her standing in the château's garden wearing a Schiaparelli dress printed with a large lobster (above, right). The infamous lobster dress was a design collaboration with Salvador Dalí that grew out of the lobsters that started appearing in the artist's work in 1934, including *New York Dream-Man Finds Lobster in Place of Phone*,

which appeared in the magazine *American Weekly* in 1935, and the mixed-media *Lobster Telephone* created in 1936 (above, left). Dalí placed the lobster amid parsley sprigs on the front of the skirt (and apparently was disappointed when Schiaparelli would not allow him to spread real mayonnaise on the finished gown), and master silk designer Sache translated the sketch to the fabric (opposite). Beaton took almost a hundred photographs during the session with Simpson, and *Vogue* devoted an eight-page spread to the results. For Dalí both the telephone and the lobster had sexual connotations. His placement of the lobster thus charged the design with erotic tension, effectively defeating the public-relations purpose of Beaton's photographs.

Schiaparelli's winter 1937–38 collection, from which
Salvador Dalí selected the Shocking pink *chullo* he
placed on his Surrealist mannequin in the 1938
Exposition internationale du Surréalisme, featured
another collaboration with Dalí, a simple black dress
and jacket in Ducharne's crêpe satin with embroidered
pockets shaped as glistening red lips (above), a
reference to Mae West's lips. The jacket was worn
with a black felt hat in the shape of a high-heeled
shoe with a Shocking pink heel, also available in all
black (right). The idea for the hat evolved from a 1933
photograph Gala Dalí had taken of her husband in Port
Lligat, in which the artist wears a woman's shoe on
his head and another on his right shoulder. Gala was
photographed wearing Schiaparelli's ensemble, but it
was generally agreed that only Daisy Fellowes managed
to carry it off successfully. The exclusive New York shop
Jay Thorpe carried the original model of the hat, which
I. Miller, the noted American shoe retailer, considered
too much of a novelty; thus a more wearable version
was offered in its millinery department.

The *Exposition internationale du Surréalisme*, held at
the Galerie Beaux-Arts in Paris, opened on January 17,
1938. Visitors to the exhibition entered the gallery
through a street lined with sixteen shop mannequins,
each dressed by a different artist or writer. Dalí's
mannequin appeared in two different forms during the
month-long installation. In the second, more menacing
version, shown above in a photograph by Man Ray,
Dalí has added Schiaparelli's Shocking pink knitted ski
helmet to the original bird headdress and fabric turban.

The helmet had been included in the couturière's
August 1937 showing for winter 1937–38 and was
inspired by the traditional Peruvian *chullo* (a knitted
wool cap with ear flaps) that she saw at the Peruvian
pavilion in the 1937 *Exposition internationale des
arts et techniques dans la vie moderne*. The same
helmet was worn by Chick Austin, the memorable
director of the Wadsworth Atheneum in Hartford,
Connecticut, for his winter 1939 surreal magic show,
"Magic on Parade."

One of the paintings in Schiaparelli's personal art collection was Dalí's *Necrophiliac Springtime* from 1936 (top, right), in which the head of the corpselike female figure dressed in a gown with torn sleeves bursts into bloom. The image was made reality by Sheila Legge in London that same year, during the New Burlington Galleries' *International Surrealist Exhibition*, when Legge was photographed in Trafalgar Square as the "Surrealist Phantom," her head completely covered in roses and wearing a long white dress shredded at the hem. *Necrophiliac Springtime* was one of three paintings Dalí made in 1936 with similar figures; the others are *The Dream Places a Hand on a Man's Shoulder* and *Three Young Surrealist Women Holding in Their Arms the Skins of an Orchestra* (bottom, right). In all three works the boundary between gown and body has dissolved, so that the torn fabric cannot be distinguished from flayed skin. This theme was developed further in the Schiaparelli-Dalí design collaboration for her Circus collection of summer 1938, presented at the beginning of February, just after the opening of the Paris Surrealist exhibition on January 17. The evening dress from that collection at left is printed with an illusion of torn animal flesh, with the trompe l'oeil effect given a third dimension in the appliquéd fabric applied to the "tent" veil. On the pale blue fabric, now faded to white, the "skin" is slashed and peeled back to reveal a magenta underlayer, the hanging pieces printed to look like fur, as if the gown were made from an animal skin turned inside out.

Yet another Dalí collaboration, the skeleton dress, was included in the Circus collection (p. 175, top), as were such Surrealist inventions as the inkpot hat and the hen hat, the latter possibly based on Valentine Hugo's engraving *Woman with Chicks* (1937).

Schiaparelli's close friendship with Jean Cocteau led to his making two drawings for her, which she used in her fall 1937 collection. Cocteau's extraordinary ability to create form by the use of a single line is evident in these designs, translated into embroidery by the firm of Lesage. The mirror image on the back of the blue silk jersey evening coat at left (now faded to lavender) is a classic example of Dalí's paranoiac-critical method, in which more than one possible meaning can be attached to the same image. Here, two faces in profile can also be viewed as a rose-filled urn set atop a fluted column. The second Cocteau design, on the gray linen jacket of a dinner ensemble (right), is of a woman's head in profile with long golden hair flowing down one of the jacket sleeves. Schiaparelli's collaborations with Cocteau included supplying costumes for the actress Jany Holt for Cocteau's play *Les Monstres sacrés* (The Holy Terrors) in 1940 (p. 119) and for actress Maria Casarès in Robert Bresson's film *Les Dames du Bois de Boulogne* (The Ladies of the Park), with dialogue by Bresson and Cocteau, in 1945.

The Swiss-German artist Meret Oppenheim sold Schiaparelli a design for a fur bracelet during spring 1936, and the couturière included it in her winter collection featuring Salvador Dalí's Surrealist bureau-drawer suits and a suit accompanied by a black felt hat with a fox-head mask perched on top. Oppenheim was wearing the fur bracelet during an encounter with Pablo Picasso and Dora Maar at the Café de Flore, leading Picasso to observe that anything could be made of fur. The remarks inspired this famous Surrealist object, Oppenheim's *Le Déjeuner en fourrure* (above), a fur-covered cup, saucer, and spoon.

Some of the most modern and original designs for footwear in the 1930s were created by André Perugia for Schiaparelli. These included ladylike high buttoned boots in pastel leathers and striped satins as well as surreal designs like these boots from Schiaparelli's 1938 Circus collection, with monkey fur cascading over the ankle to the floor. They recall a painting by René Magritte, *Love Disarmed* (1935), of blond hair spilling out of a pair of shoes placed in front of an oval mirror. A Magritte image influenced at least one other pair of shoes by Schiaparelli. The Philadelphia shoemakers Laird Schober & Company created several extreme designs for the couturière, including a black silk high-heeled boot with toes outlined in stitching for spring 1939, which referenced Magritte's image of a booted foot, *Le Modele rouge* (The Red Model). Magritte made three versions of the painting—one in 1935, one in 1936 for his first one-man show in New York (at the Julien Levy Gallery), and the last in 1953. Magritte explained the image in his 1938 lecture "La Ligne de vie" (The Lifeline), and his comments can be applied equally to Schiaparelli's unusual boots: "The problem of the shoes demonstrates how far the most barbaric things can, through force of habit, come to be considered quite respectable. Thanks to 'The Red model', people can feel that the union of a human foot with a leather shoe is, in fact a monstrous custom." Pierre Cardin, who briefly worked for Schiaparelli during the 1940s, developed Magritte's concept into men's shoes with molded toes in 1986.

The London society photographer Madame Yevonde experimented with Surrealist-inspired images during the 1930s. Among the best known is her series from 1935 in which society women are portrayed as Greek or Roman goddesses or nymphs. Lady Malcolm Campbell, for example, was photographed as Niobe in a pose reminiscent of Man Ray's well-known photograph *Glass Tears* (1930). Yevonde was a pioneer in color photography, and her *Still Life with Head of Nefertiti* (above) incorporates jewelry by Schiaparelli among its props. Yevonde also includes, in the foreground, a reference to Man Ray's famous sculpture *Cadeau* (1921), a flatiron with metal tacks affixed to the sole plate.

In 1938 New York City gallery owner Julien Levy proposed a Surrealist pavilion for the 1939 New York World's Fair. The final result after several permutations was Salvador Dalí's *Dream of Venus* installation. The pavilion's design had a number of references to Schiaparelli's work. Dalí used the couturière's signature color, Shocking pink, for the pavilion's exterior, and his image of Venus had precedents in some of her designs. Schiaparelli had dressed the Vicomtesse Benoist d'Azy as the Venus in Botticelli's painting *Birth of Venus* at the legendary Famous Paintings Ball in 1935, controversially giving her the appearance of being nude (p. 181), and she further developed the Venus theme in her

Pagan collection for fall 1938 (pp. 180–85). A series of photographs by Horst P. Horst and George Platt Lynes, commissioned to publicize the Surrealist pavilion at the World's Fair, includes an image of Dalí embracing the legs of a nude model on which a lobster plays the traditional role of the fig leaf, recalling the positioning of the lobster on the gown from Schiaparelli's summer 1937 collection (p. 134). In the picture at right, from the same series, Dalí drew over the photograph with ink, transforming the nude model, who wears Gala's candy-colored astronomical necklace of Galalith stars from Schiaparelli's summer 1939 collection, into a menacing mermaid.

The display of French haute couture at the 1939 New York World's Fair echoed the installations of the *Pavillon de l'Elégance* at the 1937 *Exposition internationale des arts et techniques dans la vie moderne* in Paris. The same architect-decorators were responsible for both exhibits, and the new displays once again presented fashion in the abstract. Twenty plaster mannequins in bas-relief were draped to represent the ideal woman, each a reflection of the aesthetic sensibility of the individual dressmaking

house. Marcel Vertès collaborated with Schiaparelli on her display, a fantasy of silk sequined fabric set against the plaster panel. Schiaparelli's fabric design may have evolved from discussions she had with Salvador Dalí in 1937 concerning costume designs for the ballet *Tristan Fou*, which Edward James was planning to stage in London. Dalí had signed a contract with Léonide Massine, but the production was put on hold and was subsequently produced as *Bacchanal* at the 1939 World's Fair, with costumes designed by Coco Chanel

and executed by Madame Karinska, the latter best known for her later work on George Balanchine's ballets. Schiaparelli's fabric bears a strong resemblance to Dalí's original costume designs for *Tristan Fou*, duplicating in sequins the effect of the artist's "mobile jewels."

Ceci n'est pas une pipe.

René Magritte created several versions of his word painting *La Trahison des images* (The Treachery of Images) between 1928–29 and 1935 (the version at left dates to 1928–29). The text—"This is not a pipe"—refers to his thesis that "an object never fulfills the same function as its name or its image," as he stated in his 1929 text "Les Mots et les images" (Words and Images) in the journal *La Révolution surréaliste*. Thus a picture of a pipe can never be a real pipe. Schiaparelli drew on *La Trahison des images* for the men's perfume she introduced in 1940, Snuff (above), in which the pipe-shaped bottle is not a real pipe but a glass flacon presented not in a real cigar box but in a container that looks like one. The scent achieved a measure of notoriety in 1965 when one of James Bond's adversaries, Emilio Largo, played by Adolfo Celi in the film *Thunderball*, was noted for his exquisitely cut sharkskin jackets and his habit of putting a dab of Snuff on his Charvet handkerchief.

Schiaparelli spent most of World War II in the United States, where she was actively involved with the Coordinating Council of French Relief Societies, helping to organize concerts, lectures, and exhibitions of French art and culture. The first of these were one-person shows of the works of Jean Pagés and Malvina Hoffman. Pagés showed a series of paintings telling the story of a French soldier from his demobilization to his arrival in New York, and Hoffman exhibited sculpture expressing the unity of mankind. In 1942 Schiaparelli, together with André Breton and Marcel Duchamp, organized the *First Papers of Surrealism* exhibition in the Whitelaw Reid mansion at 451 Madison Avenue, New York, which opened on October 14. Included were the works both of French artists transplanted to America and of American artists who had been associated with French art. Duchamp's contribution was the imaginative and inexpensive installation *Sixteen Miles of String* (actually just one mile), in which string crisscrossed the entire gallery space. According to Schiaparelli's recollections in her autobiography, the installation was designed "to form a labyrinth directing the visitors to this and that painting with a definite sense of contrast. On the opening day small children played between the legs of the rather bewildered crowd." Ann Morgan, who ran the society, was pleased with the financial result but not particularly happy with the installation, which she felt was undignified. Apparently Surrealism coupled with string was not her idea of French culture.

Metamorphosis

For the Surrealists the butterfly symbolized metamorphosis, the evolution from ugliness to beauty. Schiaparelli made that image reality in her 1937 summer collection. Women were literally transformed into butterflies. Butterflies fluttered onto printed dresses and alighted on hats and gloves. The collection included several butterfly-printed evening gowns that were worn with "cage" coats of coarse wide mesh—the butterfly caught in a net transformed into the liberated woman imprisoned. Schiaparelli made reference to the net and cage again and again in her collections. Hats had net veils or brims while handbags and even her perfume boutique were designed in the form of cages. She claimed that Picasso's *Bird Cage and Playing Cards* (below) was her favorite painting, and she used it as the frontispiece of the American edition of her autobiography, *Shocking Life*, which includes the following description: "There is a cage. Below it are some playing cards on a green carpet. Inside the cage a poor, half-smothered white dove looks dejectedly at a brilliantly polished pink apple; outside the cage an angry black bird with flapping wings challenges the sky." Friends who were well acquainted with her contradictory nature claimed it was a portrait of Schiaparelli (her dual nature is evident in her autobiography, in which she effortlessly switches back and forth between the first- and third-person voices).

In Schiaparelli's philosophy of dress the concept of transformation was central, from the small conversions of clothing with multiple functions to the metamorphosis of a woman's total look. She frequently designed clothing to have more than one use, such as a skirt that could be worn as a cape, while in the ultimate transformation clothing was employed to masquerade, concealing one facet of a woman only to reveal another. Former *Vogue* editor Bettina Ballard related in her memoirs the effect a Schiaparelli wardrobe had on its wearer's appearance: "A Schiaparelli customer did not have to worry as to whether she was beautiful or not—she was a type. She was noticed wherever she went, protected by an armour of amusing conversation-making smartness. Her clothes belonged to Schiaparelli more than they belonged to her—it was like borrowing someone else's chic and, along with it, their assurance." At its most extreme, the masquerade found expression as performance in the costumes Schiaparelli designed for herself and her friends to wear to the many fancy dress balls held during the 1930s, and in 1939 it was incorporated

into the theme of her spring collection featuring the Italian Commedia dell'arte, with designs inspired by Harlequins, Pierrots, and Columbines. Masks were a repeated motif in her collections, appearing in miniature as buttons and serving full-size as visors on hats, for example, and as fans.

Classical mythology provided Schiaparelli with a rich source of inspiration throughout her career, especially Ovid's *Metamorphoses*, with its stories of transformation. While growing up, Schiaparelli had constantly been told by her mother that she was as ugly as her sister was beautiful. As a result she was always dreaming up ways to improve her appearance, including, as a child, planting flower seeds in her throat, ears, nose, and mouth in the hope that she would be transformed into a garden. When she was twenty-one her cousin Attilio, an art critic, arranged to have her youthful poetry published by Riccardo Quintieri; the book was titled *Arethusa*, after the nymph who was transformed into a spring. The Pygmalion myth offered a model for the seventh of Schiaparelli's "Twelve Commandments for Women," in which she stated that a woman should select her wardrobe either alone or in the company of a man, a sort of Professor Higgins whose advice, approval, and finances could help mold her into a fashionable woman (one client recalled that she wore Schiaparelli because her husband liked her to look as sleek as a racehorse). The Pygmalion association was underscored by Schiaparelli's costume designs for Gabriel Pascal's 1938 film of George Bernard Shaw's play, starring Wendy Hiller as Eliza Doolittle. To illustrate Eliza's transformation from a Cockney flower seller into a duchess, Hiller's first wardrobe change has her appearing as a young schoolgirl, with her hair pulled back in a headband à la Alice in Wonderland and wearing a girlish ensemble consisting of one of Schiaparelli's short bolero jackets worn with a white blouse and a tie. Later in the film the young student "graduates" into a sophisticated young woman, clothed in a Schiaparelli design from her Pagan collection, a short-sleeved dress printed with wild strawberries, apple blossoms, and leaves. But when Eliza Doolittle makes her début at the ambassador's reception, she forgoes the more distinctive clothing of Schiaparelli and is dressed as a "duchess" in diamonds and a traditional satin gown by Worth. For Schiaparelli, making dresses was the closest she came to fulfilling her dream of being a sculptor, a Pygmalion who could bring into reality a shape previously existing only in the mind.

In her autobiography Schiaparelli relates one of her earliest successful metamorphoses, the actress Katharine Hepburn, whom she claimed to have changed from "a thin girl who seemed ugly and dowdy" to a "strikingly beautiful" young woman. To celebrate her first film, *A Bill of Divorcement* (1932), Hepburn went to Europe with her husband, Luddy, and in Paris purchased her first French couture outfit from Schiaparelli's salon—an eggplant purple three-quarter-length coat, a skirt, a blouse, and the knitted "Mad Cap"—just in case the movie was a hit. Unfortunately, the Schiaparelli image was not quite what the designers at RKO studios had in mind for their rising star. According to a report in the February 1933 issue of *Harper's Bazaar*, they were determined to wean Hepburn away from the Mad Caps she favored and make her over into a new type of Hollywood beauty. Despite their efforts, the star continued to be associated with the "Schiaparelli look" as late as 1938, when her connection with the designer provided cabaret performer Sheila Barrett with material for her act at the Beach and Tennis Club in Miami Beach. When Barrett did her impersonation of Greta Garbo, she had Garbo refer to her three rivals: Janet Gaynor, whom she called "Sex Takes a Holiday"; Marlene Dietrich, characterized as "Anemia Mistaken for Passion"; and Katharine Hepburn, given the epithet "Schiaparelli's Version of Black Beauty."

Schiaparelli would dress many film and stage stars during her career. One of the first was Arletty (Léonie Bathait), the most important French actress of the period and a star of both stage and film. Her unconventional good looks (p. 58, bottom) are typical of what would come to be known as the "Schiaparelli woman," and it is noteworthy that the designer deliberately chose Arletty to represent her clothes. She approached the actress in 1929 with an offer to dress her for the stage and subsequently provided the wardrobe for the comedy *Mistigri*, which opened at the Thêatre Daunou in 1930—the first play that Schiaparelli costumed, though she would dress many others in future years. More important, Schiaparelli provided Arletty with her wardrobe offstage as well, so that her clothes might be seen in fashionable circles. According to the modern-day couturier Azzedine Alaïa, Arletty recalled to him that every morning a car would draw up to her home to deliver a new Schiaparelli ensemble and would return at night to take it away.

Among the many women who regularly dressed in Schiaparelli, two in particular stand out—her assistant Bettina, who was married to the politician Gaston Bergery, deputy of the Frontiste party from 1936 to 1942 and one of Surrealist artist Salvador Dalí's best friends, and socialite Daisy Fellowes, the designer's *mannequin mondaine*, who reigned briefly as the Paris editor of *Harper's Bazaar*. Dalí, in his 1942 book *The Secret Life of Salvador Dalí*, described Bettina Bergery as "the soul and biology of the Schiaparelli establishment." It was she who dressed Schiaparelli's windows, making them, according to the designer, "the laughable, impudent, colorful last-born of the quartier, upsetting every tradition." Ballard, who reigned as Paris editor of *Vogue* from 1935 to 1940, speculated in her memoirs that Bergery's "uninhibited quality, plus her tall, hipless American figure, plus a true chic of her own, plus a complete lack of inhibition in wearing Schiaparelli's most daring designs, did much to help spread the popularity of Schiaparelli's follies." The personification of Schiaparelli chic, however, was the imperious Honorable Mrs. Reginald Fellowes, known as Daisy, who was described by Carmel Snow, then editor of *Harper's Bazaar*, as "the fashion leader of Paris" and who had, in the words of fashion illustrator Marcel Vertès, "the elegance of the skeleton." As with Arletty, Schiaparelli dressed Daisy for free, purely for the prestige of having her clothes circulate in society. Daisy was frequently featured in American, British, and French fashion magazines and, as "a woman of style," often had her Schiaparelli wardrobe illustrated on two-page spreads. She and her daughters, the Comtesse de Casteja and the Comtesse de la Moussaye, regularly appeared on the annual list of the world's best-dressed women during the 1930s, as did others of the couturière's clients, including Madame Arturo Lopez-Willshaw, the prominent South American socialite; Standard Oil heiress Millicent Rogers, the designer's most loyal American client; and Madame Eve Curie, the accomplished pianist daughter of the Nobel Prize–winning scientist Marie Curie and author of her mother's biography.

The acceptance of new concepts of female attractiveness during the 1930s had a parallel in the Surrealists' challenge to existing notions of beauty. André Breton's statement in his novel *Nadja* (1928) that "beauty will be convulsive or will not be at all" was developed by the Surrealists into works of art in which images of women were fragmented or doubled, or became objects of fetishism. Beauty implied harmony, but convulsive beauty took pleasure in being shocking, with an emphasis on dissonance and discordance. During the 1930s in the realm of fashion, women who formerly would have been perceived as ugly were ele-

In the photograph on page 150, taken by Horst P. Horst for *Vogue*, March 15, 1937, four oversize three-dimensional plastic butterflies alight along one side of a cardigan-style sky blue jacket, the smallest of them functioning as a button at the waist. The extra large slits for the buttonholes also serve a decorative purpose. The jacket was worn with a wine-colored wool afternoon dress and a matching narrow-brimmed straw hat on which perched two more butterflies. This model, together with seventeen additional ensembles from Schiaparelli's summer 1937 collection, was included in the spring wardrobe of Wallis Simpson, future Duchess of Windsor.

Not only did Schiaparelli assert that Pablo Picasso's 1933 painting *Bird Cage and Playing Cards* (p. 151) was her favorite painting, but she claimed in her autobiography (idiosyncratically using the third-person voice) that "she would not part with this painting for a fortune even if she were, through her supreme indifference to material values, reduced one day, as her mother predicted, to a crust of bread and some straw to sleep on in an empty room. The room would not be empty. The Picasso would be hanging on the wall!"

vated to *jolies laides*, which roughly translates as "good-looking uglies," and chic rather than prettiness became fashionable. For Dalí the image of the elegant woman closely conformed to the *jolie laide*. As he wrote in *The Secret Life of Salvador Dalí:* "In the elegant woman there is always a studied compromise between her ugliness, which must be moderate, and her beauty which must be 'evident,' but simply evident and without going beyond this exact measure." According to him this woman attained her elegance through the angled prominence of the hip bones, "which absolutely must be very prominent—pointed, so to speak—so that one knows they are there, under no matter what dress: present and aggressive." Bettina Bergery, whom Dalí said looked like a praying mantis, personified this type of "surreal" elegance. She conformed to the characteristic of the "smart" rather than pretty woman described in the article "Do You Want to Look Pretty?" in the March 1933 *Ladies' Home Journal:* "A certain sophistication of manner; features oftentimes frankly irregular; a slim polished directness that seems to emphasize angles rather than curves; hair that is sculptured close to the head; a profile that is strong; carriage that is distinguished rather than graceful."

What a number of fashion writers called the "hard chic" of the Schiaparelli woman was grounded in part on the couturière's insecurity about her own appearance and her attempts to counter it. Unlike her sister, whom an aunt characterized as having the classic beauty of Pallas Athena, Schiaparelli had a somewhat long face, strong features, straight dark hair, heavily lidded eyes, and moles on one cheek that her astronomer uncle, Giovanni, said were in the shape of the Big Dipper (the constellation Ursa Major). She did not photograph well, as a rule, and throughout her life tended to avoid having her picture taken. Dressing elegantly was a way of compensating for what she felt she lacked. Interviewed for the article "Take Your Personality with You" in 1954, she observed that "you must dress your *self*, the self you wish to show to the world, not only to friends who know you well, but to co-workers and casual acquaintances who are appraising you constantly." That her self-transformation was a success, according to her own very critical appraisal, is attested by an incident she relates in her autobiography that took place in a Munich restaurant with her friend Jerome Hill. As she mounted a staircase surrounded by mirrors, Schiaparelli noticed in the reflection a chic woman who reminded her of Paris in the crowd of otherwise shabby people: "'There,' I said to Jerome, 'at last there is a smart woman.' 'Heavens!' exclaimed Jerome, 'but don't you recognize yourself?'"

Schiaparelli can be credited, perhaps more than any other designer of the period, with putting truth to the statement that "made" beauty beats "born" beauty. Fashion journalist Alison Settle, editor of British *Vogue* from 1926 to 1933, included this observation in her 1938 book *Clothes Line:* "Schiaparelli, probably the most intelligent woman who ever designed clothes, says that the really well-dressed woman is, in her experience, seldom the pretty woman. Things come, you see, too easily to the born pretty woman. It is the woman who, not having the gift of great good looks (often with none at all), has worked to make herself attractive, who is outstanding for chic. The pretty woman doesn't want her type touched; she is afraid of change because she is so satisfied with what is now there, she thinks she knows just what suits her, she is not open to advice as is the made beauty. And the woman who does not change is never a well-dressed woman; change is the spice of good looks and good dress. Not to be pliable to the change and movement of fashion is to miss a great deal of the excitement and pleasure of at least one side of life. If you define fashion as time moving (and that is what it is) then you are not fully alive unless you are moving with it."

The substitution of chic for beauty during the 1930s was just one aspect of an entire rethinking of what it meant to be feminine. With fashion caught between two extremes—the Marlene Dietrich–type trousered lady and the seductive curves of a Mae West—the whole concept of femininity was called into question. It is interesting, given her philosophy of dress, which dared women to be themselves, that Schiaparelli was a traditionalist on the issue of trousers for women. Although she had championed the divided skirt, she was for many years vehemently opposed to women wearing trousers and man-tailored suits, calling them "hateful and ugly." She felt that they violated the fundamental principal of classical design, harmony, by betraying a woman's femininity. Fashion, Schiaparelli believed, should respect the body, emphasizing slim, simple lines and womanly sophistication over girlish prettiness. Thus her clothing appealed to women like herself—accomplished, independent women whose looks did not conform to the standards of conventional beauty but who managed to make a virtue of their defects, such as a prominent nose or a large mouth, because they were so beautifully turned out.

For summer 1937, multicolored butterflies fluttered over pale pink organza in Schiaparelli's latest evening silhouette in the new shorter length—ten inches from the floor (above and left). The waltz-length dress was worn with starched petticoats and the designer's own version of the ballet slipper, high-heeled Perugia ankle-high shoes with a lattice of straps in pastel kid. The new dress length was the sensation of the season, and the fashionable silhouette was ordered and reordered by dozens of America's smartest shops from coast to coast.

Man Ray's three-color carbon transfer print of brilliantly hued butterflies (above), made sometime between 1930 and 1935, may have provided the inspiration for the fabric Schiaparelli used for her waltz-length evening dress for summer 1937. The Man Ray photograph is colored in the same hues as Schiaparelli's textile design.

Schiaparelli's summer 1937 collection featured long "cage" coats of Ducharne's large-meshed crin (a heavy silk net) worn over evening gowns. In this sketch from Bergdorf Goodman (above), a black gown printed with large white butterflies is worn with a black mesh coat that fastens at the front with a single black butterfly-shaped clasp. Fuchsia pink crin coats closing with a pair of butterflies were worn over all-black gowns. Madame Arturo Lopez-Willshaw, Chilean wife of the South American art collector, was photographed for Paris *Vogue* in July 1937 wearing a white satin version printed with brilliantly colored butterflies and a black crin coat—a Surrealist metaphor for beauty captured.

Schiaparelli's Music collection for fall 1939 included her revolutionary "peephole" hats, which were worn perched at the front of the head and tilted forward. They had oversize transparent brims or deep, stiff, coarse veils that the wearer could see through. The collection also included hats with "cage" crowns enclosing brightly colored birds. In Horst's photograph for the June 1939 issue of *Vogue* (right), the fashionable woman, here embodied by Princess Jean Poniatowski, a loyal Schiaparelli client, is not only "caged" by her flower-trimmed hat with its veil of stiff mesh but protected by it as well.

The perfume shop in Schiaparelli's Place Vendôme salon, shown above in a 1947 photograph, was designed in the form of a gold and black birdcage by Jean-Michel Frank. The armchair on the left has a cotton slipcover printed with a pattern of the constellation Ursa Major, or Big Dipper, Schiaparelli's personal emblem, and the cone-shaped objects hanging in the cage are the perfume Sleeping, designed as a "lit" candle packaged in a conical "snuffer." Schiaparelli's perfume business was incorporated as a separate company early in 1938 under her administration as well as that of Henri Winter of Paris and Francis Cahill of London. Later that year an American perfume company was formed, owned wholly by Schiaparelli and with offices in Rockefeller Center under the direction of the

businessman Count Waldemar Armfelt. The interior of the American showroom was also designed by Frank, in gray and pale pink with nineteenth-century furniture, including quilted pink or pale blue satin chairs. The swagged window draperies were in a heavy, striped crinkled fabric in pale gray and white with white wool ball fringe, creating an effect similar to that of the Place Vendôme salon.

Schiaparelli's costumes for Gabriel Pascal's 1938 film
of George Bernard Shaw's play *Pygmalion*, starring
Wendy Hiller as Eliza Doolittle, helped to accomplish
Eliza's transformation from a Cockney flower seller
(above) into a sophisticated young woman. Among
the designs was a short-sleeved silk day dress printed
with wild strawberries, apple blossoms, and leaves
from Schiaparelli's Pagan collection (above, right),
shown in April 1938 and inspired by Botticelli's
paintings *The Birth of Venus* and *Primavera*. As with
many of Schiaparelli's costume designs for film and
stage, those for *Pygmalion* were drawn from her
current collection rather than produced specifically
for the production. The film was released in Great
Britain on October 6, 1938.

The empty baroque frame in which Horst P. Horst posed Schiaparelli for the photograph at left could alternatively be read as a mirror. The viewer sees not a reflection of herself but the image of the designer—in effect giving substance to *Vogue* editor Bettina Ballard's observation in her memoirs, *In My Fashion*, that the woman who dressed in Schiaparelli wore clothes that belonged more to the designer than to the wearer: "It was like borrowing someone else's chic." In the photograph Schiaparelli is dressed in an ensemble from her winter 1937–38 collection, which was described by *Women's Wear Daily* on August 5 as full of modern baroque whimsy. The evening silhouette was clean, crisp, and fitted and included richly trimmed jackets and tall narrow toque hats worn forward on the head. The ensemble worn by Schiaparelli was seen at many of the season's "first nights," such as the National Horse Show, and consisted of a copper-red crêpe dress worn with a darker-toned velvet jacket with pendent pockets and embroidered in bright copper. The same collection featured the couturière's Surrealist suit embroidered with lips, which was worn with her notorious high-heeled-shoe hat designed in collaboration with Salvador Dalí (p. 136, right). The collection also included the cupid and cherub jewelry worn by Nusch Eluard in her portrait by Pablo Picasso (p. 120).

Daisy Fellowes, considered to be the most fashionable woman in Paris during the 1930s, was described in the memoirs of *Harper's Bazaar* editor Carmel Snow, *The World of Carmel Snow* (1962), as "the personification of the hard Thirties chic that came in when Schiaparelli became the rage." Fellowes is seen above attending a wedding in London early in December 1934 wearing a satin evening gown. The daughter of the fourth Duke of Decazes, she was the granddaughter, on her mother's side, of the American Isaac Singer of sewing-machine fame. During the 1920s she wore Chanel but toward the end of the decade left Chanel for Schiaparelli. According to photographer Cecil Beaton in his book *The Glass of Fashion* (1954), Mrs. Fellowes's distinction of being the best-dressed woman in the world was owed not to frequent changes of clothing but to "the brilliance of her studied simplicity. Other women would often be furious to see her wearing the same dress perpetually for day and evening wear." Simplicity of dress was also espoused by Schiaparelli, who in the second of her "Twelve Commandments for Women" states that "a woman who buys an expensive dress and changes it, often with disastrous result, is extravagant and foolish" and, in the ninth, "she should buy little and only of the best or the cheapest." A sometime author and fashion writer, Daisy served as the Paris editor of *Harper's Bazaar* from 1933 to 1935. As Schiaparelli's *mannequin mondaine*, she was dressed for free so that the couturière's designs would be seen "out in the world." Her wardrobe provided the fashion magazines and society columnists with endless material for commentary, for she had no qualms about wearing some of the designer's most outrageous designs, including her infamous shoe hat (p. 137). She was immortalized by Schiaparelli in a design printed on the silk used for a blouse in her winter 1937–38 collection and on a glazed chintz available at her downstairs boutique, the Schiap Shop. The fabric design, which reproduced Marcel Vertès's illustrations for Daisy Fellowes's 1935 book, *Les Dimanches de la Comtesse de Narbonne* (The Countess of Narbonne's Sundays), included the name of the book and a pen-and-ink sketch of Mrs. Fellowes against a white ground with a faint ribbon-stripe of pink.

According to the November 1936 issue of *Vogue*, Marlene Dietrich's shopping trip to Paris for her winter wardrobe created the excitement of the season. Always the epitome of glamour, Dietrich bought six ensembles from Schiaparelli as well as two from Alix, two from Lanvin, and two from Molyneux, and five hats from Madame Agnès and four from Caroline Reboux. Among the Schiaparelli designs she purchased was the model at right, for winter 1936–37, for which she paid 1,000 francs. The black wool jacket is embroidered with gold-sequin palm trees and was worn over a short black crêpe dress and accessorized with a glycerined ostrich feather cone hat—the perfect ensemble for an evening of dinner and the cinema or cocktails and cabaret. Schiaparelli wore the same model to the premiere of the play *Fric-Frac* starring the actress Arletty, who was also a client. The palm trees, a nod to Napoleon's native Corsica, were based on those embroidered on the white satin tunic of the emperor's coronation costume, designed by the painter Isabey and portrayed in Robert Lefèvre's painting *Napoleon in His Imperial Costume for the Coronation of 1804* (1806), now in the Musée National de la Legion d'Honneur, Paris. Dietrich purchased other accessories with a Napoleonic theme on her shopping trip, including a bag from Madame Azka and Napoleonic hats from Madame Agnès. Her choices were possibly sentimental, referencing her first film, *Little Napoleon* (1922). Among the other models Dietrich purchased from Schiaparelli's winter collection were a simple black velvet evening dress with a red Tunisian belt, a plain white silk jersey evening dress that set off her emeralds, and a tailored wool coat with black fox-fur collar and "busby," or guard's hat, inspired by the coronation of Edward VIII, who later abdicated the throne to marry Wallis Simpson. Dietrich is wearing the latter ensemble in the photograph by Cecil Beaton above.

Millicent Rogers, daughter of John D. Rockefeller's partner in Standard Oil, Henry Huttleston Rogers, patronized Schiaparelli throughout the 1930s. She was described by Cecil Beaton in *The Glass of Fashion* (1954) as being "extravagantly beautiful . . . with her face like a lotus flower and her figure like a Chinese statuette." Named one of the world's best-dressed women, Rogers exhibited great flair and originality in her wardrobe, often wearing haute couture with jewelry she had designed herself or in unexpected combinations— for example, an embroidered peasant blouse and Tyrolean hat worn with a strictly tailored Schiaparelli suit. In the photograph for *Vogue* at left, Rogers (at that time Mrs. Ronald Balcom) wears Schiaparelli's dinner ensemble from winter 1938–39 with a black velvet jacket trimmed with gold *passementerie* (trimmings) and two antique crosses. *Vogue* editor Bettina Ballard described Rogers as one of several American women whose fashions caused a stir in Paris, even though the heiress spent little time in that city, preferring instead to ski in the Austrian Alps, where she spent almost seven months of the year.

Before her marriage to the Duke of Windsor on June 3, 1937, at the Château de Candé in Monts, France, Wallis Simpson selected eighteen models from Schiaparelli's summer 1937 collection (presented on February 4, 1937) for her spring wardrobe. Most of the designs she chose featured necklines close to the throat, long sleeves, and simple cuts. Among the models was the black floor-length evening ensemble with a rococo appliqué of white leather trimming the jacket that she wears in this photograph taken by Cecil Beaton at the Château de Candé (above). One of Schiaparelli's most copied designs, the outfit even appears briefly in the 1938 movie *Love Finds Andy Hardy*, where a version is worn in the opening scene by actress Mary Howard as Mrs. Tompkins. Other models selected by Mrs. Simpson included Schiaparelli's sky blue jacket with three-dimensional plastic butterflies

(p. 150), her black evening gown printed with white butterflies and worn with a black crin mesh evening coat (p. 156), and that famous Schiaparelli-Salvador Dalí collaboration, the lobster dress, which Mrs. Simpson wore in another photograph Beaton took in the gardens of the Château de Candé (p. 135). Beaton's entry for November 1936 in *Cecil Beaton's Scrapbook* (1937) describes the transformation of Wallis Simpson into a *jolie laide*, the epitome of the Schiaparelli lady: "Of late, her general appearance has become infinitely more distinguished. Not only is she thinner, but her features have acquired a refined fineness. She is unspoiled. She is like an ugly child who wakes up one day to find that it has become a beauty, but she herself has created this beauty by instinctively doing the right things." Her metamorphosis was complete.

Schiaparelli's winter 1937–38 collection featured richly embroidered fitted evening jackets in the tradition of the *habit à la française* from the last years of Louis XVI. The model at right, in "Dregs of Wine," one of Schiaparelli's "After the Storm" shades, was worn by Jane Clark, wife of Kenneth Clark (then director of London's National Gallery of Art), over a lighter, long crêpe dress to the 1939 opening-night party for the Museum of Modern Art in New York. Mr. and Mrs. Clark were photographed by Herbert Gehr in front of a Jacques Lipchitz sculpture with Salvador and Gala Dalí, who wears a Schiaparelli evening coat from the same collection (above). Both women regularly dressed in Schiaparelli. The designs worn by Gala were frequently a gift of Edward James, the Surrealist art collector and patron of Dalí. Jane Clark purchased her Schiaparelli ensembles at the designer's London salon. They included a newspaper-print silk day dress that she wore with the matching "folded" hat on an Orient Line cruise (1935); the lobster dress also owned by the Duchess of Windsor and Daisy Fellowes that she wore to dinner at Buckingham Palace on March 28, 1938 (p. 134); a blue version of the evening dress embroidered with Saint Peter's keys (p. 205) from Schiaparelli's summer 1939 collection (which she may have purchased to celebrate the 1939 publication of her husband's book on Leonardo da Vinci, who had influenced the design of Saint Peter's Basilica in Rome); and a white plush velvet coat with a mermaid button from summer 1937, a version of which was also owned by Marlene Dietrich.

Six Collections

Beginning with her Circus collection, presented in February 1938 for summer 1938, and for the next five seasons, Schiaparelli was at her most creative and inventive. Her imagination knew no bounds, moving from the circus to Renaissance painter Botticelli's maidens and then on to the heavens, the Italian Commedia dell'arte, bustled dresses of the late 1880s, and finally, in April 1939 for the fall collection, music. Gold and silver bells embroidered on jackets and gloves presciently tolled the end of an era, for France and Great Britain would soon declare war on Germany.

Schiaparelli had been presenting themed collections since 1935, when she moved her salon to the Place Vendôme. The aptly titled "Stop, Look and Listen" collection that opened the salon in February 1935 heralded the new approach. The collection looked to Schiaparelli's own past, present, and future. There was fabric printed with a collage of her old press clippings, a compact shaped exactly like a telephone dial that could be engraved with the number of the new salon or the owner's own number, and innovative evening dresses that draped around the body like Indian saris when other couturiers were showing full skirts. But while her collections revolved around prescribed themes, Schiaparelli continued to identify individual models by numbers, eschewing the practice of most fashion designers of giving fanciful names to each model, a practice initiated by the British couturière Lucile (Lady Duff-Gordon) earlier in the century.

With the introduction of her thematic collections, Schiaparelli also introduced a new theatricality into the salon presentations she gave four times a year. Staged more as performances than as the traditional parades of models, her showings had all the excitement of an opening night and were not to be missed. The front rows were filled with her smartest customers, and the crush of people, as fashion editor Kathleen Cannell vividly recalled in her unpublished

book *Paris Bouquet*, "resembled rush hour in the subway with the press practically crowded out by royalty, politicians, artists, aviatrixes, admirals, explorers, film stars, Gold Star Mothers, industrial magnates, generals, duchesses, and of course dress buyers. The mannequins had to fight their way through the salons."

Schiaparelli usually presented her collections at the end of the two weeks allotted for each season's showing and would so dazzle and delight her

audience with amusing "tricks" and innovative styles that they would forget what they had seen elsewhere. The designer was intensely interested in the response to her clothes. Although some couturiers, such as Coco Chanel, never attended their own showings, Schiaparelli invariably stood watching in the doorway by the stairs, always sensitive to the audience's reaction as each model passed by and, according to *Vogue* editor Bettina Ballard in her book *In My Fashion* (1960), "making the darkness of her humour felt if the farewell atmosphere was not enthusiastic enough."

In 1937 *Life* photographer John Phillips recorded the working of Schiaparelli's salons and ateliers for the magazine, although no article was ever published. His photographs document many aspects of her business, including the showing of the fall 1937 collection on April 29. In one of the photographs, shown opposite, the mannequin Christiane (whom Phillips happened to be dating) waits in the doorway to model the designer's newest waltz dress, floor length at the back, shorter in the front, and printed with Beatrix Potter–like rabbits and cabbages, while Roberte is already on the floor modeling her ensemble, a daytime suit with a short, fitted jacket and dramatic high hat, for a group of clients and their *vendeuses*. One of the few photographs of Schiaparelli that Phillips managed to take shows her at work in her studio, studying the charts of model numbers and fabric samples for one of her collections while dressed in her typical black and white, in this case a white wraparound work smock over a black dress accessorized with one of her favorite bracelets, a jeweled serpent coiled around her wrist.

In his autobiography, *John Phillips: Free Spirit in a Troubled World* (1996), the photographer vividly described the atmosphere of 21 Place Vendôme: "Luxury greeted me in the person of Georges, the doorman, resplendent in midnight-blue livery with twin rows of golden buttons, a golden 'S' on his cap, and white gloves. He ushered me into the ground-floor boutique, where a stylized gilt bamboo birdcage displayed bottles of Schiaparelli's famous perfume, 'Shocking.' The salons where the mannequins modeled the latest creations were on the first floor. Their high ceilings, large mirrors, heavy carpets, expensively fragile bamboo chairs and comfortable cream sofas created a feeling of understated elegance as the mannequins glided through in groups of twos and threes, the scent of Shocking trailing in their wake."

The Circus Comes to Town

Summer 1938
Presented February 4, 1938

One of the most imaginative and brilliantly conceived of the themed collections by Schiaparelli that dominated the prewar years was the Circus collection. Its February 4, 1938, presentation coincided with the *Exposition internationale du Surréalisme*, which had opened in Paris just three weeks before, on January 17. Schiaparelli described it in her autobiography as her "most riotous and swaggering collection . . . Barnum, Bailey, Grock, and the Fratellinis got loose in a mad dance in the dignified show-rooms, up and down the imposing staircase, in and out of the windows." Tall peaked clown hats vied for attention with such Surrealist jokes as a hat in the shape of a giant inkwell with a quill pen thrust through the top and a feathered toque shaped like a sitting hen. There were handbags that looked like balloons, and spats were worn as gloves. Boldly colored printed fabrics with circus-inspired designs that resembled children's drawings were used for both day and evening wear. Prancing horses embellished buttons, while a bolero evening jacket was richly embroidered with dancing elephants and acrobats swinging from a tightrope of tiny mirrors. A new lipstick, Frolic, was launched, and a new color was introduced—"Calliope" red, a shade between cherry and scarlet.

Within a week of the opening, American textile manufacturers had picked up the theme and launched their own versions of Schiaparelli's circus prints. By February 10 one manufacturer had introduced the theme to New York's notions show in the form of buttons, clips, pins, and buckles featuring clowns, prancing horses, toy balloons, drums, and clown hats, among other designs. The circus theme provided American retailers with a wealth of imagery to mine. Circus names were given to clothing, as, for example, Lord & Taylor's "Ringmaster" striped dress, while stores such as Bonwit Teller used the theme for its Fifth Avenue windows, as a background for its "merry-go-round" fashions.

The theme was visited again that summer, on July 2, when Lady Mendl held her spectacular Circus Ball at the Villa Trianon, her home in the Parc de Versailles. The ball featured pink-satin-clad acrobats, trained ponies, and three orchestras—one playing American jazz, another Cuban rumbas, and a third (all female) Hungarian waltzes. Lady Mendl dressed as the pony master, wearing a gown by the American designer Mainbocher and a green taffeta Venetian silk cape from Schiaparelli's fall 1935 collection. Schiaparelli herself wore a white Directoire-style gown embroidered in gold, with a long fuchsia chiffon scarf and white sandals with three-inch soles, and danced until five o'clock in the morning.

In this 1938 photograph, Madame Helena Rubinstein, founder of the successful beauty salon and cosmetic empire that bears her name, is seen wearing a design from Schiaparelli's Circus collection. The short-sleeved pink bolero evening jacket is completely covered in embroidery—elephants and acrobats set against a backdrop of embroidered swirls. This jacket was one of a number of Schiaparellis owned by Rubinstein.

Schiaparelli's boldly patterned crêpe evening gown with matching "circus tent" veil for summer 1938 made a brief appearance in the British spy movie *Ten Days in Paris*, starring Rex Harrison. A fashion-show sequence was filmed in Schiaparelli's salon, and the photograph above shows her with one of her models, preparing for the scene. The couturière (at left in the photograph) wears a jacket of civet fur and is holding fabric decorated with her signature lobster print, the result of one of several collaborations between her and Salvador Dalí. The motif was featured in Schiaparelli's February 1937 collection for summer, showing up on beachwear and on a white organdy evening gown that was one of eighteen garments Wallis Simpson ordered from the designer before her marriage to the Duke of Windsor in June (pp. 134–35).

The boldly colored silk crêpe evening gown printed with carousel animals shown here was accessorized with a matching "circus tent" veil that could be worn in several ways—over one shoulder (as illustrated at right), draped over the head (as in the house sketch above), or worn over both shoulders as a short cape. The motifs printed on the gown include childlike drawings of circus wagons, swans, rabbits, trains, and children riding carousel horses.

A circus sideshow freak, the skeleton man, inspired the design illustrated in this house sketch (left) of a black rayon crêpe evening dress with the skeleton's bones outlined in padded embroidery, worn with a clownlike hat in the shape of a snail and a long, black, "circus-tent" veil. The concept, which represents a collaboration between Schiaparelli and Salvador Dalí, has Surrealist overtones, resonating in particular with the images of bodies and bones explored by Dalí in several drawings he did around the same time. The actress Ruth Ford, sister of the Surrealist poet Charles Henri Ford, owned one of these gowns, which was given to her by Dalí's patron Edward James. James had also presented Miss Ford with another Schiaparelli-Dalí collaboration from the Circus collection, the "tear" dress (p. 138). Miss Ford's mother was a Schiaparelli client as well and owned the pink jacket with circus horses and draped harem skirt (p. 176, left).

This short-sleeved ankle-length dinner dress with a flaring skirt (left) is made of sheer pink silk chiffon printed with the same circus motifs used for the blue silk crêpe evening dress illustrated on page 173.

Designs from Schiaparelli's Circus collection were worn by the French actresses Arletty and Blanche Montel in the play *Cavalier Seul*, a comedy by M. M. Jean Nohain and Maurice Diamant-Berger that opened at the Gymnase in Paris in February 1938. The designs included four tailored suits, a travel ensemble, two evening dresses, two dressing gowns, and one nightgown. Among the designs worn by Arletty was the evening ensemble shown in the publicity photograph above (left), which was of light ultramarine blue crêpe with a matching bolero fastened with twelve gold buttons. The bolero was embroidered with large paisley

motifs of gold paillettes and gold and multicolored silk flowers, and the gown, in typical Schiaparelli fashion, was draped simply across the hips and worn with a tiny, snail-shaped hat tilted toward one eye. Another of Arletty's costumes was the tailored suit of dark green wool she wears in the photograph directly above, which buttoned up the front with thick round buttons of green Galalith and had scalloped pockets and revers replacing the collar. The suit was worn with a mauve silk blouse and accessorized with a small-brimmed hat and a box-shaped bag.

A leitmotif of the Circus collection was the Orient, a theme that resonated in Schiaparelli's work thoughout her career. The dinner ensemble illustrated in the house sketch above combines the themes of the Orient and the circus. The jacket, of pink silk woven with a design of prancing circus horses, fastens with flying acrobat buttons and is worn over a dark purple crêpe gown with a harem skirt. The skirt, draped upward between the ankles, leaving openings for the feet, recalls Paul Poiret's prewar Orientalist fantasies. Among the clients who purchased this model was the mother of actress Ruth Ford and the Surrealist poet Charles Henri Ford. Schiaparelli had experimented with a narrow, hobble-style skirt during her first trip to Paris as a young woman, when a family friend, the historian Alberto Lumbroso, invited her to accompany him to a ball held by the sculptor Marie Henraux-Bernières and her husband, Lucien Henraux. Having never attended a ball before or even owned an evening dress, she purchased four yards of dark blue crêpe de chine from the department store Galeries Lafayette, which she did not sew but simply draped around her body, passing it through her legs to achieve a look similar to that of the harem skirt. A yard of orange silk was wrapped around her waist as a sash, and another yard was made into a turban. Schiaparelli recalled in her autobiography that this design was her first couture failure—the pins used to fasten it gave way and her partner was compelled to tango her off the floor to safety.

The tiered sleeves associated with clowns' costumes—done in bright pink satin encrusted with silver thread, pearls, and blue brilliants—set off this evening gown in midnight blue Amoroso crêpe. In the house sketch above, the long, slim silhouette is accentuated by the mannequin's hair, arranged high on the head. Pink satin gloves completed the ensemble, which was worn by the socialite Madame Arturo Lopez-Willshaw to a Paris premiere, as reported in British *Vogue* in May 1938.

Traditionally, every fashion show ends with a bridal gown. For the Circus collection, Schiaparelli closed with a simple white wedding gown. However, as this house sketch shows, instead of the usual plain white veil, the virginal gown was paired with a white tulle veil embroidered with sapphire blue bugle beads arranged in wavy strands that resemble hair, or possibly snakes (left). It is tempting to compare this trompe l'oeil design to the mythical Medusa—a beautiful young maiden transformed into a serpent-haired demon—and to read it as Schiaparelli's commentary on marriage.

A Pagan Collection

Fall 1938

Presented April 28, 1938

For her Pagan collection, presented in April for fall 1938, Schiaparelli drew on the mythological paintings of the Florentine quattrocento artist Sandro Botticelli, in particular his *Primavera* and *The Birth of Venus*. The salon's publicity agent, Hortense MacDonald, described the Pagan collection in a narrative quoted in part by *Women's Wear Daily* in B. J. Perkin's "Glimpses of Paris" column on May 12: "Pan has piped in materials as soft as thistledown. All the colors to make one glad. The soil, the grass, the trees, the wild life of field and forest have come up to Paris from Tuscany hills. Fashion emerges in many guises as earthy and sylvan as spring itself." The collection of some seventy models was whimsical and youthful, echoing the lyricism of Botticelli's paintings. Slim evening gowns were decorated with embroidered or appliquéd leaves and wildflowers, and plastic owls and caterpillars buttoned jackets and coats. Clusters of pinks and cornflowers taken from Flora's robe in the painting *The Birth of Venus* were embroidered on a lavender gown, and apple blossoms and wild strawberries decorated a satin evening bolero that was half pink and half yellow. One of Schiaparelli's "inventions" that season was the flat collar of glasslike Rhodoid set with gold or colored enamel insects and worn with a low-necked evening gown (p. 184). Many of the floral and leaf embroideries included plastic materials to create three-dimensional garlands, and these crisscrossed the bodices of dresses modeled after those seen in the paintings (pp. 182–83). The season's boldest statement, and one that was to set a new trend in millinery design, was the intro-duction of a tiny doll-sized hat worn at an angle and tipped forward over an upswept coiffure (p. 185).

That season American manufacturers provided Schiaparelli with many of her accessories and fabrics, both for the couture collection and for the ready-to-wear items sold in the downstairs boutique, the Schiap Shop. Shoes designed by Roger Vivier were made by the Philadelphia shoe manufacturer Laird Schober & Co. Girdles and brassieres supplied by Formfit helped to ensure the necessary tall, reedlike silhouette. The advertising copy for Formfit, which read like one of Mrs. MacDonald's narratives, described the transforming power of the new "Pagan Charm" girdles and "girdelieres": "Her breasts must have the firmness of buds bursting into leaf. Her step and stance, her whole being, must be free, radiating the pagan joy of living. When you step into a Pagan Charm, a stirring thrill will go right through you—you'll look and feel years younger." Schiaparelli's arrangement with the Chicago-based company was first launched in November 1937. The American manufacturer was provided with design suggestions and advance information on her collection in the form of sketches, so that the foundation garments, each given an "Approved-Schiaparelli-Paris" label, would conform to the season's latest silhouette. Selected department stores promoted the approved corsets and brassieres in special displays. Similar merchandising arrangements were negotiated with other American and British manufacturers, with many of the items sold in the Schiap Shop. These included metallic mesh bags made by the American firm Whiting & Davis and sport and beach clothes made up in cotton-and-wool Viyella from England, linens from Ireland, and Everfast cottons from the United States. The Pagan collection was so successful that it inspired department stores to merchandise Schiaparelli-inspired designs under their own labels, such as Bonwit Teller's "Field and Forest" jewelry, featuring blown-glass grapes and enamel and glass flowers that were displayed in the store window against backgrounds reminiscent of Botticelli's paintings.

During the summer of 1935, Botticelli's painting *The Birth of Venus* inspired Schiaparelli's design for the fancy-dress costume worn by the American-born Vicomtesse Benoist d'Azy to Comte Etienne de Beaumont's *Bal des tableaux célèbres* (Famous Paintings Ball), where guests were invited to come as a famous painting or sculpture. Schiaparelli dressed the vicomtesse as the "Birth of Venus," in an Antoine wig of flowing gold curls and a provocative flesh-colored lamé costume discreetly padded at the bust and hips and ending at the top of the thighs in the front and with a train at the back (right). Upon completion of the tableau, the costume was transformed into a more demure evening dress by catching up the train in the back and adding an apron skirt of the same fabric to the front.

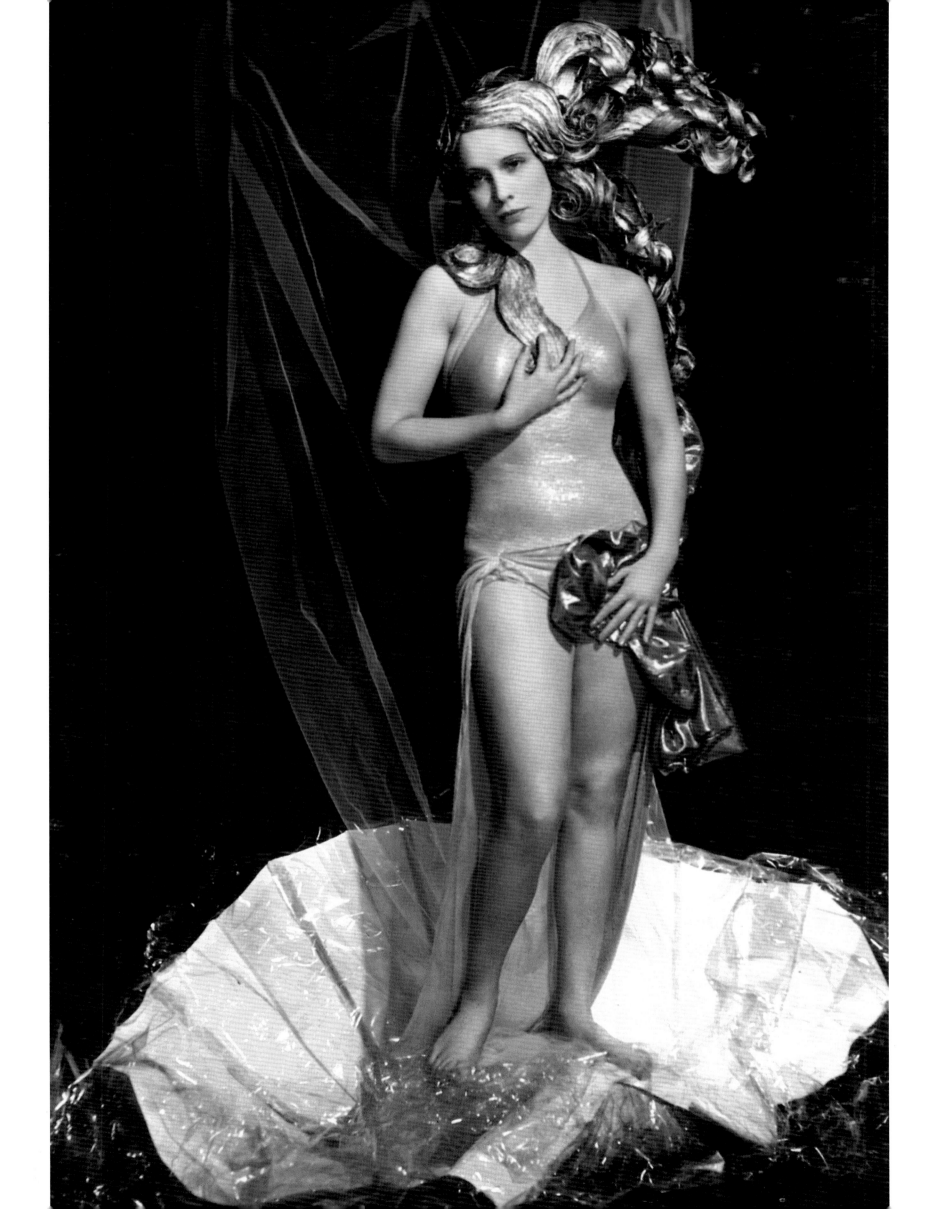

In this black crêpe evening gown the season's tall reedlike silhouette is enhanced by horizontal gathers that cling to the torso. The bodice is entwined with Lesage's inventive embroideries—semi-detached leaves and pink flowers on branches—in homage to the gowns worn by the goddesses in Sandro Botticelli's paintings.

Among the most inventive ideas in the Pagan collection were the flat collar-like necklaces, such as the one at left, once owned by Millicent Rogers. These were made from glasslike transparent Rhodoid (cellulose acetate) into which were set gold or luminous colored insects. Insects also appeared on collars and as jacket fastenings, and a violet beetle was used in the center of a Shocking pink taffeta bow on one of the doll-sized hats that Schiaparelli débuted that season. Made in black felt, the hat—worn by an unidentified model in the photograph by François Kollar at right—measured only nine inches across. Saks Fifth Avenue was the first retailer to introduce Schiaparelli's miniature hat in the United States, a mere three weeks after it was shown in Paris. The American copy, made by David Herstein, retailed for about $15.

In the painting *The Break of Day* (*L'Aurore*), 1937 (above, center), by the Belgian Surrealist Paul Delvaux, woman and tree become one. The fusion of the two had been suggested by Schiaparelli in 1932 with her introduction of the boldly crinkled rayon crêpe called "treebark," which she used for form-fitting evening gowns. In the dinner ensemble from the Pagan collection illustrated in the house sketch above, she used a brown-and-white satin print imitating wood grain. The gown's matching jacket fastened at the waist with

a green plastic leaf and was worn with a leaf-covered hat and green gloves. The ensemble once again alludes to the theme of metamorphosis. Here it is the story of Daphne's escape from the pursuing Apollo and her transformation into a laurel tree: "Her tender bosom was wrapped in thin smooth bark, her slender arms were changed to branches and her hair to leaves; her feet but now so swift were anchored fast in numb stiff roots, her face and head became the crown of a green tree" (Ovid, *Metamorphoses*, book 1, lines 549–52,

trans. A. D. Melville). Leaves were a major motif of the Pagan collection and were used in embroidery, jewelry, hat trimmings, and cutouts covering handbags. In the evening ensemble illustrated in the house sketch above, leaves made of varying shades of green taffeta are sewn to pale green organdy to make up a waist-length cape worn over a white crêpe gown printed with fauns gamboling through a boldly colored rustic setting.

Lucky Stars

Winter 1938–39

Presented August 4, 1938

Schiaparelli fondly remembered and had great respect for her famous uncle, the astronomer Giovanni Schiaparelli, director of the Brera Observatory in Milan, who is best known for his extensive observations of Mars and the comets. She recalled in her autobiography that he would allow her to look at the stars through his telescope and entranced her with vivid descriptions of the planet, sounding as though he had actually traveled there. Schiaparelli's Zodiac collection for winter 1938–39, presented in August, drew on these stories of the mysterious world of the solar system. The theme running through the collection was as usual loosely defined and required the talents of Schiaparelli's publicity agent, Hortense MacDonald, to render it a coherent whole. According to Mrs. MacDonald's commentary, the collection was defined by Euclid's *Elements*, the famous treatise on geometry. The silhouettes were thus built on the strictest measurements—slim and square shouldered, with a slightly raised waistline and feet encased in neat, Gay '90s–style high-buttoned boots. The "geometry" only changed with the added bulk of fur-trimmed capes, coats padded out with feathers, or silver fox and monkey fur hoods that tied around the head like a scarf. Materials and colors "rotated around the sun" and by extension were suggestive of the reigns of Louis XIV, the Sun King, and his successor, Louis XV. The back of a hip-length wool cape in soft "Cameo" pink was embroidered with Louis XIV's emblem, a golden-rayed sun representing Phoebus Apollo, while the front of a black velvet cape, decorated with Versailles' famous Neptune Fountain embroidered in gold (p. 191), made reference to his palace and grounds. A dinner suit was studded with "baroque" mirrors (p. 190), and a black wool evening coat had pink Sèvres-like vases for pockets (pp. 192–93). Other embroideries made more specific references to the solar system, such as a jacket embroidered with astrological signs, stars, and planets (p. 189). Strong contrasts in color were highlighted, including striking combinations, such as "Uranus" canary yellow with "aerostatic" dark eggplant purples. The drama continued with Crown Tenite cellulose acetate plastic zippers with alternating blocks of colored teeth that created a mosaic effect. Light glimmered off such fabrics as moiré silks that changed color in the shifting light and flashed unexpectedly from tiny mirror embroideries on jackets and even from battery-powered electric light ornaments that lit up handbags.

John Phillips photographed Schiaparelli and her couture house for *Life* magazine in 1937. He captured the designer in profile, showing the beauty marks that her astronomer uncle, Giovanni Schiaparelli, told her were in the shape of the constellation Ursa Major (also called the Big Dipper). Phillips was given complete freedom to photograph the couture house except for the upcoming collection, but he had great difficulty in arranging a session with the designer herself. In his memoirs, *Free Spirit in a Troubled World* (1996), he recalled this conversation with Schiaparelli: "My daily requests became more urgent and eloquent, to no avail. Finally, around noon one day, Schiaparelli suddenly emerged from her studio. She wore a wide-brimmed hat of her own design, almost certainly inspired by Bonaparte's famous bicorne. 'The shadow of Napoleon has just passed,' I exclaimed as she swept by. Schiaparelli wheeled around. 'I understand, M. Phillips, that you go out with my mannequin, Christiane.' 'Aren't you fortunate, Madame Schiaparelli,' I replied. 'Fortunate, M. Phillips?' 'Why yes. What would people say if a *Life* photographer doing a story on *la maison* Schiaparelli went out with a mannequin from Chanel?' 'You may take my picture after lunch,' Schiap said, and swept on."

References to the heavens and to astronomy were a leitmotif of Schiaparelli's collections throughout her career. Among the designs included in the summer 1935 collection, which opened her new salon at 21 Place Vendôme, was this "celestial" evening gown molding the figure with a spiral fold and accompanied by a fringed cape (above). The fabric was printed with stars configured as the constellation Ursa Major, which the designer had regarded as a good luck emblem since childhood. She incorporated the motif in her personal jewelry and also used it on fabric in her salon.

The jacket at right, originally part of a dinner costume, invokes Euclid's *Elements* in its strictly tailored "geometrical" silhouette. In keeping with the heavenly theme of the winter 1938–39 collection, it glitters with gold and silver embroidery featuring the signs of the zodiac, the planets, and the constellations (Schiaparelli's personal emblem, the Big Dipper, or Ursa Major, is on the left shoulder).

One of the most stunning ensembles of the Zodiac collection was Schiaparelli's mirror-studded dinner suit (left), originally worn with a towering ostrich-feather hat. Small rectangular mirrors set into gold-embroidered "baroque" frames recall the mirror-paneled doors and decorations of the *Salon de la Guerre* and the *Salon de la Paix* (Salons of War and Peace) on either side of the *Galerie des Glaces* (Hall of Mirrors) at the Palace of Versailles. The figurative buttons were inspired by sculptures of women from classical Greece and Rome.

Cecil Beaton photographed Lady Mendl (above) wearing Schiaparelli's black velvet cape (right) embroidered in gold sequins with a design inspired by the Neptune Fountain in the Parc de Versailles where Lady Mendl made her home. The Louis XIV theme was carried over from Schiaparelli's winter 1937–38 collection, which included jackets embroidered with arabesques and bowknots.

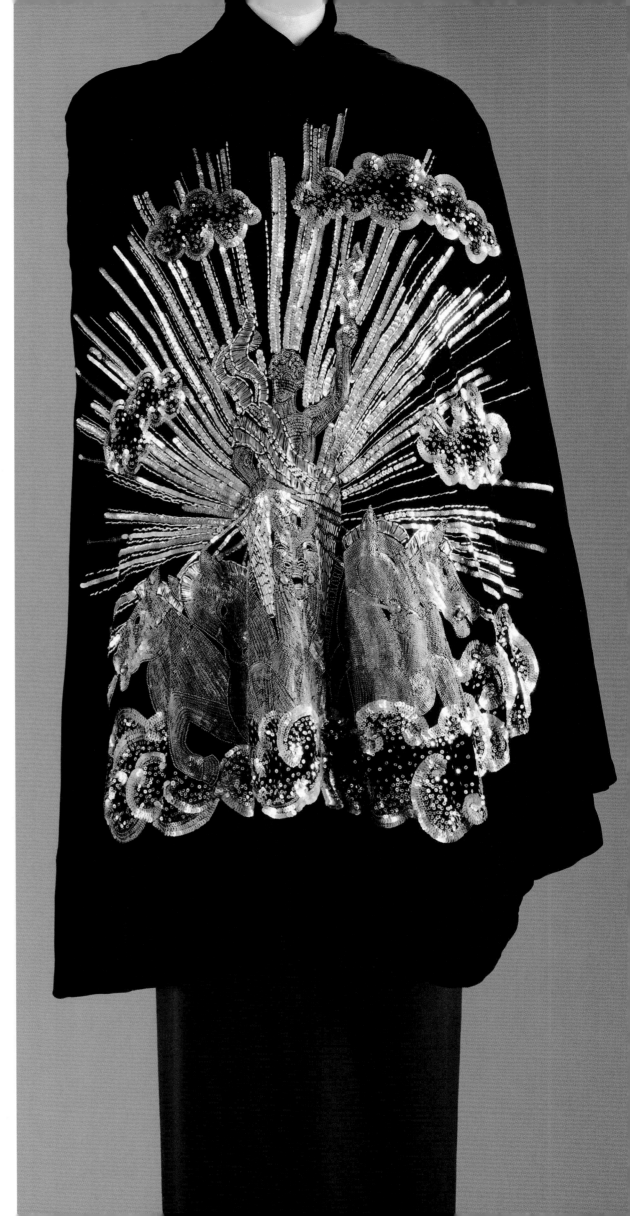

Schiaparelli's Zodiac collection for winter 1938–39 included several references to the reigns of Louis XIV and Louis XV and the palace and gardens of Versailles. In this black wool evening coat (left), the association of Louis XV with the Sèvres porcelain factory was the inspiration behind the rococo vase-shaped pockets in the factory's signature pink and decorated with gilt-edged pink-and-white porcelain flowers (right).

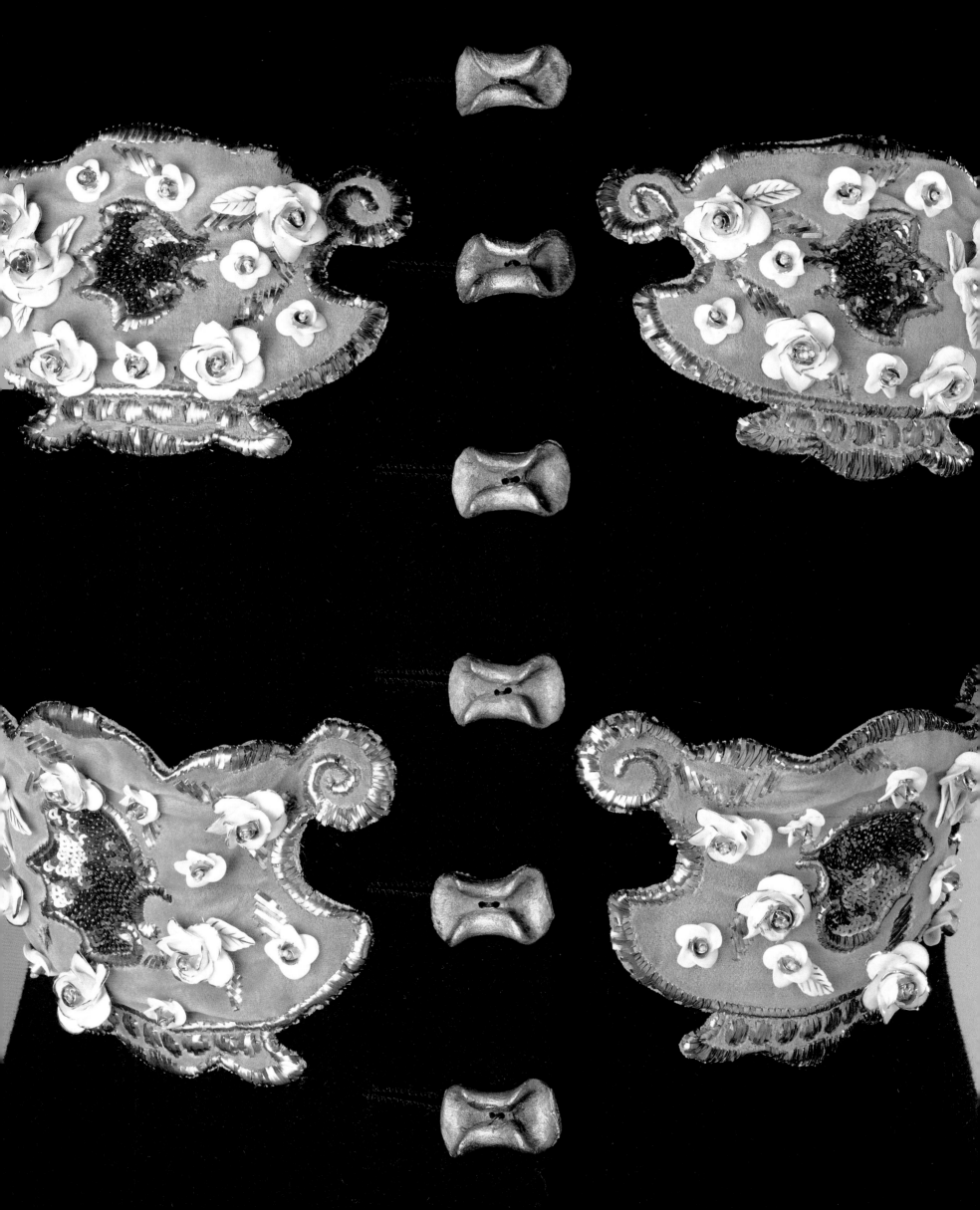

A Modern Comedy

Spring 1939
Presented October 27, 1938

Schiaparelli's fantasies continued in October 1938 with the presentation of "A Modern Comedy" for spring 1939, which brought the eighteenth-century Italian Commedia dell'arte to couture. Instead of embroideries, the collection featured multicolored harlequin patchworks on evening coats and bright satin jackets in vivid theatrical colors called Pulcinella green, Tabarin red, Pierrot blue, Mezzitin pink, and Capitan yellow worn over black dinner dresses. One of the more dramatic silhouettes included a cherry velvet asymmetric evening jacket worn over a black crêpe gown with the left sleeve ending in a large shoulder puff and, on the right hip, a pocket camouflaged by a similar large puff. At a private dinner party, Madame Arturo Lopez-Willshaw sported one yellow and one Shocking pink shoe, both with turquoise blue heels, to complement the Schiaparelli-designed harlequin dress she wore. Victorian tufted upholstery, used the previous season for hats, appeared as "Capitonne" embroidery on a dinner gown of Pierrot blue. Masks from the Italian comedy were everywhere. Schiaparelli had first used masks as evening accessories for her winter 1935–36 collection, when her mannequins carried examples designed by the British painter Derek Hill. They now appeared on buttons, belts, and the heads of hatpins, and full-size masks were used as eyeshades on beach hats.

Schiaparelli's dramatic headwear was in keeping with the theatricality of the collection. There were small Pierrot and peaked clown hats and a cuffed harlequin sport hat with a high cone crown trimmed with quills. Schiaparelli, lunching at the Ritz, wore a version of the harlequin style called "Spanish Don," in which the front and back brim turned up sharply against each other, and a hole through both held a curl of her hair. The masquerade continued with variations of a low pillbox hat called *Femme heureuse*, which was decorated across the top with a harlequin face in relief (sometimes with contrasting lips), so that the woman wearing it in effect offered two faces to the world. The hat, and the theme of the collection, fit perfectly with the latest developments in psychoanalytic theory, particularly Joan Riviere's 1929 essay "Womanliness as a Masquerade" in the *International Journal of Psycho-Analysis*, in which the author postulates that "womanliness" served to mask traits perceived as homosexual or masculine, such as intellectualism. Fittingly, Violet Trefusis, the British novelist and lover of Vita Sackville-West, hosted a costume ball in December 1938 with a Commedia dell'arte theme, at which a number of guests came dressed in Schiaparelli. The couturière wore her harlequin patchwork dress and jacket with a wig of paper curls in which little birds were perched. Daisy Fellowes came dressed in a similar costume with a lavender mask and a yellow veil, while the hostess wore Schiaparelli's large white-and-red bicorne with a white mask and a red-and-white domino, the large cloak traditionally worn for carnivals and masquerades.

The possible political implications of the collection's title should not be overlooked. "A Modern Comedy" premiered shortly after France and Great Britain's betrayal of Czechoslovakia with the signing of the Munich agreement on September 29. The agreement ceded territory to Nazi Germany and would lead to the seizure of the rest of Czechoslovakia by the German army in March 1939. Coincidentally, the October showing of the collection was followed in December by a Comédie française production of Pierre de Marivaux's eighteenth-century play *La Surprise de l'amour* (The Surprise of Love), based on the Commedia dell'arte characters.

A trio of Schiaparelli-clothed harlequins posed for Erwin Blumenfeld's photograph for *Vogue*, which appeared on December 1, 1938 (right). The photograph offers a glimpse of a bold patchwork felt evening coat and the designer's felt and velvet bicorne hats, including one with a lace mask.

Man Ray's *Le Beaux Temps* (above, right), painted in 1939, resonates with Schiaparelli's Commedia dell'arte collection for spring 1939, with the designer's patchwork harlequin coat, made up of graduated lozenges of blue, black, red, yellow, and white wool felt (opposite, and in the house sketch at upper left), coming to life in the artist's geometric-patterned figure. Schiaparelli's name for her spring collection, A Modern Comedy, presented six months earlier, is matched by Man Ray's ironic title, "The Good Times." It is interesting to note that in the following year the couturière introduced her new perfume, Sleeping, shown here in an advertisement drawn by Marcel Vertès (above, bottom left). The form of the container, designed as a burning candle with a conical "snuffer" cover, is strikingly similar to the head of Man Ray's harlequin.

One of the outstanding ensembles in Schiaparelli's Commedia dell'arte collection was a variation on the harlequin patchwork motif. The sleeves of the ruby velvet jacket at right and illustrated in the house sketch above are embroidered in silk, forming diamonds of Shocking pink, yellow, and violet. The jacket was worn over a dress that dipped low in the back and had a high, asymmetric drape at the front. The ensemble was completed by ruby velvet gloves that laced with black velvet and by yellow satin bootees that were scalloped around the top.

Black velvet patches on black wool and black buttons in the shape of harlequin masks add a touch of fantasy to this jacket from Schiaparelli's Modern Comedy collection (above), originally worn over a slinky black evening dress. In the house sketch at left, patchwork replaces embroidery on another design from the same collection, a short-sleeved mandarin-collared pink satin jacket covered with appliquéd satin patches in lavender, Tabarin red, and Capitan yellow. The jacket zipped up the front and was tipped with bows and small tinkling bells.

Return to the Bustle

Summer 1939
Presented February 6, 1939

The couture collections for summer 1939, presented in February, transformed the worldly, sophisticated woman back into the unassuming Victorian lady. *Vogue* summed up the change in their March 1 issue, declaring, "Paris has suddenly gone completely innocent, quaint, modest, girlish." In Schiaparelli's collection the new femininity was reflected in lingerie details on black dresses, rows of shirring on bodices, and apronlike effects achieved with circular tucks across the skirts of dresses. The new Victorian "angel of the house" could dress in Schiaparelli's heaven-inspired crêpes printed with tiny angels sitting on white clouds in a Sèvres-blue sky or with hands folded in prayer among wings, halos, and Annunciation lilies. Necklaces were made of acid-colored stars or gilt comets, while dinner gowns were embroidered all over with pearls forming Saint Peter's keys (p. 205). Schiaparelli, always ready to shock, abandoned innocence for sexiness in some of her designs. A slim black gown, for example, was slit up the side to reveal a leg wrapped in orange and mauve chiffon scarves, and bustled dresses stressed Mae West–inspired womanly curves. Schiaparelli had suggested the bustle in previous designs, but for summer 1939 she embraced it wholeheartedly. On June 29 a quartet of young society women wore Schiaparelli's bustled dresses when they danced a quadrille after the gala dinner held to celebrate the fiftieth anniversary of the Eiffel Tower. Schiaparelli loosely based the dresses on the fashions of the late 1880s, using striped fabrics and gathered and draped bustles, and accessorized them with short black-lace Victorian mittens or long gloves and towering ostrich-feather headdresses echoing the form of the evening's fireworks display. One slim gown made of satin fabric designed by Jean Peltier for Ducharne was printed with a Mae West–like figure dressed in the same style walking her poodle (p. 203, left).

Bettina Ballard, then fashion editor of *Vogue*, would recall in her memoirs that the Paris social season that summer was "the gayest I had yet seen. There were garden parties or big cocktail parties every day and balls or some sort of spectacle every night for all of June and well into July. I can remember thinking, as I dressed for one entertainment or another, that there would have to be some emphatic punctuation to mark the end of this season of frenzied frivolity so that Paris could start afresh on a saner social plan." Unfortunately, the frenzy would end just weeks later, on September 3, 1939, with France and Great Britain's declaration of war on Germany.

The summer of 1939 was notable for its extravagant balls, a last fling before the deluge of war. For the charity ball given in honor of the fiftieth anniversary of the Eiffel Tower, Schiaparelli designed bustle dresses for the four young society women who danced a quadrille after dinner. Three of these gowns can be seen in the photograph by François Kollar at right. The figure on the far right also wears the designer's white grosgrain-ribbon dog collar hung with gold and enamel coins.

The bustled evening dresses seen on these two pages were worn by three of the young woman who danced a quadrille at the *Gala de la tour Eiffel* (Eiffel Tower Ball). The gown on the far left was worn by Madame Propper de Gallegen, who accessorized it with an extravagant red ostrich-plumed hat and short black-lace mittens. The gown was made up in Ducharne's bold multicolored satin and white faille stripe, with the same fabric forming a fan of pleats across the front of the bodice. Jean Peltier's design for the satin fabric by Ducharne used for the bustled gown on the near left features a Mae West–style figure walking a poodle, her silhouette identical with that of the dress. The bustle on the pink-and-black-striped satin gown to the right is more tailored than in the other gowns and was created by folding in half two rectangular pieces of fabric and pleating them into the waist at the back.

In the house sketch above, Schiaparelli's bustle dress adorned with a Mae West–like woman walking a poodle is worn with a Merry Widow–style hat crowned with ostrich feathers. The printed satin fabric was designed by Jean Peltier and may be an adaptation of an illustration by Marcel Vertès of Mae West in *Every Day's a Holiday* that appeared in *Harper's Bazaar* in 1937. Between 1938 and 1940, Peltier and his wife, Suzanne Janin, designed many Ducharne fabrics exclusively for Schiaparelli.

Schiaparelli wore the dinner gown at left to the
Eiffel Tower anniversary party with a long matching
short-sleeved jacket dipping slightly at the front
and a hat trimmed with a tower of ostrich feathers.
The gown introduced Schiaparelli's newest
silhouette, which emphasized a molded sylphlike
form that was to feature prominently in her August
presentation for winter 1939–40. Here, gathers at
the side of the dress break its slim, fitted lines.
The whimsical fabric by Ducharne, one of Janin and
Peltier's exclusive designs, features a flying
swallow carrying a letter closed with sealing wax.

The summer 1939 collection also included "heaven" inspired designs like this orange rayon-silk crêpe dinner dress decorated with the crossed keys of Saint Peter, embroidered in seed pearls, diamante, and gilt thread. A lattice of seed pearls forms a yoke and neckband and is also used as bands on the slightly puffed sleeves. At its presentation the design was shown with long, pale, old-rose-colored gloves and short buttoned boots in orange and mauve striped satin. Appropriately, Jane Clark, wife of the art historian Kenneth Clark, owned a hyacinth blue version of the gown. Kenneth Clark was at the time director of the National Gallery in London and had recently published a book on Leonardo da Vinci. Da Vinci was one of the artists and architects associated with the building of Saint Peter's Basilica in Rome.

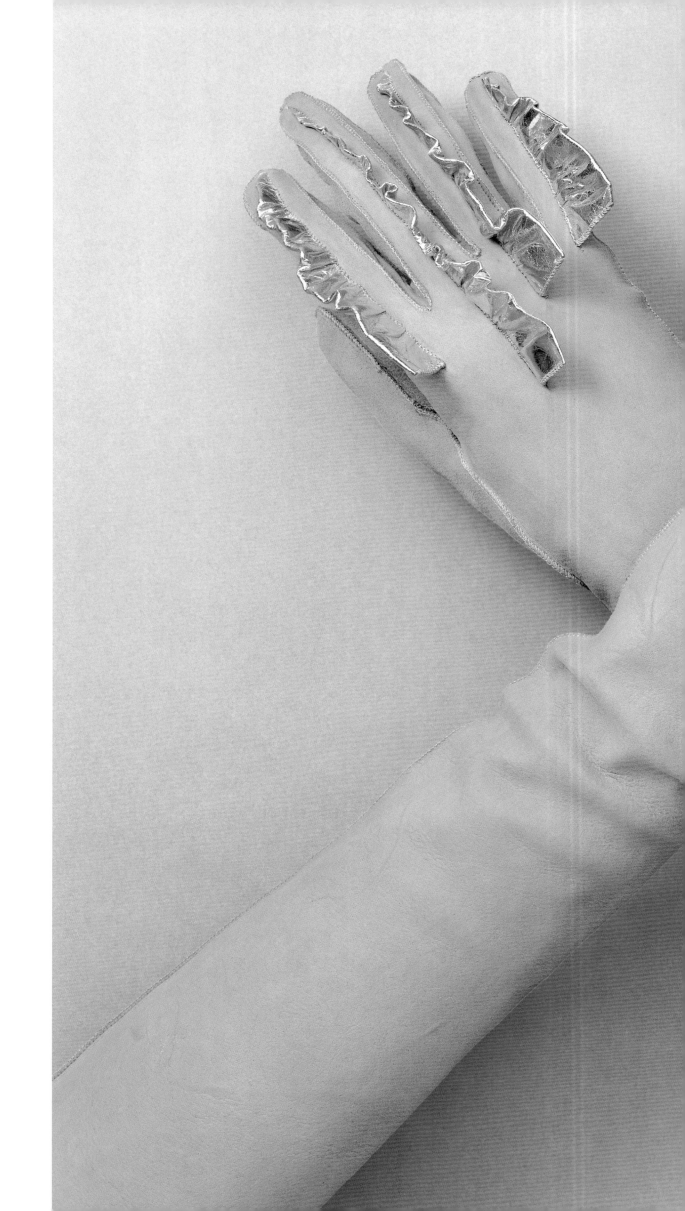

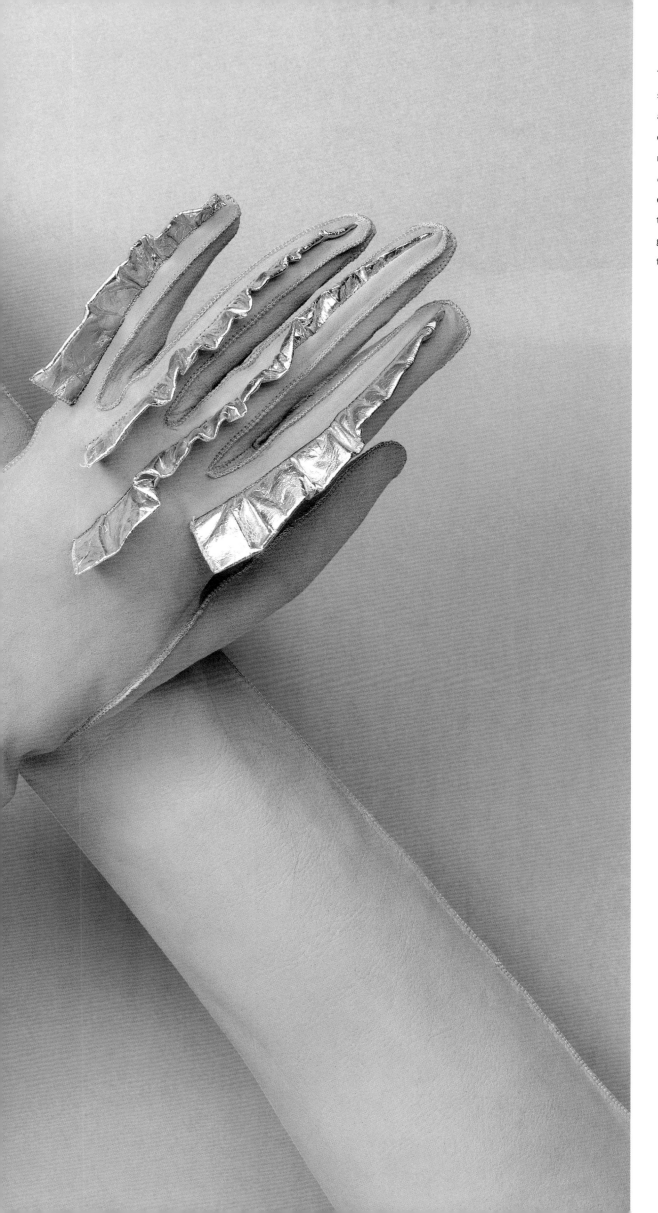

The fashions for summer 1939 ran the gamut—from sexy to ladylike to girlish innocence. Schiaparelli added a surreal note with such evening accessories as these elbow-length bright green suede gloves with gold kid ruffles running up the fingers, each recalling the Italian *corno*, or horn-shaped amulet of the Virgin Mary. Its use on the gloves can also be read as a cheeky reference to the *mano cornuta*, or "horned hand," the Italian hand gesture meant to wave off the evil eye or to indicate that a man has been cuckolded.

Music in the Air

Fall 1939

Presented April 28, 1939

Music boxes concealed in hats, bags, and belts serenaded the audience at the presentation of Schiaparelli's April collection for fall 1939. According to the show's narrative, the clothing was designed for the new woman, "a sylph-like figure whose line from neck to knee is unbroken, keeping in step with Mendelssohn" and who presented a softer, more feminine appearance: "Gone is all aggressiveness. Is she, after all, man's helpmate?" Gently flaring skirts of organdy, chiffon, and tulle on youthful dance dresses were embroidered with violins, flutes, and pianos or bars of music (pp. 212–15). See-through jackets that buttoned with tambourines were embroidered with flowers and worn over dresses that were draped at the front and back (p. 211). Embroidered gold bells rang across the surface of long, short-sleeved black or white transparent chiffon jackets (pp. 209–10), perhaps a reference to the end of the Spanish Civil War on March 28, 1939, or to Ernest Hemingway's soon-to-be-published novel set in 1937 Spain, *For Whom the Bell Tolls* (1940). Schiaparelli may have been familiar with the book prior to its publication through her connection to one of her former mannequins, Martha Gellhorn, Hemingway's wife and fellow war correspondent.

The music theme was not entirely new to Schiaparelli, having appeared in her February 1936 collection with prints dedicated to Chopin in celebration of his centenary. The theme would be picked up yet again, in 1946, on a white satin musical-theme dress she designed for the opera singer Grace Moore, who wore it for a return concert at Deauville, France, where she had first sung in 1929. The dress, which Moore called her "musical career dress," was embroidered in gold with the words and first bars of music from her favorite operas and one or two songs, transcribed by her accompanist, Ivor Newton. In the fall 1939 collection the music theme played out not just in clothing but in jewelry and accessories as well, such as lacquered vanity vases and suit buttons in the shape of piano keyboards. The latter would find an echo in the piano-body mannequin in Salvador Dalí's *Dream of Venus* pavilion at the New York World's Fair, to be unveiled in June 1939. Peephole hats had brims or veils that one could see through, continuing the emphasis on transparency. Other hats had birdcage crowns with brightly colored songbirds inside, another nod to the musical theme. Less thematic clothes included "harem skirts" for golf and bicycling, modeled after bicycle outfits from the 1890s, and town suits with bloused hems. Brightly colored gloves were worn with black dresses, and Schiaparelli offered one mauve and one yellow glove to be worn with a black dinner gown.

Louise Dahl-Wolfe photographed Schiaparelli's bell-embroidered chiffon evening jacket for *Harper's Bazaar*, July 1939, at the Museum of Modern Art during the exhibition *Art in Our Time*, which celebrated the museum's tenth anniversary. The model is posed between two Brancusi sculptures, *Bird in Space* (to the right) and *The Miracle* (left). Madame Robert Lazard was seen wearing the ensemble at the night races at Longchamp in June 1939 with a Reboux hat trimmed with black, gold, and light blue ostrich feathers, the colors matching the embroidery of the jacket.

The latest Schiaparelli silhouette was once again designed to lengthen and slenderize the figure. Long, narrow, short-sleeved transparent chiffon evening jackets dipped down in front, curved upward over the hips, and were shorter in back. They were designed to be worn with simple rayon crêpe evening dresses with subtle bustles created by layered flat flounces that were gathered slightly at the back. The black silk chiffon jacket shown here is embroidered all over with gilt metallic bells and has a flat circlet of beads and metallic embroidery at the neckline that serves as both neckband and necklace. Each of the matching black chiffon gloves is embroidered with a double bell.

This short-sleeved evening jacket in purple chiffon is embroidered with three-dimensional silk and metallic-thread flowers. Echoing the musical theme of the season's collection, it buttons down the front with silver tambourines. The jacket was designed to be worn over a dinner gown with deep, flat flounces at the front that rose into a slightly gathered bustle at the back. South American socialite Madame Arturo Lopez-Willshaw was one of the clients who purchased the model.

Although the prevailing silhouette was long and slender, Schiaparelli designed several models with fuller skirts, appealing to a younger clientele. The purple chiffon gown at left is softly gathered at neckline and sleeves. The slightly gathered skirt is embellished around the hips with an embroidered pink-and-white ribbon from which hang musical instruments—violins, cymbals, horns, and a piano keyboard. The embroidered ribbon ends in an elaborate embroidered bow at the back (pp. 212–13).

Schiaparelli's daughter, Gogo, wore the designer's musical-note evening dress with music box belt, illustrated in the house sketch at left, to a party Lady Mendl held at the British Embassy in Paris in 1939 (above). Gogo's wardrobe always made the news, and her trip to Argentina during December 1940 inspired her mother to design a line of clothing for the "Junior Miss." The American firm Horowitz & Duberman manufactured the line, which was sold exclusively through Bonwit Teller. A second promotion was planned for February, featuring a Schiaparelli-designed spring wardrobe, and another in cotton for the summer.

Schiaparelli's first trip to Tunisia was with her father, a librarian and scholar of Oriental studies, when she was thirteen years old. She visited again in 1936 and much later purchased a second home there in Hammamet. During her 1936 trip she was treated to a fashion show of women's ceremonial dress in her hostess's private quarters and was instructed in the art of sewing, draping, and veil twisting by Bedouin girls. But it was men's clothes, especially the turbans, Tuareg skirt-pants, and embroidered shirts she brought back to Paris, that were to provide a rich source of inspiration for years to come. William Vandivert, a photographer for *Life* magazine and a founding member of the international photographic agency Magnum, captured Schiaparelli and friends at a party given by Lady Mendl at the British Embassy in Paris in 1939 (above). The designer, seated at right, is wearing an ensemble influenced by her Tunisian travels. It includes a white silk faille evening coat heavily embroidered in gold (right, with the sleeves altered to elbow length) and a pale lavender gown with pearls forming a lattice across the bodice in a re-creation of the permeability of the wooden lattice windows (*moucharabia*) of North Africa (pp. 218–19).

This short-sleeved pale lavender gown has a bodice elaborately embroidered with pearls by the firm of Lesage and was worn by Schiaparelli under a gold-embroidered white silk faille coat with elbow-length sleeves (p. 217). The two side panels of the skirt are gently shirred for a draped effect, and the bottom of the skirt flares gently.

A Matter of Prestige

The summer of 1939 saw the closing of Schiaparelli's London salon, opened just five years earlier. The couturière claimed that it had become too difficult to run the two branches simultaneously because most of her time was taken up with designing. Economics certainly played a role as well, particularly the propensity of her British clients to pay "on account," postponing payment until some later date (the last of Schiaparelli's twelve commandments for women exhorts them to pay their bills). The art patron and collector Edward James, for example, who supplied Gala Dalí and the actress Ruth Ford with Schiaparelli gowns, was frequently delinquent in settling his bills, after the war even resorting to emptying his pockets of loose change whenever he dropped by the Paris salon. Several London papers, however, speculated that the major reason for the salon's closure was the activity of copyists, although Schiaparelli was less concerned about this than most of her colleagues, observing in her autobiography: "The moment people stop copying you, it means that you are no longer any good and that you have ceased to be news." The increasing feeling of insecurity in Europe also certainly played a part in her decision to close the London salon, as she would later acknowledge.

With France and Great Britain's entry into the war now seeming inevitable, the atmosphere in Paris was almost frenzied. *New Yorker* columnist Janet Flanner described the city as suddenly having "a fit of prosperity, gaiety, and hospitality." The summer saw a whirlwind of extravagant parties. In June there was a grand fête marking the fiftieth birthday of the Eiffel Tower, which occasioned Schiaparelli's revival of the bustle dress, and a number of fancy dress balls were held. These included Comte Etienne de Beaumont's July costume ball celebrating the tercentennial of the playwright Jean Racine, at which guests wore garments inspired by the court of Louis XIV; the ball was called *À la Cour au temps de Racine*, or A Court in Racine's Time. Schiaparelli

dressed the Siamese envoys to the "court" (her daughter Gogo, Eve Curie, and the Princess Poniatowsky) and went herself as the Prince de Condé. On July 14 the 150th anniversary of the fall of the Bastille was celebrated with an impressive military parade. The couture collections—the last before France entered the war—were shown at the end of July and the beginning of August for winter 1939–40 and were broadcast to the United States over NBC radio by Edna Woolman Chase, editor in chief of *Vogue*. She remarked favorably on the new

"Cigarette" silhouette Schiaparelli presented on August 3 (left), with its sleek, fitted lines, a development of the slim look the couturière had featured the previous season. Now Schiaparelli's emphasis was on materials with smooth surfaces, snugly fitting elongated jackets, hats with behind-the-ear chin straps, and lots of fur. Among the favorites of American buyers was her ruffled apron dress, pulled to the back like a bustle (p. 227). She had been using the apron form since the early 1930s, when she had appropriated the idea of the bib apron with straps crossing at the back as a model for some of her first evening dresses.

On September 3, 1939, exactly a month after the showing of Schiaparelli's collection, France and Great Britain declared war on Germany. The day-to-day operations of the couture houses were affected immediately. Most of the male workers were mobilized, including the heads of several houses: Charles Creed, Lucien Lelong, Robert Piguet, and Marcel Rochas, as well as the French managers of American buying offices. Those who could do so left Paris as quickly as possible. Schiaparelli's brilliant publicity agent, for example, Mrs. Hortense MacDonald, returned to New York. Despite the reduced workforce, the French government requested that all businesses, even those not engaged in war work, remain open. To minimize the shattering of glass during air raids, shop windows were taped up with strips of brown paper in artistic patterns over blue backgrounds. By mid-September the Paris couture was responding to the frequent air-raid warnings and the need to seek shelter by working overtime to create special ensembles for chic evacuations. One widely praised design consisted of a one-piece wide-legged wool trouser suit that zipped up the front and had four large zipper-closed pockets meant to hold identification papers, a flashlight, and other necessities. The initial *S* on each of the belt's three leather buttons left no doubt as to the designer (p. 228). It was the ideal clothing for evacuation to the air-raid shelter in the basement of Schiaparelli's salon on the Place Vendôme.

With the virtual disappearance of the couture's private clients in Europe, only American trade buyers could be relied on for sales. Soon after France's announcement of war, Schiaparelli suggested that buyers could help the French couture and its workers if they defined their needs for the next season's models, including the types of garments they desired and the approximate number they were prepared to purchase. She emphasized that with France at war the new midseason models would have to rely on simple cuts rather than novelty. Schiaparelli, along with the rest of the country, had no doubt that the couture would continue. Fashion, France's second-largest industry, employed from fifteen to twenty thousand workers in the haute couture alone, and the maintenance of the fashion houses was vital to both the country's prestige and its economy. As Bettina Wilson (later Ballard) pointed out in her article "Our Lives in Wartime Paris," written for the November 1939 issue of British *Vogue*: "The best national service the couture can do is to continue to create and to export and to bring money back to France. In the meantime, they want to use their skilled workers and their machines for making parachutes, uniforms or anything they can. They don't want the error of the last war to repeat itself—when highly trained workers lost their skill in munition factories, so that when after the war a passion for clothes swept the country, no one knew how to cut and do fine sewing. It was this, perhaps, which accounted for the chemise dress of the twenties, that needed no cutting."

By early October Lucien Lelong, who had been mobilized by mistake, was back at his business and heading the Chambre Syndicale de la Couture Parisienne. The effect of the war on the couture was evident in the October collections. Schiaparelli had been forced to cut her workforce from 600 employees to 150. Those remaining with her agreed to reduced wages and to work every other week so that a greater number of them could be kept at their jobs. Her spring 1940 collection, presented on October 26, consisted of only thirty models shown on three mannequins. It was presented, she would later state, "as a matter of prestige, to prove to oneself that one was still at work." The collection was prepared in less than three weeks and was praised for its intelligence and wearability. Its character was defined by the contingencies of war, and the military influence was apparent in silhouettes, clothing details, fabrics, and colors. Because there was no way to ensure that accessories ordered for collections would appear in time, Schiaparelli came up with creative alternatives. She replaced handbags, for example, with extra large "cash and carry" pockets and in some designs even added faux shoulder straps; there were suits with detachable patch pockets slung from real shoulder straps and others with pockets hidden in the inside of a skirt hem or concealed in the hem of a coat (p. 236). One of her more innovative ideas—and the ideal solution for the woman caught in an evening air raid—was the *robe laveuse*, or washerwoman dress, featuring a ruffled apron-like drape across the front of the skirt, which could be lowered for a quick change from street length to dinner length, recalling the French laundrywoman raising and lowering her petticoats as she worked (p. 227). Schiaparelli's colors, too, reflected wartime influences and were given names like Torch pink, Maginot Line blue, Aeroplane gray, Trench brown, and Foreign Legion red. Fabrics were equally appropriate and included waterproof wool tweeds and camouflage silk taffetas shot with splashes of blended colors.

Just a few months later the military emphasis in women's clothing had lessened considerably. Unlike their British counterparts, who quickly adopted a made-to-measure tailored uniform for war work, French women were encouraged by their government to maintain their femininity during wartime. In keeping with the new attitude toward fashion, Schiaparelli's summer 1940 collection, presented on January 26, dispensed with the military theme and instead emphasized youthfulness and femininity. Commenting on the recent collections, *Vogue* for March 15 reported: "The great news in clothes is that they are lovely, pleasing to men, and have no period throwbacks." Schiaparelli's latest silhouette for evening was very womanly. Called the mermaid, it curved in at the waist, rounded out over the hips, and drew in again at the knees, a shape helped along by an eight-ounce girdle she had designed with the American corset company Formfit. The design most talked about was her low-cut sheath made into a more proper dinner ensemble by the addition of a short bolero jacket studded with jet beads (p. 237). The only war references in the collection were to Finland, which had recently defeated the Soviet Union after being attacked at the end of November 1939. These included Finnish embroidered wedding belts (p. 242) and hand-knitted knee-length linen stockings available in Sleeping blue, Pirate red, or white and worn with Mary Jane–style patent leather slippers (p. 243). Colcombet's silk scarves printed with French regimental flags, exclusive to Schiaparelli, were made into blouses and evening dresses (pp. 240–41). Jewelry included a clip in the form of four gold swords framing a plaque with white and red hearts and a leaf-shaped lapel clip from which hung a miniature gold birdcage enclosing a gold heart. With buttons and other fastenings in short supply, Schiaparelli boldly resorted to closing a suit with a dog leash. The summer collection also marked the launch of her newest perfume, Sleeping (also the name of a new shade of vivid turquoise blue). The perfume's bottle was shaped like a candlestick with a red flame at the top

Schiaparelli developed the slim lines of her fall 1939 collection into the sleek, fitted "Cigarette" silhouette for winter 1939–40. In George Hoyningen-Huene's photograph for *Harper's Bazaar*, September 15, 1939 (p. 220), the couturière's long, tubular, snugly fitting black-and-blue-plaid velvet jacket is worn over a long black dress and accessorized with a tulle and ostrich feather hat that ties behind the ears and muffles the neck in an oversize bow. As with the bustle dresses she designed for summer 1939, which were worn in homage to the fiftieth anniversary of the Eiffel Tower, built for the Paris *Exposition universelle de 1889*, the silhouette looks back to 1889–90. The fabric, too, is a nod to the late nineteenth century, when there was a fashion for tartan plaids.

The exaggerated hats illustrated in the house sketch on page 221, made in 1942, exemplify the imaginative and extravagant forms that became synonymous with Paris millinery design during World War II.

and packaged in a container in the form of a blue cone-shaped candlesnuffer (p. 197). The design proved to be prescient, for the "City of Light" would soon find its spirit nearly extinguished by the entry of German troops on June 14.

The collection Schiaparelli designed for fall 1940, shown on April 23, was viewed by the fashion press as exceptionally wearable and becoming. Once again, war references were few, apart from a "Daily Ration" scarf printed with phrases that indicated what one could or could not buy on various days of the week but suggesting that love could be had every day: "Monday—no meat, but love," and "Sunday—everything is allowed." For fabrics, easily cleaned linens and cottons predominated. White linen choirboy jackets trimmed with lace were worn over slim evening gowns, and black wool suits had white linen pocket flaps, jacket lapels, and belts that could be removed for washing.

Meanwhile, the war continued to escalate. The Netherlands, Belgium, and Luxembourg surrendered, and much to Schiaparelli's dismay Italy entered the war against France. On June 10 the French government left Paris for Bordeaux, and four days later German forces entered the city. The resort town of Vichy replaced Paris as the capital of occupied France under Marshal Pétain. Much of Paris had fled prior to the German advance, leaving the city temporarily a ghost town. Schiaparelli, Lelong, and Molyneux, each accompanied by some of their staff, had left for Biarritz, arriving by June 20. Together they planned to work, show, and ship their collections from there to New York. But with the fall of Paris the crisis mounted. Edward Molyneux, a British national, quickly returned to England, and Schiaparelli, who had earlier signed a contract for a coast-to-coast lecture tour of the United States during the fall under the auspices of the Columbia Broadcasting Company, was urged by Lelong to leave as soon as possible if she hoped to fulfill her commitment. She departed for New York by way of Lisbon aboard Pan American Airways' "flying boat," the *Yankee Clipper*, arriving in the city on July 20. She had designed a special wardrobe to illustrate her lecture tour, "Clothes Make the Woman," and had made arrangements to have it copied by five specially selected American manufacturers. Each garment and hat would bear a label declaring it an "Authorized Schiaparelli Reproduction—Special Collection, 1940," which the manufacturers would purchase at about a dollar each. The money raised from the labels was to go to a fund administered by the Quakers to help unemployed Paris dressmakers. The designs for this ready-to-wear collection were modeled after the coats, dresses, millinery, bags, and other accessories Schiaparelli sold in the boutique of her Paris salon and made use of fabrics she had chosen expressly for the American market. Distribution of the collection was to be undertaken by the Allied Stores Corporation (formerly Hahn Department Stores), who at the time had Bonwit Teller of New York and Jordan Marsh of Boston under its umbrella.

Schiaparelli arrived in New York with only four suitcases and about $70,000 worth of jewelry. The rest of the specially designed wardrobe was scheduled to come later by ship. Unfortunately, the ship was sunk en route, a casualty of war. Bonwit Teller stepped in and generously offered its workrooms so that the missing garments could be replaced, using as models the outfits Schiaparelli herself would be wearing during the lecture tour. The project turned out to be a lesson in the difficulties and differences in producing a couture collection in the United States. In France, fabrics would have been provided to the designer on approval, but in the United States these had to be purchased outright, and individual details, such as buttons, were not supplied singly by artisans content to make only a few but had to be bought in quantity to keep costs down. Frustrated by the experience, Schiaparelli felt that the end result was not up to her usual standards, although the sixteen-piece collection was simple and wearable. It included a couple of loose coats with sloping shoulders and pockets hidden in side seams (p. 243), a dress with unpressed box pleats that could be adjusted by an elastic belt (she gave this new daytime silhouette the sobriquet "breeze blown" because the fullness was pushed to the front), and a suit with a wraparound skirt. Her signature embroideries graced a dinner suit and an evening jacket worn with pants for lounging. Only one formal evening gown was included, in black crêpe with a shirred bodice and wide shoulder straps, its skirt draped up in pocket folds at the sides. The tasseled stocking cap that she called "Peg Leg," designed to go with her day dresses, was given a U.S. patent on October 15, 1940 (p. 236).

Schiaparelli's tour took her to more than thirty cities, where she spoke to audiences ranging in size from a few hundred to twenty-six thousand in Saint Paul, Minnesota. In her lectures she defended France's style leadership, certain that despite the present circumstances it would again rise to preeminence. New York, she maintained, would never replace Paris as the center of creativity in fashion, because the premise behind American textile and fashion design was commercial rather than artistic. Naturally, many in American industry took exception to her views. One shoe manufacturer pointed out that the couturière's name had been used to promote a high-priced brand of shoes that had actually been conceived by a young American freelance designer, with the sketches merely sent to Paris for Schiaparelli's approval; no changes had been made and yet the shoes were presented as a Schiaparelli design. The shoe trade saw this as a clear indication of her lack of appreciation for American creativity. Others, however, recognized her exceptional originality and contributions to fashion, and on September 9, in Dallas, Texas, Schiaparelli became the first European designer to receive fashion's equivalent of the Oscar, the prestigious Neiman Marcus Award for Distinguished Service in the Field of Fashion, which had its beginning in 1938. According to Stanley Marcus, at that time executive vice president of Neiman Marcus, it was presented to her, the "style interpreter of contemporary life in fashion," in recognition of her "daring, originality, ingenuity, and her far reaching influence in everything she touches in the whole fashion picture from hats to shoes." The other recipients that year included the French-born American milliner Lily Daché; Edna Woolman Chase, editor in chief of *Vogue*; and Sylvan Stroock, head of the woolen manufacturer S. Stroock & Co.

By the end of her lecture tour Schiaparelli had decided that she needed to return to Paris to oversee her business interests, despite the protestations of her daughter, Gogo, who was also living in the United States, and her American friends, many of whom were in the diplomatic service. On January 4, 1941, she sailed from Jersey City on the *Siboney*, then a liner with the New York and Cuba Mail Steamship Co. (later that year the *Siboney* was acquired by the U.S. Army for transport duty and in 1944 was converted into a hospital ship, the *Charles A. Stafford*). She carried only one suitcase and a package containing thirteen thousand vitamin capsules to be distributed in unoccupied France through the American Friends Service Committee. On her arrival in Bermuda, British customs officials confiscated the vitamins, insisting that they were food and there-fore contraband—despite the fact that the vitamins had been issued a navicert by the British government (which should have prevented any search or seizure) for their delivery to the French minister in Lisbon and to American-French War Relief, Inc. News of the incident reached Europe, providing the Germans with some useful propaganda. The problem was quickly resolved, however, and on Schiaparelli's arrival in Portugal the British ambassador to Lisbon arranged for the shipment of the vitamins from Bermuda and their distribution in unoccupied France.

Schiaparelli's return to Paris in January 1941 placed her in a precarious position. She came under increasing pressure from both the Germans and the Italians, who remembered her earlier denunciations of fascism, and at the same time she found her loyalty to France questioned, although she had been a French citizen since 1931. Her stay in the city was therefore brief, and with the help of American friends in the diplo-matic service she returned to Lisbon in early May, leaving her salon on the Place Vendôme in charge of her director, Louis Arthur Meunier, and her secretary, Yvonne Souquières. Flying from Lisbon on Pan American Airways' *Dixie Clipper* with forty other passengers, Schiaparelli arrived in New York once again on May 25, this time entering the United States under the immigration quota rather than as a visitor, which allowed her to seek American citizenship, an option she would later decline. During her stopover in Bermuda on May 5 she had been interviewed by the British, who questioned her about her relationship with the Germans and her activities in the United States. The text of the interview formed the beginning of a lengthy file on the designer kept by the British Ministry of Economic Warfare from May 1941 through October 1944, in which she was classified as a suspect person. Although her interrogators found nothing incriminating in the interview, the earlier vitamin incident in Bermuda had apparently raised a red flag, creating a negative impression and suspicions. It was another interview by the British in Bermuda, during a stopover by the *American Clipper* on July 28, 1941, that started a chain of events that was to cause the couturière many future problems and was one of the sources of the "malignant force" that she felt plagued her throughout the war and afterward. This interview was with Marie Parkinson, the French wife of Schiaparelli's British director of her perfume business, George R. Parkinson, who had immigrated to the United States a year earlier. Mrs. Parkinson had decided opinions on Schiaparelli. According to the British Ministry report in the Public Record Office: "She (Mrs. Parkinson) stated that she (Schiaparelli) was and always had been very anti-British and that her feelings in this respect were well known. She was in fact spoken of as a fifth columnist. According to her Madame Schiaparelli had been extremely friendly with the Germans while she was in Paris and was one of the very few individuals who was allowed by the Germans to retain her car for personal use. On being asked if it were true that she was closely interrogated by the German authorities on her return to France regarding the confiscation of her vitamins in Bermuda, Mrs. Parkinson stated that Schiaparelli had made a great deal of fuss about this episode only in order to stir up anti-British feeling in France."

As a result of Mrs. Parkinson's denunciation, Schiaparelli was in effect blacklisted by the British. Problems with her London perfume company contributed to British animosity toward her. In particular, claims that she was diverting assets into her own pockets that should have gone to the perfume company led to British efforts to stop payments to her of profits that they claimed were wrongly distributed. As a result of the controversy, the British blocked her visa applications to the United Kingdom to work for their Medical and Surgical Relief Committee several times in 1943. In the texts of their refusals they continually refer to her as anti-British and in one letter attribute this in part to a love affair gone wrong. During her lifetime Schiaparelli remained completely unaware of the source of her troubles. If she had known, it is clear she would have been deeply hurt, for she had a great deal of affection for the British and liked to think of Great Britain as a second home.

The German Reich had in August 1940 proclaimed its intention of integrating the French couture with the German fashion industry, moving its headquarters to Berlin or Vienna. Lelong, as president of the Chambre Syndicale, resisted, and the couture houses were able to remain open but were placed under control of the new French state, together with other branches of the clothing industry. The circumstances under which they were able to continue is still not completely clear. In Schiaparelli's case, a hint can be gleaned from the business registration records in the Archives of Paris and the salon's bankruptcy papers filed in 1954. In February 1942 Schiaparelli's Paris salon was placed under a German administrator. This was apparently done as a result of the Nazis' ordinance of September 27, 1940, which defined Jewish identity and commanded that a yellow poster reading "Jewish Business" be placed on all Jewish shops. Schiaparelli's limited liability company had two Jewish associates, Charles Kahn and Charles Blumenthal, who together contributed the major share of the capital. The business was thus identified as Jewish, despite the precautions Schiaparelli appears to have taken to safeguard against this possibility by having herself designated president director in May 1941, prior to leaving for New York for the second time. M.D.C. Crawford, writing in 1941 in *The Ways of Fashion*, recalled a rumor current at that time: "An eye witness said that he had seen an anti-Aryan sign pasted on [Schiaparelli's] house in Paris." The business would not be re-registered with Schiaparelli as president director general until January 21, 1946.

During the four years Schiaparelli was in the United States, her salon was managed by Irene Dana, who was married to a Russian nobleman, Count Hayden, and had worked with several prominent designers before joining Schiaparelli. (Dana would open her own couture business in London after the war.) Together, the couture houses that remained in operation provided fashions to some twenty thousand women during the Occupation, including those made wealthy by trading on the black market in butter, eggs, and cheese (*beurre*, *oeufs*, and *fromage*; they were thus known as BOFs) as well as wives and favorites of the Nazis. Beginning in July 1941 these women had possession of a special "designer card" that gave them access to the collections, which were strictly regulated as to the number of designs that could be produced and the amount and type of fabrics and trimmings used. The French were each allotted one hundred ration points a year for clothing, and to obtain one new suit, thirty points and at least one worn suit had to be surrendered. The card-holding customer of the haute-couture houses, however, needed only fifteen points to purchase an entire season's wardrobe. The only additional requirement was that the customer contribute five percent of the purchase price to the National Emergency Relief. Although fabric was being rationed, the haute couture's allocation of material was not fixed at thirty percent of their level of consumption in 1938, as was the case with other branches of the clothing industry. Even in 1943 the haute couture received enough fabric to fill the regular rations of fifty thousand people, although it actually went to fewer than half that number.

In February 1943, Joseph Goebbels, Hitler's minister of propaganda, ordered the Paris fashion houses closed, but Lelong was able to persuade the Germans to keep them open, saving thousands of workers from being conscripted. A year and a half later, on August 25, 1944, Paris was liberated by the Allies, and the couture immediately set to work preparing new collections. Restrictions were placed on the number of models per collection—forty instead of 150. Only fifty percent of the models could be made in fabric containing just thirty percent wool. Yardage was limited to 3.25 meters per dress, 3.75 meters per suit, and 4.25 meters per coat. The house of Schiaparelli, still under Dana's management, presented its collection on October 5, ending with a tricolor "Liberation" ensemble consisting of a wide blue moiré cloak over a white dress with large red panels. The new couture collections were decried by the American fashion press as being too exaggerated and extravagant for a world still at war. On November 15, 1944, *Vogue* published an open letter from Lelong written in response to the criticism, in which he explained that the new fashions were conceived in a very short amount of time following Paris's liberation. The collections, he stated, were intended to be sold to Parisians and provincial dressmakers, not to the Allies, and, further, that after the presentations many of the exaggerated designs had been eliminated and replaced with simpler styles more in keeping with wartime austerity. Drastic shortages and curbs on raw materials, transportation difficulties, and bans on the use of electricity and gas made it impossible for the couture to resume its exports after the city's liberation, even though foreign buyers were eager to place orders. The domestic market absorbed what was available. At the rate of exchange then in place, it is likely that foreign markets would have found the French goods too expensive, for prices were as much as four times 1939 levels.

The March 15, 1945, presentation of the house of Schiaparelli was again designed by Dana. The restriction on the number of models that could be produced had been raised to sixty, new yardage limits were in place, and prices were still controlled to a certain extent. No American buyers attended the March showings, and their Paris representatives were only able to look, since there was still uncertainty about the ability to fill orders as well as concern over the high prices. Fortunately, private clients were not put off by the price increases, and rumors of further fiscal restrictions yet to come fueled buying. Besides, selling was not really the point. The collections were viewed by the couture mainly as a way of keeping the creative juices flowing. This was especially true of designs for evening, since there was no place to wear them, as balls and parties were still things of the past and few had the money or spirit for gala nights out. Some of the couture models in any case exceeded American and British fabric restrictions and could not have been reproduced in those countries. Although the foreign press had been allowed to attend the openings, representatives of the overseas buying groups were restricted. No photographs were allowed, and no sketches could be published until after April 15 in order to protect legitimate buyers from premature production and stop piracy. The Chambre Syndicale was now more interested in catering to a private clientele than to manufacturers and retailers.

The ruffled apron pulled up high at the back of the black dress at right adds a note of domesticity and femininity to the "hard chic" for which Schiaparelli was famous. The designer called these *laveuse*, or washerwoman, dresses because by changing the position of the sash they could be transformed from street length into a longer length for evening, echoing the way a washerwoman would raise or lower her skirt as she worked. In this photograph by Jean Moral for *Harper's Bazaar*, September 1939, the dress is pictured with a pale turquoise-blue velvet hat with a shirred velvet chinstrap. The dress was a favorite of American buyers and was imported to the United States by the New York fashion house Hattie Carnegie.

Eleven days after France and Great Britain's declaration
of war with Germany, *Women's Wear Daily* reported that
Parisian designers were busily creating functional but
fashionable air-raid-shelter suits that women could quickly
slip into before rushing out to a shelter. Schiaparelli's
designs included this version photographed by François
Kollar—a one-piece wide-legged trouser suit that zips
up the front and has large zippered pockets designed
to hold a flashlight and identification papers (left). The
model in the photograph also carries a sturdy handbag
large enough for a gas mask and first-aid kit, as well
as a powder puff and lipstick. The house sketch above
illustrates another Schiaparelli design, a purple woolen
trouser suit camouflaged by a pale blue transparent
oilskin overall. The hood was designed to slip easily
over a gas mask.

Fur appeared in all the couture collections for winter 1939–40. One of the season's most talked about ensembles, illustrated in the house sketch at left, was Schiaparelli's matching leopard-skin jacket, hat, and bootees. Bands of navy velour bordered the sleeves and lower edge of the long, smoothly fitted jacket, whose buttons, with tiny holes and little balls under glass, mimicked a type of child's toy. The dress worn with the jacket had a navy façonné silk top, navy suede belt, and wool velour skirt with a ruffled apron-like panel at the front, the edge of which extended below the bottom of the jacket. In the spirit of 1889–90, the little toque hat dips over one eye in the sketch and ties behind the ears with a shirred black velvet chin strap that forms a jabot at the neck. Among the accessories shown that year, the leopard-skin bootees that fastened up the side with four small buttons made the biggest splash. The well-worn examples seen above were part of the designer's personal wardrobe and one of her favorite pairs of shoes. She was even known to wear them bowling (opposite).

High-buttoned kidskin boots inspired by the shoe styles of the 1890s were first shown by Schiaparelli and Maison Paquin at the summer presentations of the winter 1938–39 collections. Designed to be worn with formal costumes, Paquin's black boots were presented with afternoon ensembles, while Schiaparelli's bright yellow, green, or mauve versions were worn with matching gloves and contrasting gowns. The following season Schiaparelli offered a new look—ankle-high satin bootees that were scalloped around the top and closed with tiny mother-of-pearl buttons (above) and a multicolored, striped leather version with platform sole (opposite). Both pairs were designed by André Perugia for Padova of Paris (Perugia designed much of Schiaparelli's footwear). The pink bootees with pencil-thin green and white stripes matched Schiaparelli's ankle-length satin harem-skirted evening gown for winter 1939–40, seen in the house sketch at left, a formal version of a skirt style introduced the previous season for town and sports suits.

A Matter of Prestige

In December 1939 Schiaparelli arrived on the *Dixie Clipper* for a two-week stay in New York City. According to *Vogue* for January 15, 1940, she arrived with "limited luggage, unlimited chic." Four frameless, zipper-closed bags contained an entire wardrobe, the basis of which was black, apart from a warm brown wool suit and a blue corduroy sport dress. The ensembles in black included three simple day dresses, a wool suit, three slim evening dresses, and two jackets that could be worn with either day or evening dresses. One of those jackets was the black rayon crêpe with gold embroidery and oversize pockets shown at left, from Schiaparelli's collection for spring 1940. The designer reported to the American press that despite the war in Europe, the Parisian couture would continue to do all it could to supply the American market. During her visit, *Women's Wear Daily* reported on December 15 that she had been approached by representatives of the Museum of Modern Art to direct a division of modern commercial design.

Schiaparelli's midseason collection, shown in October 1939 for spring 1940, introduced a military theme, inspired by France and Great Britain's recent entry into the war. The gadgetry the designer was known for was kept to a minimum, with the emphasis instead on smart, simple silhouettes and accessories. Extra large "cash and carry" pockets on suits and coats eliminated the need for handbags, while for evening there were oversize mufflike pockets, such as those seen on the black crêpe long-sleeved tunic jacket of this dinner ensemble that François Kollar photographed for *Harper's Bazaar*, December 1939 (above). The jacket is worn over a cap-sleeved sheath dress and is accessorized with a gold-spangled turquoise scarf tied in a bow under the chin and a tricorne hat lined in the same fabric.

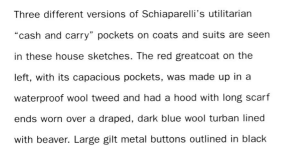

Three different versions of Schiaparelli's utilitarian "cash and carry" pockets on coats and suits are seen in these house sketches. The red greatcoat on the left, with its capacious pockets, was made up in a waterproof wool tweed and had a hood with long scarf ends worn over a draped, dark blue wool turban lined with beaver. Large gilt metal buttons outlined in black

were embossed with the designer's initials. On the black wool suit at center, a band that runs at a diagonal across the front and back simulates the strap of a handbag, a role filled by the large pocket on the left side of the jacket. The suit is worn with the designer's new wool jersey scarf-hat, where the scarf is of a single piece with the crown rather than coming

from the sides of the brim. In the right-hand sketch, the pocket is hidden underneath a divided panel that simulates a front pleat on the skirt of the olive green wool suit, which was worn with the designer's latest hat, a toque suggestive of the so-called Scotch cap.

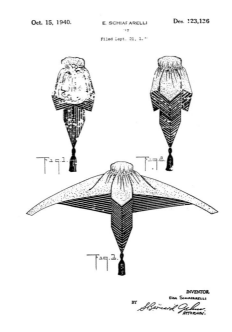

In October 1940 Schiaparelli received an American patent for a knitted jersey stocking cap that wrapped around the head like a turban. The striped cap was originally worn with a matching purple-and-green-striped wool sports dress with unpressed box pleats and an adjustable belt. This ensemble was one of sixteen garments Schiaparelli designed to wear during her American lecture tour in 1940, all of which were to be copied and sold at moderate prices throughout the United States. When the ship carrying part of the collection was sunk, Bonwit Teller generously offered the use of its workrooms to reconstruct the wardrobe. In contrast to the way of doing things in France, where all materials were sent on approval, in the United States every change of fabric or details resulted in a loss of revenue. The entire endeavor turned out to be very expensive, and despite good intentions and the efforts of Bonwit Teller's workers, the collection did not live up to Schiaparelli's expectations.

This slim, black, low-cut evening gown for summer 1940, with a scalloped neckline edged with jet beads, was covered by a very short, high-necked, jet-embroidered bright pink bolero jacket, turning the sultry silhouette into a proper dinner ensemble, as illustrated in the house sketch above. The smooth, molded line of the dress, dubbed the "mermaid," was tight at the waist, rounded out over the hips, and drew in again at the knees before flaring at the bottom. An eight-ounce corset Schiaparelli had designed in collaboration with Formfit helped to achieve the required curves, and a jet-encrusted black tulle evening hat worn tipped forward over the brow completed the ensemble. The jacket was also available in Sleeping blue, Schiaparelli's newest color.

At her January 26 presentation for summer 1940,
Schiaparelli featured a tiny hat ruched with tulle and jet
coils planted among the gathers. As illustrated in the
house sketch above, it was worn perched forward on
the head and was shown with a street-length black
afternoon dress and a linen jacket trimmed with Sleeping
blue velvet and embroidered with silk-and-metallic-thread
flowers. The jacket closed with two gilt buttons in the art
nouveau style emblazoned with swans (left). These appear
to be remounted old stock dating from the beginning
of the century, probably used because of the difficulty of
procuring new findings during the war. Schiaparelli also
launched a new lipstick and a new perfume with her
summer collection, linking both by name to her two newest
colors, Pirate red and Sleeping blue.

Schiaparelli designed a group of evening gowns and blouses for summer 1940 made from silk scarves printed with adaptations of the flags of famous French regiments, which the textile manufacturer Colcombet had made exclusively for her. Man Ray's photograph for the March 1940 issue of *Harper's Bazaar* (right) shows an evening dress made from scarves printed with the flag of the Scottish Ogilvy regiment (established in France in 1745). The gown on the left in Schiaparelli's new Sleeping blue, also illustrated in the house sketch shown above, is printed with the flag of the Royal des Vaisseaux. Both gowns were imported to the United States by Bonwit Teller.

Marking the Soviet invasion of Finland at the end of 1939, many of the designs at the couture openings in January 1940 had a Finnish theme. Molyneux offered prints featuring the arms and emblems of Finland, while Bruyère included floral needlepoint belts with designs taken from Finnish peasant costumes. Schiaparelli contributed penguin-print day dresses and a brightly colored embroidered Finnish wedding belt, worn with a black moiré taffeta jacket in the photograph by François Kollar at left, which was taken in Schiaparelli's apartment. In the photograph above, shot by Jean Moral in front of her salon, lacy Finnish hand-knitted linen stockings that were available in a trio of patriotic colors referencing the French flag—Sleeping blue, Pirate red, or white—are worn with patent leather Mary Jane–style slippers. The blouse under the suit is made from one of the regimental scarf prints Colcombet designed exclusively for Schiaparelli.

Schiaparelli's revolutionary red coat (above) was notable for its loose fit and sloping shoulders, definitively marking the end of shoulder pads. *Harper's Bazaar* for March 1, 1941, reported that the design was based on a nineteenth-century nightdress owned by the noted theatrical designer Aline Bernstein. During a visit to the United States, Schiaparelli spent a weekend at Bernstein's country house in Armonk, New York. While there, she made a tracing of a detailed drawing that Bernstein had done for her book *Masterpieces of Women's Costume of the 18th and 19th Centuries*, published posthumously in 1959. The coat was included in the wardrobe Schiaparelli designed for herself to wear on her American lecture tour.

During the German occupation following the defeat of France in 1940, the Vichy government embarked on a program of renewing the French moral climate. "Work, family, fatherland" became the new symbols of France, with roles for men and women rigidly defined. The ideal was no longer the career woman or the fashion plate of the decadent 1930s but rather the wife and mother. Women's vanity and affectations, it was claimed, had contributed to France's defeat; by embracing the simple life, women could now contribute to the country's recovery. Schiaparelli's design for this dinner ensemble for summer 1941 offers a witty observation on the changing role of women. The wool and velvet jacket simulates an eighteenth-century waistcoat of the *ancien régime* (France prior to the revolution of 1789) and is decorated with produce from the French kitchen garden—embroidered vegetables and fruit and three-dimensional buttons in the form of carrots, cauliflower, and a white radish (right). The jacket was worn over a long gown with a Lastex shirred bodice and a ruffle that extended across the front and partly down the sides of the skirt to form a mock apron, as illustrated in the house sketch above. The collection, presented in February, was the last Schiaparelli designed before leaving Paris for the United States on May 11, 1941, for the duration of the war.

L'AMANTE DI C

CON: **ARLETTY** • JEAN TISSIER • PIERRE LARQUEY

The French actress Arletty was dressed by Schiaparelli in films and on and off the stage. During the German occupation of Paris she continued to appear in films, including *L'Amant de Bornéo*, released in February 1942. The ensembles she wore in this movie were designed by the house of Schiaparelli, which in Schiaparelli's absence was directed by Irene Dana. In this Italian poster for the film, Arletty wears a dinner suit, its jacket buttons emblazoned with the *coq gaulois* (Gallic cock), with an oversize striped satin turban. Arletty was imprisoned as a collaborator after World War II because of a love affair she had had with a German officer. After her release she resumed her film and stage career.

Themes and Variations

Schiaparelli returned to Paris in July 1945 after a four-year hiatus from couture. Despite a number of proposals, she had rejected all offers to design while in the United States. According to the explanation given in her autobiography, she saw her role as defending the dressmaking traditions of France and thus was unwilling to offer any competition, however slight, to the struggling Paris couture. Instead, she spent the war years acting as a judge for a national sewing contest; working two days a week as a nurse's aid at the New York Hospital and an additional full day at the Red Cross blood bank; volunteering as a hostess at a canteen for French sailors run by Ann Morgan (daughter of banker and financier J. P. Morgan), who had headed a war-relief organization in France during World War I; joining the Rochambeau unit of woman volunteers for North Africa and France in 1943; and arranging concerts and art exhibitions for the Coordinating Council of French Relief Societies, including, with Marcel Duchamp, the *First Papers of Surrealism* exhibition in New York, organized by André Breton in 1942.

Schiaparelli's complete separation from the world of fashion during those four years left her unprepared for the current Parisian styles. In her autobiography she described the clothes she encountered on her return as ugly and the hats as an "incredible horror." The women of Paris had responded to the restrictions imposed by the Germans during the Occupation with eccentric exaggerations in their clothing, which they wore as a sign of defiance. The fashions of 1943–44 were particularly overstated, featuring towering turbans, over-trimmed hats, and short, extravagantly skirted garments with bulky shoulders. By the time of Schiaparelli's return in summer 1945, fashion had become less extreme but was still exhibiting enough bravado for Schiaparelli to resolve to remake Parisian women, taking them back to what *Vogue* editor Bettina Ballard described as the "hard, highly individual chic" of the years before the war. Regrettably, the type of elegance Schiaparelli remembered was long dead. "I fell into step not with what had happened in between, but with myself in 1940," she recalled in her autobiography.

Schiaparelli found her workrooms still intact but reduced to eight rooms from the twelve she had left behind. Ballard, who returned to Paris immediately after the Liberation, described in her memoirs the atmosphere in Schiaparelli's salon, noting that the rooms were badly in need of paint and heat and that the saleswomen looked pinched and worried. Monsieur Meunier, Schiaparelli's business

administrator, had written to her in New York that he had lost fifty-five kilos and at age seventy-two had the waist of a young man of thirty. Among the other staff remaining were Irene Dana, who had designed the clothes in Schiaparelli's absence; Madame Gilberte, her *première* (workroom supervisor); and René, renowned for the best tailoring in Paris. Many of the *midinettes*, or sewing girls, had left to join the city's growing throng of "little dressmakers," aware that they could earn nearly three times as much on their own as they could by continuing to work for the couture.

There were many additional changes and obstacles for Schiaparelli to overcome. In an interview with *Vogue* published in November 1945, she described some of the challenges she faced while preparing her September collection, the first she had designed in five years. Fabrics were in short supply, and as a result toiles (mock-up models) could not be made up in the traditional way from muslin but had to be pieced together from scraps of material or from paper. Although the Chambre Syndicale had agreed in 1945 on a limit of sixty models (an ensemble of a coat and dress counted as one), the couture was guaranteed only enough fabric to make ten copies of each design. In addition, fabrics were no longer confined exclusively to a specific couturier but had to be shared. The quality of materials also suffered. Synthetics, usually rayon, were substituted for wool and silk, which were in short supply. Sewing supplies, too, were limited, such as pins and the buckram used to stiffen collars and suit shoulders. The cost of producing a new collection had skyrocketed, reflecting the latest increases in wages and the costs of materials. Fabric prices had jumped upward of seventy percent, with rayon double-faced satin, for example, costing four times the price of silk satin in 1939. The cost of a garment was calculated on a customer's measurements and the amount of material used, to the inch. One of the ways to keep prices down was to cut overhead by increasing productivity, but production itself was slowed, not only by shortages of materials but by equipment and machinery that were frequently unreliable and in need of servicing, by periodic interruptions in electricity service, by poor-quality fabrics and workroom supplies, and, not least, by the fatigued and undernourished workers.

In the absence of foreign buyers, the only people purchasing couture were provincial buyers and private clients, who could buy as much as they liked with a special card that could be obtained by presenting a kilo of old wool plus two hundred francs and one's ration card. To the already high cost of garments were added taxes of forty percent, including five percent that went to the Returned Prisoners Fund, which also received the kilo of wool. Despite the absence of foreign buyers, the Paris couture still found itself "exported" through private clients. American G.I.s, for example, would send model hats and other small items to their wives and girlfriends back home, which were often copied by American manufacturers and exclusive retail stores.

For her return to couture with her September 13 presentation, Schiaparelli took inspiration from her own past rather than from her American experiences, as everyone had anticipated. She once again looked back to the Directoire period and the slim lines she had favored throughout the 1930s. But the look seemed new when contrasted with the short, full-skirted silhouettes still seen on the streets of Paris. The most remarked-on design was her elongated silhouette, the "Talleyrand," with its narrow skirt, short stiff jacket, and square shoulders. The suit was worn with a high top hat and a Directoire-style plastron, or dickey, which was slightly padded and tied around the neck, covering the nape, the chin, and the bottom of the cheeks (p. 261). The ensemble was reminiscent of the designs Schiaparelli had presented for fall 1934, which were strongly influenced by the Directoire and featured stiffly starched lace scarves that stood up over one's mouth and chin (p. 260).

For the February 1946 showing, her first collection to be exported since the Liberation, Schiaparelli received advance orders from a number of American buyers who, because of transportation difficulties, were unable to attend. The collection's Indo-Chinese influences, inspired by France's engagement in the Indo-Chinese War, vied with amusing dress prints reviving the Gay '90s textile designs that Schiaparelli had featured in 1939 with her bustle dresses. This was her take on the general trend in couture that season toward a reinterpretation of the fashions of the early 1900s. Schiaparelli's textile design *Les Vieux Beaux* (The Old Beauties; p. 262), drawn by the master silk printer Sache, featured boulevardiers wearing top hats, derbies, or straw boaters and holding canes. Her collection looked to the future as well. One of her most prophetic ideas—and the sensation of the collections—was the packable "Constellation" wardrobe, designed for air travel and named after the popular Lockheed aircraft used for transcontinental and trans-atlantic flights. Composed of six dresses, a reversible coat, and three folding hats, the wardrobe fit neatly into what the *New York Times* described on February 21 as "the largest handbag known to woman" and altogether weighed barely twelve pounds.

Few houses offered anything new in the spring midseason collections for 1946, shown in late April and early May. Traditionally, the spring and fall collections launched the trends that would follow in the main seasonal openings. Like the majority of the houses this season, Schiaparelli chose not to use the spring collection to test the waters, instead offering her prewar staple, embroidered jackets worn over simple untrimmed gowns. The silhouette gave no indication that with her August 29 presentation for winter 1946–47 she would once again revive the bustle of the 1880s, as she had before the war. In this latest version the illusion of curves was tailored and built over a smooth, rounded, bowler-like form. It was seen on short jackets, princess coats, and evening dresses, where the fullness fell softly in flares at the back of the skirt (p. 263). Schiaparelli once again offered innovative ideas for the traveler's wardrobe. Amply sized swing coats with large suitcase-sized waterproof pockets near the hem solved luggage problems by holding pajamas, underwear, and a pair of folded slippers. Schiaparelli refurbished her boutique and launched a new perfume, Le Roy Soleil (the Sun King), in a sumptuous gold and crystal bottle designed by Salvador Dalí and made by Baccarat (p. 264).

American buyers were unanimous in their opinion that, with the August collections, Paris had made a comeback and that the new models were sure to influence American spring styles. Unfortunately, the high prices prompted the majority of retail buyers to purchase models only for style guidance. They did not plan to offer the models for resale but would return them to France or would export them to Canada or South America to avoid paying duty on what were already very expensive goods. Only those stores with dressmaking departments that were equipped to make copies, such as Bonwit Teller or Bergdorf Goodman, could afford to sell the original models. Meanwhile, the couture continued to have production problems. There was still a labor shortage, and it was difficult to obtain fabrics because much of the textile production continued to be allocated to utility garment programs. With the couture midseason openings for late October through early November 1946 in sight, there was increased apprehension that shortages of

Schiaparelli was photographed by Hans Oswald Wild at home at 22 rue de Berri in 1947 (p. 248), two years after her return from the United States. During the war her home had been occupied for a time by the Germans, and after the liberation of Paris it served briefly as home to Angier Biddle Duke and other American officers. Schiaparelli had purchased the eighteen-room *hôtel particulier* in 1937. It had once been the home of Princess Mathilde, a niece of Napoleon Bonaparte and a first cousin of Napoleon III. Jean-Michel Frank and Maison Jansen assisted Schiaparelli with the interior decoration, which was an eclectic mix of treasures she had gathered over the years, from chinoiserie tapestries by François Boucher to English china to contemporary paintings, which were placed anywhere, including on chairs and the floor. Among her most treasured possessions was the screen in the background at left, which held an honored place in her drawing room. It was painted for her by Christian ("Bebe") Bérard around 1935 for her house on the rue Barbet-de-Jouy and consisted of three panels illustrated with the Virgin Mary and her attendants in the style of an Italian fresco. Schiaparelli described it as "magnificent" and felt that it was one of Bérard's best works. She particularly valued the artist's friendship, noting in her autobiography that "to be approved and admired—and sometimes befriended— by Bebe was a consecration in the artistic, social, and intellectual world of Paris."

The house sketch on page 249 illustrates an ensemble celebrating the liberation of Paris. Presented in October 1944 for spring 1945, the collection was by Irene Dana, who designed for the house of Schiaparelli during the couturière's four-year absence. The plain black afternoon dress is worn with an oversize, quintessentially French beret and incorporates bands of leftover fabric (Colcombet's silk scarf prints adapted from the flags of the old French regiments) that had been used by Schiaparelli during the summer of 1940 for evening dresses and blouses (pp. 240–41).

dyestuff would also slow fabric deliveries, especially of rayon, and that measures to conserve electricity would force workrooms to close for part of the week. Luckily, Schiaparelli was able to present her collection on November 8, just three days before electricity restrictions were enacted. The collection continued the emphasis on fullness at the back, and she paid homage to Louis XIV in one of her most striking ensembles, a dinner suit that consisted of a black crêpe cocktail jacket bordered with a broad band of jet-embroidered cyclamen pink taffeta along the front and continuing toward the back, where it ended in an oversize bustle-like bow (pp. 265–67).

The spring 1947 openings took place later than usual in February. There were fewer American buyers than there had been the previous season, and buying continued to be conservative. The prices were still prohibitively high, so that once again buying was cautiously relegated to token purchases that had prestige value and could be used for in-store promotions back home. Only one presentation shook up the season's openings. On February 12 Christian Dior, with the backing of the cotton magnate Marcel Boussac, presented his Corolle Line, which resembled a flower in full bloom, with a long, slender waist and a full skirt blossoming out over padded hips. Proclaimed the "New Look" by Carmel Snow, editor in chief of *Harper's Bazaar*, the revolutionary silhouette was just what Paris needed to revive itself as the undisputed center of fashion. By contrast, Schiaparelli's newest silhouette was straight and tubular, with ribbons or shirred bands that spiraled around the body.

At her April midseason showing for fall 1947, Schiaparelli featured cotton, bestowing glamour on the modest fabric by using it for elaborate evening gowns. As she observed in her autobiography, "cotton can be even more beautiful than brocade." The attendance by American buyers at the couture openings for winter 1947–48, held in late July and early August, was the largest since the war, no doubt spurred by anticipation of new things to come, after Dior's spectacular opening in February (he had not presented in April). Schiaparelli again retreated to the slim lines of the Directoire but added a new silhouette, a barrel outline that belled out over the hips and then curved in again at the thighs on jackets and in dinner suits and, on evening dresses, curved in at the ankles. In November, the barrel moved to the back as a bustle, in a collection for spring 1948 that the *New York Times* described as "particularly handsome and wearable" (pp. 268–69). Among the many new ideas Schiaparelli presented was a striking "pudding-bowl" hat formed from a ring of fur, coarse net, and dramatic blue, yellow, and black kingfisher feathers (p. 270), while monkey fur covered the front and back of the black wool jersey bodice of a long, chic dinner gown (p. 271).

The mood of the late January through early February openings for summer 1948 was unabashedly romantic and picturesque, and the collections were rich in new ideas and silhouettes. Schiaparelli's contributions were sleeves that ballooned below the natural shoulder line in a silhouette reminiscent of the riding habits worn by the "Amazons" (horsewomen) of the early nineteenth century. In April she celebrated the centenary of France's Second Republic (1848–52) with sleeves that ballooned even larger, using them especially for evening capes and coats, some in solid black but with spectacular yellow linings. Period influences continued in the August showings for winter 1948–49 with Schiaparelli's introduction of the cone-shaped "hooped" skirt for daytime, its form achieved by boning running through the narrow flared hem, recalling her parachute-skirted dresses of 1936 that billowed around the ankles as one walked (p. 92, left). "Jungle" furs appeared in the collection, including a revival of Schiaparelli's Perugia monkey-fur boots from 1938 with fur spilling out from the cuff to the heel (p. 143), which now had matching, similarly trimmed coats. A new, sweet and musky perfume was introduced, in a bottle designed to be shocking. Zut (the word is an expletive in French) came in a bottle shaped like a woman's legs seen from the back with her skirt fallen around her ankles, revealing her undergarments.

As the couture prepared its collections for the openings in late January through early February 1949, it was clear that prices for models would likely escalate. This increased the anxiety about American buyers, who the couture feared would purchase muslin toiles rather than actual models made from expensive French fabrics. Schiaparelli's "Hurricane" silhouette, shown that season (p. 272), was perhaps prophetic of the stormy weather ahead for the couture. Continued inflation and the elimination of black-market currency conspired to keep tourists away during the spring of 1949, and the higher costs of hotels, car rentals, and restaurants meant that fewer American buyers attended the presentations in late April and early May. Not all designers held midseason showings that year. Dior and Balenciaga, for example, were conspicuously absent. Schiaparelli presented her collection, however, and her theme was points. There were pointed arched collars inspired by the graceful curves of the calla lily and, on dresses, uneven, jagged décolletages looking like broken eggshells.

On July 27, 1949, some fourteen thousand *midinettes* went on strike in Paris after their wage increases were rejected by the employers association. The strike happened just as the couture was finishing preparations for the season's showings, which were scheduled to start the following week. Although most of these were delayed a few days, Schiaparelli was determined that hers would take place on August 7 as advertised. Only her tailor, *première*, saleswomen, and mannequins remained in the workrooms and salon. As she recalled in her autobiography: "All present worked in a fever, as if for a huge bet, in the best of humor. We showed as I wanted at the scheduled time, but what a show! Certainly as a publicity stunt it was sensational. Some coats had no sleeves, others only one. There were few buttons, certainly no button-holes, for these were difficult to make. Sketches were pinned to the dresses, pieces of material to the muslins to show what colors they would eventually be. Stately evening dresses cut in muslin were made to spring to life with costume jewelry. Here and there explanations were written in a bold hand. It was the cheapest collection I ever made but it sold surprisingly well." The next day the sewing girls returned to work.

The collection received unanimous praise from the press. The headline of the review in the *New York Times* read "Striking," and Schiaparelli even made the cover of the September 26 issue of *Newsweek*. In the article, titled "Schiaparelli the Shocker," the magazine commented that her August 1949 collection had "reasserted her mastery." Its simple silhouettes were transformed by unusual lines and techniques. One of the most daring creations was the evening dress called Forbidden Fruit (p. 273). (By this time Schiaparelli was giving each of her designs a name rather than referring to them only by number, as she had before the war.) *Newsweek* described the gown as "a frisky evening dress in black shot with gold with a slanting décolleté, revealing a pale pink brassiere embroidered in gold and dripping with crystals," for which women were willing to pay $382. It was also announced in the magazine that the designer was making arrangements for the production of ready-to-wear suits and coats to be sold for $100 or more throughout the United States. The new company, Schiaparelli Inc., was to be organized by the New York wholesaler and manufacturer Henry Mandelbaum, who would oversee the manufacturing and negotiations for retail outlets, which would be limited to one per city.

Schiaparelli's November midseason collection was once again full of new ideas. A number of dramatic hats were introduced, including irregularly shaped "cookie cutter" caps, big draped berets, and even a red satin visored evening cap with a peephole for the eye and a Van Cleef & Arpels diamond clip for the eye-brow (p. 275). Among the most startling designs were "House of Cards" coats, including a gold-embroidered ruby red velvet topper with its lower edge held out by a wire and dipping to a large point on each side; it was worn over a matching street-length dress with its hem wired to the same shape (p. 274, left).

The points, angles, and asymmetrical effects that dominated the Paris couture during the November 1949 midseason collections were dropped the following season for softer, more supple lines. For her February 1950 showing, Schiaparelli introduced full coats with wide, short bell sleeves (p. 277, right) or wide, circular back panels that could be draped over the arms like a shawl. In honor of the Roman Catholic Holy Year initiated by Pope Pius XII, she introduced the "Cardinal's Cap," appropriately made in red satin to match a boat-necked dress. On one finger of the long navy blue gloves worn by the mannequin was a large ring recalling those worn by church dignitaries. The *New York Times* commented that the accent in the Schiaparelli collection was on modernity rather than the past.

The designer's silhouettes remained unchanged in her May presentation, which included seventy designs. One model, however, stopped the show—a white cotton net evening dress with a dramatic hemline in which two fan-pleated panels dipped to the back from a huge pink bow centered on the front of the gown, the silhouette giving the mannequin the appearance of gliding like a swan. The dress made an appearance at the June charity ball held at the Hôtel Lambert, where the ballerina Nathalie Philippart wore it for the divertissement from *Swan Lake* she danced that evening with Jean Babilée (p. 278).

Schiaparelli was said to offer the best-tailored suits in Paris, and for August 1950 she featured stiff, pyramid-shaped peplums that broke the long-stemmed silhouette she consistently favored. The collection was named The Front Line, a reference both to the Korean War and to the flat line produced by an oval wooden paddle six inches by three inches that slipped into a pocket over the stomach of the girdle (p. 276). One of the season's standouts was her street-length evening dress in white satin heavily embroidered in gold. Its hem, shorter in front than in back, revealed a bright red lining, and it had a standing collar slashed narrowly at the front to reveal the décolletage. Schiaparelli wore the gown over a longer underdress in June 1951 to the couturier Jacques Fath's *Le Bal des tableaux vivants* (Ball of the Living Pictures), the theme of which was the French court in the eighteenth century.

At the beginning of November, Schiaparelli Inc. presented its first suit and coat collection that interpreted for the New York wholesale market the models originally presented by the couturière in August. The suit with the pyramid-shaped peplum was adapted for the mass market, as were collarless boxy toppers and loosely fitting coats. Publicity for the new endeavor was garnered from a benefit showing in the United States of half of the November couture collection, prior to its presentation in Paris. The collection premiered at a charity showing in Beverly Hills, California, for the John Tracy Clinic, founded in 1942 by the actor Spencer Tracy and his wife, Louise, for the education of deaf children. An additional fashion show, this time for the public, was held at the Beverly Hills Hotel. For the showing in Paris, Schiaparelli added an additional thirty models. The two collections complemented one another, the Hollywood group stressing bright springlike colors and unusual contrasts, while the Paris models featured black and were darker hued.

The highlights of the late January and early February 1951 showings for summer were Schiaparelli's cape costumes, which featured tailored hip-length capes with large, flat pockets at the front, worn over pencil-slim skirts. The involvement of the United States and the United Nations in the Korean War led her to include references to both war and Asian culture in her collection. Camouflage dresses were cut so that colored sections bisected the figure to make it appear slimmer, as in a dress with a white front and red sides. A Chinese-lantern effect was created on evening dresses by organdy pleated overskirts thrown toward the back of the skirts (p. 279). Coats and jackets had oversize buttons and pagoda sleeves and slits for the hands, so that the sleeves hung unused. Satin hats with chignons at the back completed the "Oriental" look. Political references continued, and for the July 29 collection for winter 1951–52 Schiaparelli dubbed the silhouette "SHAPE" (p. 280), after the Supreme Headquarters Allied Powers Europe, which had been established on April 2, 1951, by General Eisenhower. The effect was once again "Oriental," with harem hemlines, turbans, Persian-patterned brocades, and ornate costume jewelry. Full sleeves were again emphasized, although now they were also incorporated as huge balloonlike cuffs on gloves. Meanwhile, Schiaparelli's boutique was making a name for itself with prêt-à-porter glamour and was soon taking in more money than the couture business. It was headed by Hubert de Givenchy, who had joined Schiaparelli in 1947 and would soon leave to set up his own couture house, premiering his first collection on February 2, 1952. His "defection," as Schiaparelli saw it, led to a falling out between the two, and they reportedly never spoke to one another again.

In her February 1952 couture collection Schiaparelli presented a navy blue, tightly corseted taffeta evening bodice with a décolleté neckline like an inverted heart that was described by *Vogue* on March 15 as the "most exciting evening bodice in Paris" (p. 283). Its slim skirt was draped with red paper taffeta that wrapped across the front, ending in a huge bustle set high in the back. In the weeks leading up to the showing of her next collection, for winter 1952–53, Schiaparelli had on display in the window of her salon on the Place Vendôme an enormous green satin grasshopper. The significance of the display became evident at a gala midnight opening on July 31 at her home, where the new collection was unveiled in a private showing. The smooth, sleek lines of the grasshopper and katydid, with their wings folded over their backs, had a counterpoint on her garments in "jut outs"—projecting collars and peplums that gave movement to the designs. Schiaparelli's midseason collection, shown in November, numbered only twenty models, a significant descrease from the sixty to seventy she usually presented, and represented a continuation of the styles she had shown in August. The reduction was a reflection of her financial difficulties, which were worsening. The profit she had made from the boutique in 1951, with Givenchy still designing, turned in 1952 to a substantial loss. In part, this was brought on by the Korean War and its effect on her American customers, which led the designer to expand her licensing arrangements with American manufacturers, building on the ties she had established in the United States at the very beginning of her career. The franchises for all licensed products were handled by Schiaparelli Inc., which also coordinated the sales of the designer-sponsored goods in American stores.

The ready-to-wear coat and suit collections Schiaparelli had licensed in 1949 had been joined in 1951 by Schiaparelli Couture Lingerie (p. 281). The line included slips, gowns, peignoirs, negligees, chemises, and panties and was produced in the United States by McKay Products Corporation and merchandised by Daniel F. Sheehy and Company. By February 1953 Schiaparelli had licensing arrangements with eleven American clothing and accessory manufacturers who were applying her name to products that she endorsed but that were actually the work of American designers. Schiaparelli Separates, for example, were designed by Pat Sandler, who freelanced for New York ready-to-wear firms before establishing his own label of moderate to higher-priced clothing. Altogether, these manufacturers sold $18 million worth of "Schiaparelli" merchandise that year. The ready-to-wear line was expanded to include menswear. In May 1953 it was announced that Schiaparelli had agreed to create a line of robes, sports shirts, and swimwear for Peerless Robes and Sportswear, a menswear manufacturer. A line of men's ties was produced by Bachrach Company. In an article on contemporary necktie design (including those by Salvador Dalí) in the *Saturday Evening Post*, Arthur Bachrach related how he brought out the line. He had been looking for a line of neckties that would compete with the exclusive ties designed by Countess Mara in New York and so approached Schiaparelli, who was more than happy to take a commission. ("Countess" Mara was also Italian, born in Rome three years after Schiaparelli, and was married to an American singles tennis champion.) When visiting New York, Schiaparelli would come in to criticize the designs and colors, which were based on the palette she featured each season in her Paris collections. At times, she would have some of her *modélistes* send sketches that might be adapted by David Crowell, who designed the ties under the Schiaparelli signature.

The financial situation of Schiaparelli's haute-couture business became more and more critical, until the perfume business and licensees were in effect bankrolling the couture, which was organized separately. In an effort to stimulate sales, Schiaparelli presented four wardrobes in October 1953 in addition to her couture collection, each selling at "budget" prices ranging from $575 to $1,400. Models could be purchased singly, but the sum of the individual pieces was much more than the price of the complete wardrobe. The groups were color coordinated and interchangeable, so that it was possible to be well dressed throughout the day at relatively little expense. Unfortunately, neither the collection nor the wardrobes sold well, and Schiaparelli once again ended the year with a loss.

By mid-March 1954 it was rumored that Schiaparelli would be closing her couture house and that she was reorganizing the business toward private clients to enable her to reduce prices and streamline her production methods. In an interview conducted during one of her business trips to New York, she commented in the *New York Times*: "Life has changed for elegant women. Even people with money aren't spending it they way they used to. Today only a feeble minority of women will pay the prices we are forced to ask." She continued that henceforth she was banning the words "super deluxe" and "exclusive" to describe her collections and would instead substitute the words "de luxe confections." Despite her evident plans for the future, she would not design any further collections. The severity of her financial situation led her to close her couture business precipitously on December 13, 1954. The collection she had presented earlier that year, on February 3, turned out to be her last. Ironically, it had been followed two days later by her old rival Coco Chanel's return to couture after an absence of fifteen years.

Although she had left the world of haute couture, Schiaparelli's legacy continued. It is present today not only in the many firsts with which she is credited, from the designer boutique to designer eyewear, but also in the way she revolutionized fashion by giving it a modern sensibility and relevance. She took fashion out of the closet and turned it into "dressing with attitude." The looks she created were widely imitated and adapted, and continue to be so. Many, such as wraparound dresses and lavishly embroidered evening jackets, have become so much a part of the mainstream of clothing design that her influence is not even recognized and goes unacknowledged. Always ahead of her time, Schiaparelli consistently tantalized with new ideas, even during her last years of designing. Her passion was fueled by her artistic sensibilities and by what she referred to in her autobiography as "imagination, initiative, and daring." It was this, above all, that inspired new generations of designers, from Geoffrey Beene to Zandra Rhodes to Yves Saint Laurent, and continues to influence today's *enfants terribles*, among them John Galliano and Jean Paul Gaultier. Schiaparelli chose an ancient Chinese quotation to open her autobiography. It was an apt choice, for not only does it express a truth about an individual life; it also reaffirms her influence on fashion and recognizes a fundamental reality about haute couture—its continuity and frequent cross-generational impulses.

Birth is not the beginning,

Death is not the end.

The *Chuang Tzu*, c. 390 B.C.

As a gift to his wife, U.S. army captain Sidney Williams brought back from the house of Schiaparelli the first hat to arrive in the United States from Free Paris. His wife reportedly took it to Nan Duskin, the owner of an exclusive Philadelphia dress shop of the same name, who then showed it to *Vogue*. Schiaparelli, still in America in the fall of 1944, was asked to model the hat in New York, where she was photographed by Cecil Beaton for the November 1 issue of *Vogue* (left). The striped silk surah hat, in Shocking pink and white, could be worn two ways—with the knot at the center of the head and the loose ends hanging free, as in the photograph, or tilted at an angle, with the short ends tucked in to give the effect of a turban and the longer ends wrapped around the neck like a scarf. Copies of the hat were available to order at Nan Duskin.

The first collection presented by the house of Schiaparelli after the liberation of Paris on August 25, 1944, included several outfits for bicycling, the primary means of transport during the war and immediately after, necessitated by gasoline shortages. The ensemble seen above was photographed by Lee Miller for *Vogue*, November 15, 1944, to illustrate an article chronicling the new winter collections, shown the month before. The model wears a light tan, wool tweed fur-lined coat with patch pockets over brown fur culottes attached to a silk yoke and an emerald green velvet jacket. A matching green velvet helmet with fur halo completed the ensemble.

While on a U.S.O. (United Service Organizations) tour during World War II, in November 1944, Marlene Dietrich posed while "inspecting" the troops in Namur, Belgium, wearing a Shocking pink silk evening coat by Schiaparelli woven with a design of British lions (above). The original caption for the news photograph read "'the gal with the million dollar legs' ponders the issue at hand before she ventures an opinion as to which GI's sport the shapeliest gams." *Vogue* noted in its December issue that French women would wear the coat as a dressing gown. The inference was that the style was too informal for evening wear.

During the March 1945 presentation of the house of
Schiaparelli's collection, designed by Irene Dana, the
front row was filled with servicemen and young American
women in uniform. Although the collection retained the
classic wartime silhouette—short, full skirts and broad
shoulders—it was updated with bright colors, such
as turquoise, pinks, and yellows. The slim-fitting rayon
crêpe jacket seen above and in the house sketch at left
was worn over a matching street-length dress
and featured a softly scalloped Chinese-inspired collar
delicately embroidered with pastel silk and gilt threads.

The hats shown above and in the sketch at left are from the house of Schiaparelli's March 1945 collection. Reminiscent of clown's collars, they look back to the designer's landmark 1938 Circus collection. Wartime shortages of fabrics and trimmings led Irene Dana to imaginative solutions. These hats were cut economically from a semicircle of black satin scalloped around the edge and tied at the top with a ribbon bow. The one above is decorated with feathers dyed pink, yellow, and purple, while the version illustrated in the sketch is festooned with blue ostrich feathers and polka dots of pink, yellow, and purple feathers and is shown with a full-skirted coat that reflects continued wartime influences.

The first collection Schiaparelli designed after her return to Paris in July 1945 following four years in the United States was presented in September for winter 1945–46. The collection looked to her own past, updating the silhouettes she had used previously. Her latest, the "Talleyrand," was inspired by one of her favorite periods, the Directoire, and contrasted with the full, bulky forms that had characterized wartime fashions. The dandified suits and coats she presented were worn with high-crowned hats

and the season's most striking accessory—padded neckwear in the tradition of the muffler worn by the consummate English Regency man-about-town, Beau Brummel. The plain or striped satin dickey tied around the neck and covered the chin, the bottom of the cheeks, and the nape of the neck, as seen in the photograph on the right by François Kollar, recalling the stiffly starched lace scarves Schiaparelli had shown for fall 1934, illustrated above in a Bergdorf Goodman fashion sketch.

Schiaparelli's February 1946 showing for summer featured many amusing dress prints, including a design called *Les Vieux Beaux* (The Old Beauties), used for a ballet-length rayon dinner dress with a wide, wavy, off-the-shoulder collar (left). The fabric print, by the master silk designer Sache, features fin-de-siècle boulevardiers twirling canes and wearing derbies, top hats, or straw boaters. Sache provided designs to all the great haute-couture houses, from Balenciaga to Worth, and was responsible for translating Dalí's design for a lobster onto silk organza for Schiaparelli in 1937 (p. 134).

For her August 1946 collection for winter 1946–47, Schiaparelli returned to the bustles she had featured in 1939, but she modernized the silhouette by giving it a dramatic arching curve. This time the fullness was produced not by the addition of draped fabric but by drawing up the skirt in back, as can be seen in this evening dress of black satin with cut velvet

flowers. The dress was originally worn with a little jacket stiffly rounded at the back, made of black velvet with cyclamen pink facings, and was accessorized with cyclamen pink buttons and gloves. In the photograph above, taken for a French fashion magazine, the ensemble is worn with pink chiffon flowers and black velvet ribbons in the hair.

The bottle for Schiaparelli's 1947 perfume Le Roy Soleil, an homage to Louis XIV, the Sun King, was designed by Salvador Dalí and produced in a limited edition of two thousand bottles by Baccarat and packaged in oversize gilded metal seashells (above). The flacon's sun-shaped stopper rises and sets over a rock lapped by waves. Dalí, in typical fashion, created an optical illusion, having the sun transmute to sky with birds in flight that in turn can be read as the features of a face. The photograph was taken by Hans Oswald Wild for *Life* magazine.

The most dramatic design Schiaparelli showed in November 1946 was a short-skirted dinner suit featuring a black crêpe jacket faced with Shocking pink taffeta and elaborately embroidered in a Baroque-inspired pattern of jet beads. As can be seen in the photograph at right, by Horst P. Horst, the pink fabric draped to the back of the jacket, culminating in a wide, jet-encrusted bow. The courtly ensemble, with its tall, feathered, fontange-like headdress, once again paid homage to the fashions and luxury of France's Golden Age, the reign of Louis XIV, the Sun King. The designer's latest perfume, Le Roy Soleil, named after the monarch, was launched at the same time.

Schiaparelli owned this version of her spectacular ensemble for spring 1947 (above and left), presented in November 1946 (p. 265). The sumptuous jet embroidery over the pink taffeta on the front of the jacket and ending in a bow at the back forms three-dimensional flowers on curling stems. Schiaparelli wore the dinner suit during a trip to New York, and it was subsequently described by *Vogue* on February 15, 1947, as "a sort of summary of her designing tradition" because it was a dinner suit combining black with her signature Shocking pink and was bustled.

Schiaparelli emphasized magnificent fabrics, color, and silhouette rather than elaborate embroidery in her November 1947 collection for spring 1948. The ensemble shown here reaffirms the barrel outline that she had introduced in August. The bronze-and-black striped satin jacket is cut away at the front, bells out over the hips, then curves and turns in at the back (left). The striped fabric is used again on the bodice to emphasize the contours of the bosom. The dress's dramatic full skirt, although flat at the front, ties up into a slight bustle at the back. Its bronze-and-black rayon damask fabric is woven with a sweeping design of elongated tulips, and the ensemble was accessorized with a striking feather headdress, as illustrated in the house sketch above. The photograph at right was taken at the Louvre by Horst P. Horst in front of Henri de Toulouse-Lautrec's painting *La Danse Mauresque* (1895). It appeared in the December issue of *Vogue*.

Schiaparelli's newest idea in millinery, shown in
November 1947, was this striking "pudding bowl"
hat with a fur halo surrounding a net crown dramatically
trimmed with yellow and blue kingfisher feathers. The
hat's design was in keeping with the general tenor of
the collection and its emphasis on color, form, and
texture rather than decorative detailing.

In her November 1947 collection for spring 1948 Schiaparelli reintroduced monkey fur, which she had used during the 1930s for coats and boots. Some of the new furs were dyed tortoiseshell blond and made into sleeveless sweaters that were accessorized with matching fur berets. This wool jersey top (above) zips up the sides and is trimmed in black monkey fur on the front and back. It was originally worn with the dinner gown illustrated in the house sketch at left, adding a touch of warmth and chic to the ensemble.

Schiaparelli revived the blown-back look that had been so revolutionary in 1933–34 in her summer 1949 collection, presented on February 6. The new "Hurricane" silhouette was expressed in dresses with folds that wrapped around the body, throwing the fullness to the front or to the back, as seen in the slim black-and-white satin evening gown at left. The concept was also carried through in colors such as "Storm" gray and electric "Lightning" blue and in fabrics with blurred flower prints, such as that shown here.

The praise that Schiaparelli's August 1949 collection for winter received, along with the announcement that she was to mass-produce coats and suits in the United States, landed the designer on the cover of the September 26 issue of *Newsweek*. Dior's "New Look" had suddenly become old, and Schiaparelli filled the void with a collection that, according to the magazine, "reasserted her mastery." The *New York Times* for August 12 described it as "challenging, sometimes sound, sometimes bizarre." This tightly fitting taffeta evening dress in dark maroon blended with red, a color

named "Forbidden Fruit," was photographed on Shari Herbert by *Life* photographer Nina Leen (above). Its bodice is cut at a slant to reveal a pale pink gold-embroidered brassiere dripping with crystal, and the skirt draws in sharply at the knees and is cut short in front, flaring out in a pink-lined train at the back. According to *Newsweek* it cost $382. The August collection was produced under the most difficult circumstances. Paris seamstresses were on strike, and Schiaparelli showed garments unfinished, with pins and basting stitches still in place.

In her November 1949 collection for spring 1950, Schiaparelli stressed interesting cuts rather than a radical change in silhouette. In the photograph above, the angled hemline seen on both the loose topper and the matching street-length dress of the richly embroidered ruby red velvet evening ensemble, called House of Cards, is held in place with wire.

Schiaparelli's November 1949 midseason showing was full of surprises, including hats with cutout sections, as seen in the photographs on these two pages. Some had cookie cutter–like shapes around the perimeter, while others featured peepholes for the eyes. The visor of the red satin evening hat at right dips down on one side and has an elongated hole for

the eye and a diamond clip from Van Cleef & Arpels for an eyebrow. In the sportier version modeled above, the open crown over the nose has two large triangular openings for the eyes.

Schiaparelli called her August 1950 collection for winter 1950–51 the Front Line, and its centerpiece was a flat, oval piece of wood six inches by three inches that the mannequins slipped down the front of their girdles to achieve a flat stomach. In the suit at left, photographed by Irving Penn for the September 1 issue of *Vogue*, the look was reinforced by a stiff, fan-shaped peplum that lays close to the body in the front and juts out at the sides. Simply cut, the suit closed on the diagonal,

its peplum hiding a flat, curved pocket. The Duchess of Windsor was photographed by Cecil Beaton wearing the same model (above, left), which she had modified into a more conservative silhouette by eliminating the front pocket, paring down the angle of the peplum, and setting the buttons farther apart.

The summer 1950 collection that Schiaparelli presented in February was inspired by modern travel and included this full coat with large, short bell sleeves, photographed by Genevieve Naylor (above). In white wool, the design was an updated version of the "revolutionary" loose-fitting coats with sloping shoulders that the couturière had included in the collection she presented in Paris just before leaving for the United States on May 11, 1941.

The costumes worn by the ballet dancers Jean Babilée and Nathalie Philippart in the divertissement from *Swan Lake* that preceded the charity ball held at the Hôtel Lambert in June 1950 were designed by Schiaparelli (above). The ball, one of the highlights of the social season, was attended by eight hundred people, including the Duke and Duchess of Windsor, and was photographed by Robert Doisneau for the July–August issue of French *Vogue*. The design for Miss Philippart's costume was similar to the show-stopping model Schiaparelli included in her May 1950 collection—a theatrical, snowy white cotton-net evening dress with an enormous flat pink bow at the center of

the front hemline, the skirt spreading toward the back into two fan-pleated sections that slanted upward. The effect was such that as the mannequin walked she appeared to glide like a swan, which in the divertissement was reinforced by the dancer's swan headdress. In her February 1951 collection for summer, Schiaparelli used pleats to create even more dramatic effects with striking color combinations and contrasting textures. In the ethereal strapless evening dress on the right, photographed by Horst P. Horst for *Vogue*, the pleated violet silk organdy overskirt is thrown back on itself, creating Chinese lantern–like curves that reveal a plum organdy underdress.

For her winter 1951–52 collection, presented on July 29, Schiaparelli called her silhouette SHAPE after the Supreme Headquarters Allied Powers Europe. For evening there were daringly paired color combinations—pistachio green with ruby red or Shocking pink with gray—and gowns with fabric draped dramatically across the front of the skirt and ending in a giant bustle of enormous loops at the back, as seen in the example at left, photographed by François Kollar.

On June 12, 1951, Schiaparelli introduced her first ready-to-wear lingerie collection, designed in Paris and manufactured in the United States. The collection included a luxurious bed jacket trimmed with rabbit and the white nylon peignoir with mink shawl collar seen in this photograph for *Life* magazine (above). The collection was distinguished by simple tailoring and a good fit, especially evident in nightgowns with shirred bodices that fit closely at the waist. The first showing of the collection took place at Hess's department store in Allentown, Pennsylvania.

Schiaparelli's February 1952 collection for summer retained the slim lines of her silhouette from the previous season and continued to emphasize the natural waist and molded hips. New details were added, however, including the daringly low, wide-open inverted heart-shaped neckline on the strapless navy blue taffeta evening gown at right, with its enormous draped and twisted bustle in red paper taffeta. Henry Clarke photographed the dress for the March 1952 issue of *Vogue*.

In her last collaboration with the American movie industry, Schiaparelli designed the costumes that Zsa Zsa Gabor wore in the role of Jane Avril in John Huston's 1952 Oscar-winning film, *Moulin Rouge*, the fictional account of the life of the artist Henri de Toulouse-Lautrec. She based her designs on Toulouse-Lautrec's lithograph posters advertising the performances of Avril, a famous dancer. In the publicity photograph shown above, Miss Gabor wears a design derived from a five-color poster printed in 1893 to publicize Jane Avril's début at the Moulin Rouge. Avril was the only dancer allowed to wear red, and Schiaparelli chose to use the color for her costume. Among her other designs was a dramatic "snake" costume that featured a sequined serpent winding itself around Gabor's body. Again, the design was based on a famous lithograph by Toulouse-Lautrec, this one from 1899 and never actually used

as a poster. In the film the dress is purchased by Jean Avril at Madame Paquin's couture house, opened in 1892. Madame Paquin was the first woman to achieve success in the French haute couture. Two other costume designers, Julia Squire and Marcel Vertès, worked on *Moulin Rouge*, whose two Academy Awards were won by Vertès for set decorations and costumes.

In the photograph above, taken by *Life* photographer Bob Wendlinger, Schiaparelli poses with two of the Gabor sisters—Eva on the left and Magda on the right—at a party she gave on September 23, 1952, at the Roof of the Saint Regis Hôtel. She had recently finished the costume designs for the third sister, Zsa Zsa, to wear as Jane Avril in the film *Moulin Rouge*. The designer is wearing the latest silhouette from her August collection, inspired by the grasshopper and katydid and featuring a sleek, smoothly rounded body, irregularly cut décolletages, and "folded wings" at the back.

The April showing of Schiaparelli's midseason collection for fall 1953 included formal evening wraps of "angel hair"—long, glistening rayon threads knotted into a loosely scattered fringe that moved as one walked. For the white coat at left, worn over a pink organdy dress, the threads are shaded from white to pink.

In the photograph above, taken in Schiaparelli's salon in 1953, a mannequin poses between two Air France stewardesses in front of a collage designed for the Schiap Shop. Made by Marcel Vertès, who in 1952 had received Academy Awards for set decoration and costume design for the film *Moulin Rouge*, the collage is a summary of Schiaparelli's most significant designs, with the images cut from fashion magazines

and incorporated into a surreal landscape of dinosaurs and butterflies. The passenger balloon in the upper-right corner is a reference to the postwar fancy dress ball that Schiaparelli held during the summer of 1949 in the garden of her home. Called the *Bal du ballon*, or Ball of the Balloon, it celebrated the achievements of the balloonists Auguste and Jean Piccard and the Montgolfier brothers.

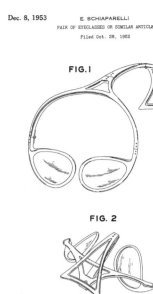

Dec. 8, 1953   E. SCHIAPARELLI   Des. 171,056
PAIR OF EYEGLASSES OR SIMILAR ARTICLE
Filed Oct. 28, 1952

FIG.1

FIG. 2

INVENTOR
Elsa Schiaparelli
BY
ATTORNEYS

SCHIAPARELLI

During the 1950s Schiaparelli's creativity extended to inventive designs for eyewear, including these sunglasses with lenses trimmed with long blue eyelashes, photographed by Gordon Parks in February 1951 for *Life* magazine (above, left). Among her other designs were folding eyeglasses inspired by the logo for the Vespa motor scooter in 1952 and, in 1953, sunglasses attached to cellophane pigtails. In 1952 Schiaparelli entered into an agreement with the American Optical Company, launching the first designer signature eyeglass collection, Schiaparelli Lunettes, which included ninety uniquely ornamented styles, each with a French name to add cachet. In 1955 the company introduced the most expensive frame ever made, an exclusive Schiaparelli model called The Crown Jewel. At the time, the diamond-studded platinum frame was valued at $10,000.

In her 1954 autobiography, Schiaparelli noted the changes that had occurred in the Place Vendôme, where her salon was located, since the war: "From my windows I notice especially the increasing number of cars, parked so tightly that one wonders how their drivers will remove them. There are Packards, Cadillacs, and Rolls-Royces, and, sneaking amongst them, small Austins, Simcas, and Citroëns, fewer Mercedes and Alfa Romees [*sic*], but squeezed in corners the steadily growing Vespas." The legendary Vespa motor scooter made its début in Rome in 1946 and quickly rose from its status as a convenient and inexpensive means of transport to a Hollywood icon after it "starred" with Audrey Hepburn in the 1953 film *Roman Holiday*. Schiaparelli, too, became enamored of the scooter and ingeniously incorporated its logo into the silhouette of a pair of folding goggle-like

eyeglasses for which she filed a French patent on May 7, 1952, and a U.S. patent on October 28 (above, center). The 1954 Vespa 150 in particular caught Schiaparelli's eye, and she featured it in the window of the Schiap boutique being ridden by one of the house's wooden mascots, Pascaline, dressed in cashmere and pearls, as the photograph on the right shows. The scooters parked in front of Schiaparelli's establishment also appear to have attracted the attention of the young Andy Warhol, who sketched two Vespas during his first trip abroad in the summer of 1956 (above, right) and captioned the drawing "Schiaparelli."

Dressing for Film and Stage

Between 1931 and 1953 Schiaparelli costumed at least thirty-two films and thirty stage productions, usually dressing the leading ladies. The "hard chic" for which she was famous was often chosen for actresses playing divorcees, "man-eaters," seductresses, or scheming women. Her first work for the theater was in 1930, dressing Arletty in the play *Mistigri*, in which the French actress wore one of the designer's newly-introduced evening gowns. In 1931 she dressed her first British film, *A Gentleman of Paris*, and also designed costumes for the young dancer Tatiana Riabouchinska (who was to become one of George Balanchine's "baby ballerinas") to wear in her appearances as Diana the Huntress and Primavera in the London production of Nikita Balieff's revue *Chauve-Souris*. Her designs for Riabouchinska were such a hit that Lux took notice and profiled Schiaparelli in an advertising campaign to promote their soap flakes. That same year, *La Revue du cinéma* asked Schiaparelli for her opinions on "le cinéma et la mode" (film and fashion), calling the designer the youthful face of Paris couture; others interviewed included Coco Chanel (who in 1929 had been invited to Hollywood by Samuel Goldwyn to costume MGM's leading ladies), Jean Worth (who was not interested in the cinema), Chéruit, and Paul Poiret, among others. In the interview, Schiaparelli stated that she saw film as a vehicle for transmitting fashion and commented that she did not design for specific roles but felt that the choice of clothing should be more spontaneous and reflect the times as they were then lived: "Le cinéma est la vie. Je veux rester dans la vie" (Cinema is life. I want to stay in the moment). In another interview, published in *Women's Wear Daily* on November 2, 1933, Schiaparelli indicated that she much preferred dressing films to the theater, since in films the garments were seen in their pristine freshness while those worn onstage night after night quickly looked shopworn and reflected badly on the couturier. She also observed that directors were able to exercise much more control over film costuming; onstage the actresses tended to choose clothes they liked with little regard for the parts they played.

In France, rather than having a couturier design for a particular role, selections were usually made from a salon's existing models. Arlette Marchal and her cameraman, for example, chose a satin "aeroplane"-silhouette evening dress from Schiaparelli's October 1933 collection for the film *La Femme idéale* because of the way its fabric reflected light. The practice of drawing costumes from the current collections continued after the war as well. In 1945 Robert Bresson personally selected the clothes worn by Maria Casarès, Elina Labourdette, and Lucienne Bogaert in the film *Les Dames du Bois de Boulogne* from Schiaparelli and Madame Grès, using the garments to help create a psychological portrait of each of the actresses. This practice had its pitfalls, however, for the fashions worn onstage were also those currently being ordered by a couturier's clients, which could occasionally cause conflicts. Marlene Dietrich's purchase of a navy blue evening dress and cape for fifty guineas from the collection Schiaparelli showed in October 1936 at the London salon was returned on January 27, with an accompanying letter expressing her annoyance: "Fortunately, I have not worn it for which I am very glad, as a few nights ago at the play 'Heart's Content' I saw the same dress being worn by an actress with only a very small part in the play. I cannot understand, therefore, why you did not tell me this when I ordered the dress, as you must know I would never have ordered it for myself had I known it would be worn on the stage in such a way." The actress Dietrich was referring to was Kathryn Hamill, who wore the Schiaparelli gown in Act II of the Shaftesbury Theatre production of *Heart's Content* in London. According to the *Evening Standard* of December 24, 1936, Miss Hamill's character, Lorna Hesaltine, was "a perfect portrait of a young woman for whom man is spelt with a capital M."

When Schiaparelli made her first visit to Hollywood in March 1933, the rivalry between that city and Paris was at its peak, and the question of who influenced whom was the subject of numerous articles in fashion trade papers and Hollywood film magazines. In an interview with Schiaparelli in the December issue of *Motion Picture*, she was introduced as "the most copied couturier in Paris." Her influence on costume for Hollywood films was already making itself felt in the broad padded shoulders that the costume designer Adrian had adapted for Joan Crawford from the Schiaparelli designs the actress wore offscreen. Schiaparelli believed that Hollywood would never replace Paris as the creative center of fashion, because in Paris inspiration came not just from ideas but also from the beautiful materials to which the Paris couturier had access, from silks and laces to feathers and jewelry. She readily acknowledged, however, that film was a powerful aid in launching new styles and that American stars were the ideal models for her sports clothes because they had healthy, athletic bodies—just the type of figure she designed for. Among Schiaparelli's earliest private clients were the American film stars Clara Bow and Ina Claire, and throughout her career she contributed to the personal wardrobes of many European and American actresses, including Annabella, Arletty, Madeleine Carroll, Danielle Darrieux, Marlene Dietrich, Ruth Ford, Greta Garbo, Miriam Hopkins, Dolores del Rio, and Fay Wray. Even Hollywood costume designer Edith Head was seduced by the transforming power of a Schiaparelli gown. She recalled in her autobiography, *The Dress Doctor*, that when she was named head designer at Paramount Pictures in 1938, replacing Travis Banton, she went to Paris to acquaint herself with the haute couture and decided to completely make over her image. She purchased a black Schiaparelli dinner suit embroidered with pink and yellow sequins and accessorized with long lemon-yellow gloves that reached to the shoulder. Unfortunately, the expensive ensemble did not transform her into "Madame Edith" as she had hoped. The effect was so awful and so unlike her that she reverted back to "Miss Head" and her old look—tailored suits worn with her trademark round glasses and bangs, a style she followed until her death in 1981. The Schiaparelli dinner suit was tucked away in her closet and was still in her possession in 1959 when her memoirs were published.

The opening of the London branch of Schiaparelli's couture house in 1934 created more opportunities for film and theater work. During the years 1934 and 1935 alone, she provided costumes for the leading ladies in five British films and ten British stage productions. Although the majority of Schiaparelli's theater work was for the London stage, she dressed Tallulah Bankhead in two New York productions, *Dark Victory* in 1934 and *The Circle* in 1938 (the clothes were Schiaparelli designs supplied by Hattie Carnegie). She designed period costumes for only a few stage and screen productions. The first was the Empire gown worn by Lesley Wareing in the 1934 film *The Iron Duke*, and for Roger Vitrac's 1936 stage production *Le Camelot*, Schiaparelli spoofed the fashions of 1919, 1924, and 1928. Her most influential period costumes were represented in the turn-of-the-century wardrobe she designed for Mae West to wear in the 1937 film *Every Day's a Holiday*, which set a fashion for bustle dresses and dinner costumes worn with "Merry Widow" hats.

The most sumptuous historic costumes Schiaparelli created were for the last film she would dress, the 1953 Oscar-winning movie *Moulin Rouge*, for which she copied directly from Henri de Toulouse-Lautrec's posters to create the ensembles worn by Zsa Zsa Gabor as Jane Avril. Her clothes also made appearances in fashion sequences in the so-called fashion films of the 1930s (in which a fashion show was staged as part of the production), including the 1938 comedy *Artists and Models Abroad*, whose costumes Edith Head designed, and the short *La Mode rêvée*, which premiered as a promotional film for the Paris haute couture at the New York World's Fair in 1939. Although she continued to dress films after the war, she only worked on two plays. In 1951 she realized the costumes for Jean-Paul Sartre's *Le Diable et le bon Dieu*, which were designed by twenty-eight-year-old Francine Galliard-Risler. The collaboration was fraught with difficulties and discord, and Schiaparelli lived up to her reputation of being temperamental. The young designer's costumes originally were to be made up in the workshops of a Russian costume maker, but the set designer, Félix Labisse, insisted that Schiaparelli make them instead. Schiaparelli took Galliard-Risler's sketches and had Hubert de Givenchy, her assistant at the time, redesign the costumes according to her own ideas. Galliard-Risler was forbidden by Schiaparelli to visit the workrooms, but the play's two stars, Maria Casarès and Marie Olivier, refused to try on their costumes unless Galliard-Risler was present. Schiaparelli in turn refused to speak to the designer. On the day of the dress rehearsal, Galliard-Risler was asked to go to the Place Vendôme workrooms to salvage the costumes, which the director, Simone Berriau, would no longer permit Schiaparelli to touch.

Films Costumed by Schiaparelli

Child actress Nova Pilbeam in the film Little Friend, *1934*

1931

A Gentleman of Paris
Directed by Sinclair Hill. Produced by Gaumont-British Picture Corporation, Great Britain. Dressed Vanda Greville as Paulette Gerrard and Phyllis Konstam as Madeleine.

1933

Je te confie ma femme
Directed by René Guissart. Produced by René Guissart and Yves Mirande, France. Dressed Arletty as Totoche and Jean Aquistapace as Thorel.

Coralie et Cie
Directed by Alberto Cavalcanti. Produced by Films Jean Dehelly, France. Dressed Françoise Rosay as Madame Coralie.

La Femme idéale
Directed by André Berthomieu. Produced by Films de France. Dressed Arlette Marchal as Madeleine.

1934

Little Friend
Directed by Berthold Viertel. Produced by Gaumont-British Picture Corporation, Great Britain. Dressed Nova Pilbeam as Felicity Hughes.

The Iron Duke
Directed by Victor Saville. Produced by Gaumont-British Picture Corporation, Great Britain. Dressed Lesley Wareing as Lady Frances Webster.

1935

Brewster's Millions
Directed by Thornton Freeland. Produced by British and Dominions Film Corporation, Great Britain. Dressed Lili Damita as Rosalie (seven ensembles).

King of the Damned
Directed by Walter Forde. Produced by Gaumont-British Picture Corporation, Great Britain. Dressed Helen Vinson as Anna Courvin.

The Tunnel
Directed by Maurice Elvey. Produced by Gaumont-Michael Balcon, Great Britain. Dressed Helen Vinson as Varlia Lloyd.

1936

Aventure à Paris
Directed by Marc Allégret. Produced by Productions André Daven, France. Dressed Arletty as Rose de Saint-Leu.

The Beloved Vagabond
Directed by Curtis Bernhardt. Produced by Columbia Pictures and Franco London Films, Great Britain. Dressed Betty Stockfeld as Joanna Rushworth and Margaret Lockwood as Blanquette.

Le Vagabond bien-aimé
Directed by Curtis Bernhardt. Produced by Toeplitz Productions (French version of *Beloved Vagabond*). Dressed Betty Stockfeld as Joanna Rushworth and Hélène Robert as Blanquette.

The Ghost Goes West
Directed by René Clair. Produced by London Films, Great Britain. Dressed Jean Parker as Peggy Martin.

Love in Exile
Directed by Alfred L. Werker. Produced by Capital Films and Gaumont-British Picture Corporation, Great Britain. Dressed Helen Vinson as Countess Xandra St. Aurion and Mary Carlisle as Emily Stewart.

Two's Company
Directed by Tim Whelan. Produced by British and Dominions Film Corporation, Great Britain. Dressed Mary Brian as Julia Madison.

I'd Give My Life
Directed by Edwin L. Marin. Produced by Paramount Pictures, United States. Dressed Frances Drake as Mary Reyburn. One of six designers dressing Miss Drake; others included Jeanne Lanvin, Edward Molyneux, George Creed, and Victor Stiebel.

Navy Born
Directed by Nate Watt. Produced by Republic Pictures Corp., United States. Dressed Claire Dodd as Bernice Farrington and Dorothy Tree as Daphne Roth.

1937

Jump for Glory (or *When Thief Meets Thief*)
Directed by Raoul Walsh. Produced by Criterion, Great Britain. Dressed Valerie Hobson as Glory Howard.

Every Day's a Holiday
Directed by Edward Sutherland. Produced by Paramount Pictures, United States. Dressed Mae West as Peaches O'Day.

1938

Hôtel du Nord
Directed by Marcel Carné. Produced by S.E.D.I.F., France. Arletty, as Raymonde, carried a Schiaparelli handbag.

La Chaleur du sein
Directed by Jean Boyer. Produced by Héraut Films, France. Dressed Arletty as Bernadette.

Pygmalion
Directed by Anthony Asquith and Leslie Howard. Produced by MGM, Great Britain. Dressed Wendy Hiller as Eliza Doolittle.

Artists and Models Abroad
Directed by Mitchell Leisen. Produced by Paramount Pictures, United States. Provided gown for the Palace of Feminine Arts.

La Mode rêvée (premiered in 1939)
Directed by Marcel L'Herbier. Produced by Atlantic Films, France. Provided gown for the "living painting."

1939

Ten Days in Paris (or *Missing Ten Days* or *Spy in the Pantry*)
Directed by Tim Whelan. Produced by Columbia Pictures and Franco London Films, Great Britain. Provided gowns for the fashion-show sequence.

1942

L'Amant de Bornéo
Directed by Jean-Pierre Feydeau and René Le Hénaff. Produced by Compagnie Commérciale Française Cinématographique (C.C.F.C.), France. Irene Dana, for the house of Schiaparelli, dressed Arletty as Stella Losange.

1945

Les Dames du Bois de Boulogne
Directed by Robert Bresson. Produced by Films Raoul Ploquin, France. Dressed Maria Casarès as Hélène, Elina Labourdette as Agnès, and Lucienne Bogaert as Mme D.

1948

Sombre dimanche
Directed by Jacqueline Audry. Produced by Codo-Cinéma, France. Dressed Barbara, a Schiaparelli mannequin.

1949

Un Certain Monsieur
Directed by Yves Ciampi. Produced by Eclectique Film, France. Dressed Hélène Perdrière as l'Index.

1950

L'Inconnue de Montréal (or *Fugitive from Montreal* [U.S.A.] or *Son Copain* [France])
Directed by Jean Devaivre. Produced by Eclectique Films, France, and Quebec Productions, Canada. Dressed Patricia Roc as Helen Bering.

1951

Topaze
Directed by Marcel Pagnol. Produced by Les Films Marcel Pagnol, France. Dressed Hélène Perdrière as Susy Courtois.

1953

Moulin Rouge
Directed by John Huston. Produced by Romulus Productions and United Artists, United States. Dressed Zsa Zsa Gabor as Jane Avril.

Plays Costumed by Schiaparelli

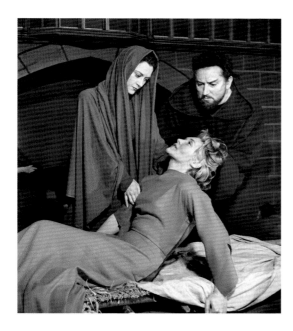

Maria Casarès, Pierre Brasseur, and Marie Olivier
in a scene from Le Diable et le bon Dieu, *June 1951*

1930
Mistigri
By Marcel Achard. Opened at the Théâtre Danou, Paris, in December 1930. Dressed Arletty as Fanny.

1931
Chauve-Souris (The Bat Theatre of Moscow)
Nikita Balieff's Franco-Russian vaudeville. Opened at Cambridge Theatre, London, on November 20. Costumed (with Madame Agnès) Tatiana Riabouchinska as Diana in sketch no. 6, "Diana Hunts the Stag," and in sketch no. 12, "Primavera."

1934
Vintage Wine
By Ashley Dukes, Seymour Hicks, and H. Fowler Mear from the play *Der Ewige Jungeling* by Alexander Engel. Opened at Daly's Theatre, London, on May 29; moved to the Victoria Palace Theatre, London, on June 22, 1935. Dressed Clare Luce as Nina Popinet.

Happy Week End
Book and lyrics by Dion Titheradge; additional lyrics by Arthur Stanley. Based on the Hungarian musical play *Die Katz' im Sack* by Ladislaus Szilágyi. Music by Michael Eisemann. Opened at Duke of York's Theatre, London, on May 30. Dressed Louise Browne as Polly Petworthy in Act I and Act II, scene 1.

The Private Road
By John Carlton. Opened at Comedy Theatre, London, on May 31. Dressed Dorothy Dickson as Sylvia Ashwin in Acts I and III.

Sour Grapes
By Vincent Lawrence. Opened at Comedy Theatre, London, on July 22. Dressed Constance Cummings as Alice Oreton.

Admirals All
By Ian Hay and Stephen King-Hall. Opened at the Shaftesbury Theatre, London, on August 6. Dressed Laura La Plante as Gloria Gunn.

Murder in Mayfair
By Ivor Novello. Opened at the Globe Theatre, London, on September 5. Dressed Edna Best as Auriel Crannock.

Yes, Madam?
By Jack Waller and Joseph Tunbridge. Book by R. P. Weston, Bert Lee, and K.R.G. Browne. Lyrics by R. P. Weston and Bert Lee. Music by Jack Waller. Opened at the Hippodrome Theatre, London, on September 27. Dressed Binnie Hale as Sally Ganthony.

Dark Victory
By George Brewer and Bertram Bloch. Opened at the Plymouth Theater, New York, on November 7. Schiaparelli London dressed Tallulah Bankhead as Judith Traherne.

1935
Duet in Floodlight
By J. B. Priestly. Opened at the Apollo Theatre, London, on June 4. Dressed Madeleine Carroll as Julia Chertsey.

The Two Mrs. Carrolls
By Martin Vale. Opened at St. Martin's Theatre, London, on June 12; moved to the Garrick Theatre, London, on February 24, 1936. Dressed Elena Miramova as Sally Carroll, Joan Maude as Cecily Harden, and Netta Wescott as Mrs. Lathan.

Call It a Day
By C. L. Anthony. Opened at the Globe Theatre, London, on October 30. Dressed Valerie Taylor as Beatrice Gwynne.

L'Inconnue d'Arras
By Armand Salacrou. Opened at the Comédie des Champs Elysées, Paris, on November 22. Dressed Yolande Laffon (Schiaparelli was one of four dressmakers supplying Laffon's costumes).

1936
Process Faukner
Supplied "widow's weeds." (No further information available; mentioned in "Fashions in the News," *Women's Wear Daily*, February 10, 1936.)

Le Camelot
By Roger Vitrac. Opened at the Théâtre de l'Atelier, Paris, on October 7. Dressed all the female actresses, including Jenny Burnay.

Heart's Content
By W. Chetham-Strode. Opened at the Shaftesbury Theatre, London, on December 23. Dressed Kathryn Hamill as Lorna Hesaltine in Act II.

1937
Sarah Simple
By A. A. Milne. Opened at the Garrick Theatre, London, on May 4. Dressed Leonora Corbett as Sarah Bendish.

Yes, My Darling Daughter
By Mark Reed. Opened at St. James Theatre, London, on June 3. Dressed Margaret Bannerman as Constance Nevins.

A Lady's Gentleman
Adapted by Hylton Cleaver from the play *Jean* by Ladislaus Bis-fekete. Opened at the Vaudeville Theatre, London, on December 12. Dressed Margaret Scott as Katrinka.

1938
The Circle
By Somerset Maugham. Opened at the Playhouse, New York, on April 18. Dressed Tallulah Bankhead as Elizabeth (costumes executed by Hattie Carnegie from Schiaparelli's February collection).

Cavalier Seul
By Jean Nohain and Maurice Diamant-Berger. Opened at the Théâtre du Gymnase, Paris, in March. Dressed Arletty as Danièle Jorselin and Blanche Montel (character not identified).

Married Unanimously
By Frederic Carlton. Opened at the Phoenix Theatre, London, on May 10. Dressed Leonora Corbett as Kathleen Lady Glenby.

Happy Returns
By Charles B. Cochran. Opened at the Adelphi Theatre, London, on May 19. Dressed Beatrice Lillie as a bad-mannered "first nighter" in skit 7, "The Rival Hamlets."

1939
Design for Living
By Noel Coward. Opened at Theatre Royal Haymarket, London, January 25; moved to the Savoy Theatre on December 12, 1939. Dressed Diana Wynyard as Gilda in Acts II and III.

Behold the Bride
By Jacques Deval. Opened at the Shaftesbury Theatre, London, on May 23. Supplied all costumes, including those worn by Luise Rainer.

1940
Les Monstres sacrés
By Jean Cocteau. Opened at the Théâtre Michel, Paris, on February 17. Dressed Jany Holt as Liane.

1951
Le Diable et le bon Dieu
By Jean-Paul Sartre. Opened at the Théâtre Antoine, Paris, on June 7. Costumes designed by Francine Galliard-Risler and realized by Schiaparelli.

1952
La Duchesse d'Algues
By Peter Blackmore; French adaptation by Constance Coline. Opened at the Théâtre Michel, Paris, on May 16. Dressed Gaby Sylvia.

Stylistic and Historical Chronology

Elsa Schiaparelli wearing a short satin evening gown and matching skullcap with chignon at the back from her November 1950 collection for spring 1951

1890
September 10: Elsa Luisa Maria is born in Rome to Maria-Luisa and Celestino Schiaparelli. She is the second of their two children, both girls.

1892
December 17: The first issue of a new weekly magazine, *Vogue*, is published in New York City.

1901
The magazine *Femina* is founded in Paris.

1903
Elsa travels with her father to Tunisia, where, at age thirteen, she receives a marriage proposal from an influential Tunisian.

1906
The couturière Chéruit moves her salon to 21 Place Vendôme, Paris, the future premises of Schiaparelli.

1907
One of the first completely synthetic substances is discovered by New York chemist Leo Hendrik Baekeland and is given the name Bakelite.

1910
The Chambre Syndicale de la Couture Parisienne is founded to oversee the Paris couture.

1911
A book of Schiaparelli's poetry, titled *Arethusa*, is published by Quintieri in Rome.

1912
Gabrielle (Coco) Chanel opens a millinery business in Paris.

1913
February 17–March 15: The work of more than three hundred European and American avant-garde artists is on display at New York's 69th Regiment Armory.

Marcel Duchamp renounces painting and signs his first readymade.

Schiaparelli leaves Italy to care for the children of her sister's friend in London, stopping in Paris on the way. There she attends her first ball, wearing an ensemble she designs herself.

1914
She attends a lecture by Wilhelm Wendt de Kerlor, a young theosophist, and they marry shortly afterward in a London registry office.

June 28: Archduke Franz Ferdinand, heir to the Austrian throne, and his wife are assassinated in Sarajevo, an event that precipitates World War I in August.

The Italian Futurist Giacomo Balla publishes a manifesto on men's clothing.

1914–16
Schiaparelli resides in Nice with her husband, who has family there. She spends time at the casinos in Monte Carlo.

1916
Her father leaves his post as chair of the school of Oriental studies in Rome, which he has held since 1895.

The literary and artistic movement Dada is launched in Zurich.

Schiaparelli and her husband leave for New York City aboard the *Chicago*. Among the other passengers is Gabrielle Picabia, wife of the artist Francis Picabia, who will be one of the core group of Dadaists active in New York.

1917
Schiaparelli travels to Cuba with aspiring opera singer Ganna Walska, who débuts in *Fedora*, to disastrous reviews.

c. 1917–18
She meets Blanche Hays, wife of the renowned American lawyer Arthur Garfield Hays.

1918
November 11: The Armistice is signed at Compiègne, France, ending World War I.

1919
Benito Mussolini founds the Fascist party in Italy.

October 25: Schiaparelli's father dies in Rome.

c. 1919
She and her husband reside on Charles Street in Boston.

c. 1919–20
Her daughter, Maria Luisa Yvonne Radha (Gogo), is born.

1920
The manufacture of cellophane starts a craze for plastics around the world.

August 26: The Nineteenth Amendment to the U.S. Constitution is ratified, guaranteeing American women the right to vote.

Schiaparelli meets Man Ray, then a member of the Dadaist group in New York, and is photographed by him in his studio.

1920–21

Winter: While living on Patchin Place in Greenwich Village in New York City, she does translations and part-time work for importing houses, watches ticker tape for a Wall Street broker, and works as a stand-in for a film being made in New Jersey.

1921

July 14: Man Ray arrives in Paris.

Edith Wharton becomes the first woman to win the Pulitzer Prize, for her novel *The Age of Innocence*.

Summer: Schiaparelli takes a holiday in Woodstock, New York, known for its colony of artists.

In Paris, Chanel introduces her perfume Chanel No. 5.

1922

June: Schiaparelli, who has separated from her husband, returns to Paris, where she and Gogo reside briefly with Gabrielle Picabia and then share an apartment with Blanche Hays on the boulevard Latour-Maubourg.

1923

Edna St. Vincent Millay wins the Pulitzer Prize for poetry, for *The Ballad of the Harp Weaver*.

1924

January 25–February 4: The first winter Olympic games are held in Chamonix, France.

The first issue of the periodical *La Révolution surréaliste* is published in Paris and will continue through 1929.

May 4–July 27: Paris hosts the summer Olympics, at which American swimmer Gertrude Ederle wins three medals.

December 24: Schiaparelli attends couturier Paul Poiret's midnight party celebrating his salon's move from the rue Saint-Honoré to his ultramodern house at the Rond-point des Champs Elysées.

1925

Modern decorative arts are on display at the landmark *Exposition des arts décoratifs et industriels modernes* in Paris.

Josephine Baker enthralls Paris in the Revue Nègre at the Théâtre des Champs-Elysées.

An American friend of Blanche Hays, a Mrs. Hartley, opens a small dress house, Maison Lambal, with Schiaparelli as the designer.

1926

Although Schiaparelli's designs have received favorable mention in *Women's Wear Daily*, Mrs. Hartley closes Maison Lambal for financial reasons.

Chanel's "little black dress" is called "fashion's Ford" by American *Vogue*.

August: Mussolini dictates fashion for Italy, aiming to create a national dress.

1927

January 10: Fritz Lang's futuristic film *Metropolis* premieres in Germany.

January: Schiaparelli presents her first solo collection, "Display No. 1," in her apartment at 20 rue de l'Université. It includes hand-knitted sweaters with black and gray stripes, small black dots on beige, and white rectangles on brown. The sweaters are featured in the February issue of French Vogue.

March 10: She shows hand-knitted sweaters with pointed or square necklines, bold blocks of color or small all-over designs, and metallic and wool yarn mixtures. To the sweaters she adds matching scarves and sport socks that repeat the sweaters' designs on the cuffs. These are worn with crêpe de chine skirts with front pleats and narrow, matching belts.

May 20–21: Charles Lindbergh completes his first solo flight across the Atlantic.

May 23: Schiaparelli shows hand-knitted wool sweaters with geometric patterns in shades of gray or with modern floral decoration near the shoulder, some metallic and wool yarn mixtures, and hand-knitted wool cardigan jackets with grosgrain ribbon edging worn with matching hand-knitted pullovers and wool skirts.

August: She presents sweaters with modernistic skyscraper patterns and trompe l'oeil bowknots. The bowknot sweater is a smashing success.

September 14: The modern dancer Isadora Duncan dies when her scarf is caught round the wheel of her car.

October 6: The first "talking picture," *The Jazz Singer* with Al Jolson, is released.

November 1927: Wm. H. Davidow Sons Co. is named the exclusive American distributor of Schiaparelli sweaters and prints an advertisement for her trompe l'oeil bowknot sweater.

December 5: Schiaparelli registers her company in France in partnership with Charles Kahn, capitalized at 100,000 francs.

December 15: The bowknot sweater is illustrated in *Vogue* magazine; meanwhile Schiaparelli moves her salon and apartment to attic rooms at 4 rue de la Paix.

1928

In Great Britain women are granted equal voting rights.

Radclyffe Hall's controversial novel *The Well of Loneliness*, about a "sexually inverted" young woman, is published; at a subsequent trial in London it is condemned as obscene.

January 31: Schiaparelli presents her collection for summer 1928. Bathing suits and beach pajamas are added to hand-knitted sweaters, circular skirts, and crocheted berets. The sweaters feature seaside motifs, nautical themes, and inset belts and collars, including a fichu effect with a little bow to one side.

February 11–19: The second winter Olympics are held at Saint-Moritz, Switzerland. The fifteen-year-old Norwegian Sonja Henie, the "Pavlova of the Ice," wins the first of three consecutive gold medals in figure skating.

American anthropologist Margaret Mead publishes *Coming of Age in Samoa*, which becomes a bestseller.

April 25: Schiaparelli presents her collection for fall 1928, featuring black-and-white English tweed sports suits; hand-knitted sweaters with knit-in collars, ties, fichus, and jabots; and two-piece linen dresses with insets in contrasting colors.

At the summer Olympics in Amsterdam, women, wearing shorts, compete for the first time in track and field events.

June: Schiaparelli's hand-knitted bathing suits with ship silhouettes and fish motifs are featured exclusively at Saks Fifth Avenue in New York.

June 18: Amelia Earhart, flying with two others, becomes the first woman to cross the Atlantic in a plane.

August 3: Schiaparelli's collection for winter 1928–29 features plaids for hand-knitted sweaters and dresses; wrap-over coats with printed velvet scarves; collarless suits with leather fastenings; three-piece weekend costumes; Roman toga-like evening wraps; novelty woolens, such as wool woven with ostrich feathers; and large colored cut-glass chokers and matching bracelets. She launches her first perfume, S.

November 5: For spring 1929 she shows skiing suits with sweaters and matching caps, scarves, and gloves; pigskin trimming on bathing suits and ski costumes; lacquered leather sports jackets with fur linings; and beach pajamas.

November: Schiaparelli's bowknot sweater has become so ubiquitous that *Ladies' Home Journal* publishes a pattern for knitting it, without crediting the designer.

1929

Joan Riviere's essay "Womanliness as a Masquerade," in which she argues that women are mimicking ideal feminine behavior to disguise their "masculine" traits, is published in the *International Journal of Psycho-Analysis*.

February: Schiaparelli presents her collection for summer 1929, featuring hand-knitted bathing suits with tattoo designs; coats with dropped shoulder lines and bouffant sleeves with long cuffs fitted from elbow to wrist; tailored tweed sports suits worn with hand-knitted or crêpe de chine tuck-in blouses with rolled-up sleeves and skirts mounted on crocheted hip yokes; and organdy scarf collars.

April: Her collection for fall 1929 features reddish brown tweed coats and jackets with raglan sleeves; straight wrap-over coats and jackets; wraparound skirts with back fastenings worn with a one-piece crêpe blouse-culottes combination; and apron-style linen beach dresses with jackets.

August: For winter 1929–30 she retains the straight silhouette and features coats with kimono and raglan sleeves; tweed ensembles; and tennis costumes with the top and straight-hanging trousers cut in one piece.

September 11: She creates a group of eight beach pajama costumes in Cheney Brother's "Staccato Prints" to publicize resort wear. They are shown in Cheney's New York showroom.

Schiaparelli's clever publicity director, Mrs. Hortense MacDonald, wearing a suit with an amusing horseshoe-print blouse from the designer's summer 1937 collection

October: Schiaparelli's collection for spring 1930 features three-piece linen beach ensembles with terrycloth-lined sleeveless coats and beach bags that unfold into beach rugs; skiing costumes emphasizing comfort and freer arm movement with metal zippers that extend the full length of the sleeves and wool armhole yokes on leather jackets; three sweaters in different colors worn one over the other, with the three colors overlapping at neck, wrist, and waist; and narrow skirts with back slits.

October: The stock market crashes in New York, depressing markets worldwide and precipitating the Great Depression.

November 9: Schiaparelli sails for New York on the S.S. *Berengaria* for a month-long visit.

November 20: In New York she presents a sports collection modeled by her friend Comtesse Gabrielle di Robilant at Stewart & Co. It includes an aviation suit and a tennis costume worn with green hand-knitted cuffed sports socks.

1930

February: Schiaparelli's collection for summer 1930 features scarf collars on coats and dresses; beach costumes consisting of two different-color half-dresses, each with a single armhole and tying at the side like an apron; "prystal" (phenol formaldehyde, a material similar to Bakelite) necklaces and cuff bracelets; multicolored wooden jewelry; and multicolored zigzag Galalith or silver necklaces. Presented with the collection are examples of American-made colored Westcott Fabrimode Costume Hoisery, which will be marketed in the United States with a "Schiaparelli" label sewn in.

March: *Ladies' Home Journal* publishes an article by Schiaparelli titled "Smartness Aloft."

Madame Agnès's hats are shown with Schiaparelli's ciré satin dresses at the milliner's spring presentation.

April 14: Mahatma Gandhi leads a civil-disobedience revolt against British rule in India.

May 14: In her collection for fall 1930 Schiaparelli emphasizes a high waistline and wrap-over coats. The collection includes her most successful evening gown, in black crêpe de chine with a short, white wraparound jacket that ties at the side.

June: The Hawley-Smoot Tariff Act raises U.S. tariffs to historically high levels.

August 4: Schiaparelli's winter 1930–31 collection features padded shoulders on coats and suits; draped or twisted girdles in contrasting shades on tuck-in blouses and dresses; wide, diagonal knitted ribbed collars and glove cuffs worn over coat or jacket sleeves; openwork hand-knitted yokes on dresses; detachable boleros; afternoon ensembles consisting of three-quarter-length black coats of rough wool worn over wool dresses with crêpe yokes, sleeves, and hip bands; black-and-white reversible satin for evening gowns; and silks in a dull black that is widely noticed.

November 4: She presents her collection for spring 1931, with a focus on costumes for tennis and winter sports, including removable bolero tops and tunic effects; printed linen beach pajamas; sequin embroidery on evening gowns; and open mesh yokes on day dresses.

December: Schiaparelli's white porcelain "aspirin" necklace, designed by Elsa Triolet and sold at Emmet Jones, New York, is illustrated in *Harper's Bazaar*.

She is asked to design the official sweater of the Corviglia Ski Club at Saint-Moritz.

1931

Margaret Sanger's *My Fight for Birth Control* is published in New York.

January: Schiaparelli wears Antoine's short lacquered wigs at the winter resort Saint-Moritz—blond for skiing and silver for evening.

February 4: She presents her collection for summer 1931, which exhibits strong influences from the forthcoming Exposition coloniale internationale in Paris, including rustic woolens resembling Moroccan hand weaves, heavy wood and silver jewelry, and bold color combinations like bright pink with purple. The open-mesh crocheted yokes of the previous season continue, and the collection also features metal clips and rings replacing buttons; novel armhole and shoulder treatments; divided skirts for evening (replacing the evening pajama); hand-knitted stocking caps matching hand-knitted pullover sweaters; and an invisible soutien gorge (brassiere) used with a backless bathing suit.

April: Lili de Alvarez shocks the London tennis establishment by wearing Schiaparelli's divided skirt while competing in the North London tournament.

May 1: In New York City, the Empire State Building, then the tallest building in the world, is officially opened.

May 6: The *Exposition coloniale internationale* opens in Paris.

May: Schiaparelli presents her collection for fall 1931, featuring a white evening gown with trompe l'oeil pleats painted by the Swiss Art Deco designer Jean Dunand, worn with a white coq-feather evening cape. Clip fasteners continue from the previous season, appearing on lamé evening gowns fastening with diamond "snow boot" clips, and there are printed afternoon dresses with divided skirts.

June: Surrealist artist Salvador Dalí has his first solo exhibition, at the Galerie Pierre Colle in Paris.

June: The American Mrs. Hortense MacDonald, formerly with the shipping company United States Lines, takes charge of publicity for Schiaparelli, succeeding Mrs. Tr. de Caraman Chimay, who moves to Chanel.

American designer Elizabeth Hawes exhibits a collection of gowns in Paris with the aim of showing how American women dress.

August 5: Schiaparelli's collection for winter 1931–32 introduces high-waisted "First Empire" evening gowns with draping trains that hook up under the waist for dancing; metal rings and S-shaped fasteners replacing clip fasteners; belts of twisted wire; square, padded shoulders on coats and jackets with detachable fur collars, some of them double breasted and with "curtain ring" clips; and celluloid collar necklaces. Divided skirts continue for sports, and featured fabrics include "Riboulding" crêpe silks and ribbed corduroy velvets.

October: The popular priced American company M. C. Schrank announces that Schiaparelli is among those who will design cotton pajamas for them.

October 17: Schiaparelli becomes a French citizen.

October 27: She presents her collection for spring 1932, featuring gold dollar-sign clips; wool dresses worn with a long scarf made of three different-colored scarves braided together; beach pajamas that, when removed, become a loose scarf to be worn over a hand-knitted bathing suit; and wraparound surplice backs on one-piece pajamas that fasten at the side with clips. Featured colors are pink and dark red.

November: She provides costumes for two sketches for the London performance of Nikita Balieff's revue *Chauve-Souris*.

December 1: Saks 34th Street in New York City presents the entire Schiaparelli midseason collection of fifteen models, twelve of which have been copied for immediate sale while others are available on special order.

Schiaparelli writes an open letter to the English press on the subject of Paris models and English tariffs, complaining that increased duties on British fabrics used by the French couture will make French models prohibitively expensive.

December 21: Paul Poiret retires from active participation in his salon, and Schiaparelli's *modéliste* Henri Delcourt leaves to take over Poiret's position as artistic director and *modéliste* in partnership with Madame Apolline.

1932

January 9–29: The exhibition *Newer Super-Realism*, the first major exhibition of Surrealist art to be held in the United States, is on view at the Julien Levy Gallery in New York.

February 5: Schiaparelli presents her collection for summer 1932, emphasizing crinkly fabrics and ribbons; apronlike wraparound dresses with back fastenings; blouses and sweaters ending just below the bust; triangular and cylindrical metal clips clasping edges of garments in place of buttons; three models in American-made woolens from Walther Manufacturing; wide shoulders achieved with padding, wide cuts, and folds; washable "paper" necklaces; white deep-velvet plush for evening wraps; and pre-washed uncrushable linens. Featured colors are "Cardinal" red and "Beetroot" brown.

March: She opens a small shop within her salon that carries ready-to-wear garments, scarves, necklaces, and bags at prices slightly lower than in the main showroom. Her premises are expanded to include the second floor.

March: Hattie Carnegie opens a small men's department carrying ties, bathrobes, cigarette cases, and pajamas in New York. Schiaparelli does buying for her in England.

April 29: Schiaparelli's collection for fall 1932 includes extended shoulders, created by using detachable yokes that pass around the tops of sleeves; big fur collars on coats; white ciré peu d'ange *jersey evening dresses; thick, square, nickel buttons; and black shield-shaped clips. Featured colors are "Stone" beige and "Ice" blue.*

May 20: Amelia Earhart becomes the first woman to fly solo across the Atlantic Ocean.

June: Le Bal blanc (White Ball) is held in Paris and is attended by a number of women dressed in Schiaparelli. The designer herself is present, wearing a white dress with coq-feather collar boa.

August 5: Schiaparelli's collection for winter 1932–33 features a "Speakeasy" silhouette for day and evening that consists of gathered back fullness in the form of a "shelf" at the back waistline; exclusive novelty silk and synthetic jerseys; shiny fabrics; discreetly patterned woolens; wired fur collars forming "wings"; pouched elbow-length gloves; and swagger coats. She discontinues clips and chalky crêpes. New fastenings include copper slides, large pyramid-shaped buttons, and small hooks. Featured colors are "Cabbage" red, "Hyacinth" blue, yellow, and brown.

October 26: In her collection for spring 1933 she returns to a normal waistline and includes ski suits worn with knickers and mannish gaiters and tweed-like cottons for sportswear. Featured colors are green and yellow, and there are three-color combinations for town and sports clothes.

December 20: Schiaparelli is granted a U.S. patent for a backless bathing suit.

1933
January 30: Adolf Hitler becomes chancellor of Germany.

February 6: Schiaparelli presents her collection for summer 1933, which emphasizes wide shoulders with "shoulder trays" and retains a molded bodice and narrow silhouette. Other features are sharply peaked "circus hats" (soft cone-shaped hats with raffia or knit cuffs); slide fastenings and huge tortoiseshell bar fastenings; loose three-quarter-length coats; a

twine-lace afternoon dress; feather collars on coats; plaid crinkled-ribbon jackets; capes fitted with sling straps inside to help keep them on; and Irish Vale of Avoca tweeds dyed in the fleece. Featured colors are "Eel" gray, "Wheat" yellow, and "Mussel" blue.

February 8: The Boeing 247, the first all-metal monoplane, makes its inaugural flight.

February 24: Schiaparelli arrives in New York aboard the Conté di Savoia, her first trip to the United States since the autumn of 1929.

February 28: She speaks at a Fashion Group luncheon in New York on trends in pants and fabrics while wearing a shoulder-tray coat with a deep fringe of monkey fur and a "circus hat." During the talk she expresses disapproval of trousers for the street, discusses shiny fabrics and cottons, and endorses wide shoulders.

March 4: U.S. President Franklin Delano Roosevelt launches the New Deal to combat the Depression.

March 11: Schiaparelli is caught in an earthquake while visiting Los Angeles.

March 23: Schiaparelli, Inc., is chartered in Delaware and New York State.

April: On a tour of Europe, Duke Ellington and his orchestra play Paris.

April 28: Schiaparelli presents her collection for fall 1933. Wide shoulders continue in the form of big, pointed lapels ("angel wings") or upward curves like those on costumes worn by Siamese dancers. Also featured are added puffs on the upper arms; elastic insets on skirts replacing fastenings; and leather piping and fastenings on coats. Featured colors are "Pansy" blue, "Water Lily" green, "Navy-cut" brown, and verdigris.

June: Schiaparelli wears a curved heron-feather collar on a black evening dress to Lady Mendl's party.

Mae West, starring as Lady Lou in She Done Him Wrong, takes Paris by storm.

August: The Honorable Mrs. Reginald (Daisy) Fellowes, who will become one of Schiaparelli's main customers, is named Paris editor of Harper's Bazaar.

August 7: In Schiaparelli's collection for winter 1933–34, padded, rounded shoulders replace the exaggerated shoulder line. Also featured are a pencil-slim silhouette; low-cut evening dresses with narrow straps; a Tyrolean inspiration in hats; mandarin necklines and quilted hip-length capes; bold, crinkled "treebark" rayon crêpes and flannel-backed silks; American-made products (Ameritex-Sudanette cotton for Palm Beach and Walk-Over Shoes); knitted caps and hats; and Armada quilted taffeta. Featured colors show Chinese influences: "Granite" gray, "Tibetan" brown, "Peiping" red, "Gobi" beige, and "Cathay" blue.

October 30: Her collection for spring 1934 features a winged-hip "Aeroplane" silhouette for evening; a windblown "Stormy Weather" silhouette for coats, with winged collars and skirt fullness pushed to the front; squared box shoulders; and bicorne berets. Featured colors are green-blue and bright lemon yellow.

November: Schiaparelli opens a London branch of her salon at 6 Upper Grosvenor Street.

December 5: Prohibition is repealed in the United States.

1934
February 5: Schiaparelli presents her collection for summer 1934, introducing the "Typhoon" silhouette for day and evening, with front and back windblown drapes and "fish" and "bird" silhouettes for evening; frothy elastic tulle evening capes; nursery-printed linens for sports clothes; and Walk-Over shoes. Featured colors are bright red, "Hyacinth" blue, pale pink, and a dark warm gray. Three perfumes are launched with the collection: Salut, Soucis, and Schiap.

April 1: Mrs. Virginia Chandler Lemmon retires as Schiaparelli's representative in charge of American public relations.

April 23: Schiaparelli's collection for fall 1934 features Spanish "Goya" influences reflected in bell-shaped evening skirts; "chichi" ruffled tucked crêpe; metal-striped gauzes; "King Kong" feather pile fabrics for evening wraps; black lace accents; suits with boxy jackets; toreador-style beach hats with back veils; white plastic hands used as fastenings on coats; and Scottish tams and tartans for sports clothes. Featured colors are black with white, light "Flower" pink, pale grayish mauve, and dark grayish brown.

June: She dresses two London plays, Vintage Wine and Private Road.

Schiaparelli visits Holland.

The fourteen-year-old Indian princess Karam of Kapurthala visits Paris, where her beauty is greatly acclaimed. Her clothing will influence Schiaparelli's 1935 collection.

Schiaparelli opens a millinery department with Madame Marcelle as designer.

August 6: Her collection for winter 1934–35 includes a synthetic "glass" dress; stiffened peplums and postilion capes; evening dresses with hoops in their hems; sleeves ballooning slightly just below the shoulder; huge hairpin fastenings on belts; "peasant" evening dresses with drawstring backs; parachute-capeleted coats; black fabric with shaggy gold and silver hairs; and horses' and dogs' heads on wooden clips. Featured colors are bright violet, "Geranium" pink, pinkish gray, "Lapis" blue, gray blue, and "Cedar" green. Schiaparelli has her first formal showing of hats: poke bonnets and "François Villon" hats.

August 13: Schiaparelli appears on the cover of Time magazine. The caption reads "Mme Elsa Schiaparelli . . . glorifies the gadget, persecutes the button."

October 16: Leading an army of two hundred thousand, Mao Tse-tung sets off on his "Long March" from Jiangxi, China, to Yan'an in the Shaanxi province.

October 29: Schiaparelli's spring 1935 collection features soft, feminine silhouettes; draped shoulders on coats; a "spun-glass" apron over evening dress; cellophane belts; and "Dutch" bonnet scarves. Featured colors are "Inky" plum, "Mango" orange, "Horizon" blue, and "Ginger" brown.

The inimitable René, Schiaparelli's head tailor, adjusting a coat collar, 1937

1935

King George V and Queen Mary of England celebrate their Silver Jubilee.

Margaret Mead's *Sex and Temperament in Three Primitive Societies* is published, challenging sex-role assumptions.

January 1935: Schiaparelli moves her salon from the fourth floor of 4 rue de la Paix to 21 Place Vendôme. Designer Jean-Michel Frank decorates it using cotton dress goods.

February 5: Schiaparelli presents her collection for summer 1935 (the "Stop, Look and Listen" collection), which features a "Celestial" silhouette with soft spiral folds draping the figure, including sari dresses with ihram scarves. There are also large floral prints; cellophane "glass" fans and parasols; transparent "glass" belts; gilded egg-shaped vanity handbags dangling from wrist straps; "Hot and Cold" ensembles with two coats, silk for warm days and wool for cold; and a "Television" hat (a black high-crowned hat with tassel trimming). Print themes include newspaper clippings and the Big Dipper constellation. Featured colors are "Carbon" blue and "Desert" rose. The collection opening is broadcast to the United States by radio.

April: Schiaparelli provides the bridal retinue and trousseau for the wedding of Lady Duff Assheton-Smith (the Honorable Joan Marjoribanks, daughter of Lord and Lady Tweedsmuir) from her summer 1935 collection.

Spring: She is asked to endorse Anchor Tricoton yarns in England for sports and knitwear, in recognition of her contributions in these areas.

April 30: Her collection for fall 1935 includes harem trousers for evening; flower visors on filet mesh caps; head veils influenced by Italian primitive paintings attached to jeweled caps for evening; "Venetian" evening capes in heavily crinkled "Simoun" taffeta; vanity cases shaped like telephone dials; and hemplike printed linens.

May: The Stresa Front, an informal alliance between Great Britain, France, and Italy, is formed for the purpose of keeping Nazi Germany from extending beyond its borders.

May: The exhibition *L'Art italien*, sponsored by Mussolini, opens at the Petit Palais in Paris.

May 29: The S.S. *Normandie*, the largest ocean liner yet made, makes its maiden voyage from Le Havre to New York.

June: Daisy Fellowes holds her Oriental Ball. Schiaparelli dresses Daisy Fellowes, Baron Eugene de Rothschild, and Lady Mendl, among others.

July: Schiaparelli visits Vienna and Hungary. She makes arrangements with Swarovsky to use their rhinestone-studded material for evening capes and gowns.

Comte Etienne de Beaumont holds his Famous Paintings Ball. Schiaparelli dresses Comtesse Benoist d'Azy as the Venus from Sandro Botticelli's painting *The Birth of Venus*.

She provides the trousseau for Lady Daphne Finch-Hatton, who is marrying Whitney Straight, the well-known race-car driver.

August 8: Schiaparelli presents her collection for winter 1935–36, featuring Royalist and Republican clothes. There is a coq gaulois (Gallic rooster) motif; gold franc buttons; coxcomb hats; Hungarian-style embroidered suits and dresses; padlock fastenings on coats and handbags; "sealing-wax" buttons; elbow-length fox fur gloves; colored plastic zippers; net snoods for evening; plaster mask fans with real feather eyelashes; draped evening skirts revealing contrasting trousers; hooded evening capes; vividly colored Irish tweeds; petit point vests; enameled mesh bags and belts; and golden "Easter egg" vanity bags. Featured colors are rouge gaulois, "Royal" blue, and "Imperial" violet.

September 1: The cutter and fitter for Schiaparelli's London salon, Albert Cezard, leaves to join the designer Norman Hartnell, prompting litigation by Schiaparelli, who eventually loses the case.

October: Schiaparelli designs blue-and-white cotton dresses, aprons, and caps for the waitresses at the luxury roadhouse Kingshead, near London.

October 29: Her collection for spring 1936 features long, slender silhouettes; perfume-filled jewelry; man-styled "shirttail" flannel topcoats; smock-style waterproof raincoats; straw hats with cellophane visors; and gold chains holding up trains of evening gowns. Print themes center around wild horses and Chopin, whose centenary will be celebrated in 1936 (motifs include musical notes). Featured colors are reddish violet, "Orchid" pink, dull red, and "Peacock" green.

November: She participates in the French luxury trade show in Moscow, showing a specially designed costume for the Russian working woman.

An international exhibition of Chinese art opens at the Royal Academy in London.

1936

Paintings of Napoleon are on view at the Petit Palais in Paris in an exhibition of works by Baron Antoine-Jean Gros.

January: Schiaparelli visits Vienna, where she is the guest of honor at a government ball.

January 20: King George V of England dies.

February 5: Schiaparelli presents her collection for summer 1936, introducing a "Parachute" silhouette; high-waisted tunic suits; "Empire" evening dresses; whimsical Victorian accessories; derby-style hats; smooth shoulders; lovebird fasteners on coats; and love letters, cancelled postage stamps, crazy patchworks, and enormous leaf or flower patterns as print themes. Featured colors are "Spice" brown, rouge originale, "Helieum" oyster white, and "Russian" lilac.

March: She creates metal mesh bags for the American manufacturer Whiting & Davis, in an agreement that lasts through 1938.

April 30: Her collection for fall 1936 includes a transparent evening raincoat with a long, pointed "hangman's hood"; black lacquered kid "ormolu" accessories with white hand-stitching; "Liane" soft fabric headbands worn with draped or pleated "Roman" evening gowns with tunics; slim princess-style evening gowns; and three-pointed raffia beach parasols. Print themes are La Crise (The Depression, a patchwork print), hand-painted roses and leaves, thermometers to register a wearer's passion, and "Speed," combining signs of telegraph, radio, and so on. Featured colors are "Opaline" rose, blue-green, yellow, and "Rebellion" red.

May: Amy Mollison (née Johnson) sets a record flying solo from England to Cape Town, South Africa, while wearing a wardrobe created by Schiaparelli.

June 11: The *International Surrealist Exhibition* opens at the New Burlington Galleries, London.

June 19: Schiaparelli launches "Phrygian" bonnet styles, based on the symbol of emancipated slaves in ancient Rome and adopted by the revolutionary *Sans Culottes* upon the fall of the *ancien régime* in 1792.

July: Spanish general Francisco Franco leads an army revolt in Morocco, beginning the Spanish Civil War.

July 18: The U.S. duty on imported zippers increases from 45 percent to 66 percent, threatening to delay the export of Schiaparelli's collection.

July 26: The Second Congress of the International Federation of Business and Professional Women is held in Paris. Schiaparelli gives a presentation at the session on "Women's Contribution to Business," read by a representative of her salon.

August 6: Schiaparelli's collection for winter 1936–37 features Surrealist-inspired suits with bureau-drawer pockets designed with Salvador Dalí; dark floor-length tweed evening coats with richly embroidered lapels or brightly colored linings; gold- and stone-embroidered evening jackets; hats with tiny coronets perched on the crown of the head; gloves with red fingernails or blue veins; brightly feathered cone hats with rolled bands;

high chechia (a cylindrical cap) hats; and leather chain-link fastenings. Featured colors are "Danger" red, "Chateau Neuf du Pape" wine, "Moor" green, "Heather" purple, and "Gorse" tawny yellow. The opening is attended by Dalí, author Louis Bromfield, and Edward James, Dalí's patron.

October 3: Italy invades Ethiopia, a former colony.

October: Schiaparelli announces that the firm Drucker-Wolf will act as the American agent for her printed silk fabrics.

October 28: She presents her collection for spring 1937, showing low-cut evening gowns with sweeping trains; waist-length fitted jackets; long capes with sequin and stone embroidery; velvet trousers with embroidered jackets; "gold ingot" fastenings; high hats; sun-shielding accessories, such as fabric face masks; American-made Everfast cotton for beach clothes; English Viyella for day dresses; and casquette (cap) and open crown "cartwheel" hats.

November: William Hollins & Co. Ltd launches thirty-six "Schiaparelli Viyella Fashion Fabrics" in Great Britain.

November 18: Schiaparelli sails on the S.S. *Europa* for New York.

December 10: Edward VIII abdicates the British throne to marry the American divorcée Wallis Simpson.

December 13: Schiaparelli arrives in New York on the S.S. *Europa* with a plan to indulge in a shopping spree at five-and-dime stores. While there, she launches a "tie-in" with Formfit foundations.

December 28: She returns to France on the S.S. *Normandie*.

1937
Cristóbal Balenciaga opens a couture house at 10 avenue George V in Paris.

February 4: Schiaparelli presents her collection for summer 1937, featuring the butterfly theme; an hourglass figure with corseted waist; and a new evening silhouette evident in short, bell-skirted dresses worn with starched petticoats and high-heeled ballet slippers. Other elements include a lobster motif on cotton beachwear (a collaboration with Dalí); metal-stripped gauzes for evening; short gloves with butterflies perched on wrists or embroidered rings; butterfly fans; Perugia ankle bootees with open-work straps; fastenings that include plastic mermaids, ship's prow figures, and tiny umbrellas; tinted mother-of-pearl and celluloid flower trimmings; funnel hats; and wide horsehair mesh evening coats worn over plain or printed dresses. Print themes are Greek statues, famous autographs, horseshoes, chess figures, and lovebirds. Featured colors are "Seine Sunset" and "Seine Sunrise."

April 10: Schiaparelli designs a wedding dress with a headdress of white birds for Marie Françoise Argence's marriage to Pierre Ducharne of the silk-manufacturing family.

April 29: The theme of her collection for fall 1937 is "Paris 1937," a reference to the forthcoming Exposition internationale des arts et techniques dans la vie moderne. Also present are Mae West

influences; slim, straight silhouettes; "Exposition" dinner ensembles consisting of slim floor-length dresses worn with fitted jackets; dramatic flaring hats with metal "feather" ornaments; designs by Jean Cocteau for an evening coat, dinner costume, and evening dresses; flaring ballerina-style dance dresses that are short in front and long in back; and tulle evening capes. Print themes are rabbits, flower-seed packets, Caribbean designs, and landscapes. The perfume Shocking and the color "Shocking" pink are launched.

April 30: Wallis Simpson selects eighteen models from Schiaparelli's fall collection for her trousseau.

May: Schiaparelli throws a coronation party for George VI in London.

She begins the Viyella fabric campaign, making the cotton and wool fabric fashionable.

May 25: The *Exposition internationale des arts et techniques dans la vie moderne* opens in Paris. Schiaparelli visits and is influenced by the Peruvian pavilion, which will inspire her August collection.

June 3: Wallis Simpson and the Duke of Windsor are married at the Château de Candé in Monts, France.

June: Schiaparelli opens her birdcage-inspired perfume boutique designed by Jean-Michel Frank.

June 25: Her winglike beret, called "Wing Spread," is inspired by Amelia Earhart, and "His Honor" hat, by a hat worn by the Lord Mayor of London to the opening of the British pavilion at the Paris exposition.

June: The French couture pavilion opens at the Paris exposition, with Schiaparelli's controversial display featuring a naked mannequin.

July 7: Amelia Earhart is lost over the Pacific during an attempt to fly around the world.

July: Maurice de Rothschild gives a costume ball in Paris, with the theme "Italian Comedy."

August 5: Schiaparelli's collection for winter 1937–38 features scanty, slim silhouettes with front slits to enable walking; snugly fitting gowns with brassiere bodices; a black suit with pockets embroidered with lips worn with a high-heeled-shoe hat (another collaboration with Dalí); gold cupid earrings and cherub-head pins designed by Jean Schlumberger; high "windblown" hats; and coats with Louis XV or Chinese-style embroideries. Featured colors are "Yankee Blood" red; "Della Robbia" blue, "Sultry" rose, and "After the Storm" dark reds and blues. The models wear shoes by Joseph Casales for the American manufacturer Laird Schober & Co.

September: French actress Danielle Darrieux selects a Schiaparelli wardrobe for her trip to Hollywood to star in *The Rage of Paris*, with costumes by Vera West.

October 28: Schiaparelli presents her collection for spring 1937, which includes flaring bust-length jackets; brassiere-cut evening dresses; tufted Shocking pink satin pillbox hats; long embroidered gloves with velvet garters at the top; clips; Victorian-inspired buttons representing little hands holding flowers, candlesticks with tapers, spoons, or flowers under glass paperweights; and a large necklace of gold leaves.

November 29: She sails on the *Queen Mary* to New York, where, on December 2, she is honored at the all-male 721 Club's annual party at Bonwit Teller.

December 7: She hosts a cocktail party and press reception at the new showrooms of Parfums Schiaparelli in New York.

December 8: Schiaparelli returns to France on the S.S. *Normandie*.

December 18: The American film *Every Day's a Holiday* opens, with Mae West wearing costumes designed and made by Schiaparelli.

1938
January 17: The *Exposition internationale du Surréalisme* opens in Paris.

February: Parfums Schiaparelli is organized as a separate company, with capital of 200,000 francs, under the administration of Schiaparelli and Henri Winter of Paris and Francis Cahill of London. The perfume business moves from 21 to 12 Place Vendôme (where Chopin died in October 1849).

February 4: The theme of Schiaparelli's collection for summer 1938, the circus, is reflected in designs, embroideries, and trimmings. There is a dinner dress decorated with a skeleton silhouette padded to shape; evening dresses with tent veils; Chinese cuts in coats; harem skirts; tall, peaked hats; an inkwell-shaped hat with a quill pen sticking out the top; satin drawstring bags from which flowers emerge; mitts buttoned up the sides like gaiters; and gold "ear" earrings. Featured colors are "Calliope" red, "Monseigneur" purple, and "Imperial" blue.

March 6: Designs from Schiaparelli's Circus collection appear in the play *Cavalier Seul* in Paris, worn by actresses Arletty and Blanche Montel.

April 28: Schiaparelli's collection for fall 1938, called "A Pagan Collection," features Botticelli-inspired and spring themes: leaves, apple blossoms, wild strawberries, and insects. There are also doll-sized hats; three-dimensional petal and leaf embroidery; and a flat collar necklace of Rhodoid set with insects.

July 2: Lady Mendl holds her Circus Ball.

August 4: Schiaparelli presents her collection for winter 1938–39, whose theme is the zodiac. There are Louis XIV influences in sun-ray embroideries, Sèvres porcelain–shaped pockets; mirror-embroidered dinner jackets; electric-light ornaments on handbags; changeable moiré evening coats; fur hoods; Crown Mosaic zippers; and high-buttoned shoes. Featured colors are "Cameo" pink, "Aerostatic" purple, "Sooty" blue, and "Salt Water" green.

September 29: Great Britain, France, and Italy, hoping to avoid war with Germany, sign the Munich Agreement, ceding to Germany the Sudeten region of Czechoslovakia.

October 27: The theme of Schiaparelli's collection for spring 1939 is the Commedia dell'arte. Included are "Femme heureuse" and "Spanish Don" hats; buttoned bootees worn with evening clothes; harlequin patchwork embroideries; masks on buttons and jewelry; tufted "Capitonne" embroidery; and zippers tipped with tinkling bells.

Monsieur Louis Meunier, Schiaparelli's financial administrator, 1937

1939

February 6: Schiaparelli's collection for summer 1939 emphasizes the "ladylike." There are long slim gowns; bustle drapes for evening; moiré-ribbon dog-collar necklaces with dangling coins; gloves with gold ruffles on the fingers; pastel dinner jackets with Louis XVI or Chinese embroideries; pearl-mesh embroidered necklines on evening dresses; comet and star necklaces; starched lace trimmings; apron dresses; evening sandals with heels made of three gold balls; and embroidery in the form of Saint Peter's keys. Print themes include red ladybugs, zebras, string beans, hands joined in prayer, Annunciation lilies, and naive angels drawn by a Chinese refugee child.

February: The *Golden Gate International Exposition* in San Francisco opens. The theme of the French pavilion is "how the haute couture has been inspired by the great painters of Paris," featuring dresses inspired by the paintings of Henri Matisse, Georges Rouault, Pierre-Auguste Renoir, and others. The installation "Souvenir de Paris" includes clothes by Schiaparelli and Jeanne Lanvin and is designed by Etienne Kohlman. Schiaparelli sends her wooden mannequin Pascal, dressed as a French cyclist.

April 1: Having subdued the rest of Spain and occupied the capital of Madrid on March 28, General Franco officially declares an end to the Spanish Civil War.

April 28: Schiaparelli presents her collection for fall 1939, featuring a musical theme that is reflected in music-box belts, a handbag that plays "Rose Marie, I Love You," and evening dresses embroidered with musical instruments. Also shown are mesh peephole hats; hats with birdcage crowns with birds inside; slim silhouettes with long, tight bodices and jackets that curve down in front and up in back; and a bloused hem used on town suits and sports knickers.

April–May: The New York World's Fair opens. Schiaparelli collaborates with Marcel Vertès on her installation, a plaster slab with sequined fabric.

May 17: She dresses Queen Charlotte's Ball, a mass gathering of British debutantes in London.

May 20: She designs a hat for the westbound maiden voyage of Pan Am's "flying boat," the *Yankee Clipper*, which is featured in the window of Saks Fifth Avenue in New York.

June: Four young women wear bustle dresses designed by Schiaparelli for the gala in Paris celebrating the fiftieth anniversary of the Eiffel Tower.

June: Schiaparelli arranges with the Spool Cotton Company of New York to promote Boilfast six-cord mercerized crochet cotton; she has for the past couple of seasons promoted their Crown Mosaic zippers.

June 30: Comte Etienne de Beaumont holds his ball celebrating the tercentenary of Jean Racine. Schiaparelli attends.

July: André Durst holds a *Bal de la forêt* (Forest Ball) at which Chanel dances with Schiaparelli and almost sets the younger designer's costume alight when she pushes her into a candelabra.

End of July: Schiaparelli closes her London branch, allegedly because of the actions of copyists, though she later states that she considers it a compliment when her designs are pirated.

August 3: Her collection for winter 1939–40 introduces a "Cigarette" silhouette, seen in slim, sleek lines broken by soft bias gathers. There are jackets with pouch pockets; apron effects on dresses; bloused hemlines; long, tubular jackets with discreet back drapes; fur "Guardsmen" hats with chin straps, influenced by British guards parading in Paris on Bastille Day; Victorian-influenced hats with behind-the-ears chin straps; buttoned fur ankle bootees; a leopard-skin fedora hat, buttoned bootees, and bracelet; shoulder-high velvet gloves for evening; and bib necklaces made of coins.

September 1: Germany invades Poland.

September 3: France and Great Britain declare war on Germany.

September 14: Paris couturiers design special clothing to be worn by women during air raids.

September 19: Schiaparelli proposes that American buyers help the couture through a difficult time by specifying their needs very clearly.

October 26: In her collection for spring 1940 the military theme appears in "cash and carry" saddlebag pockets on slightly flared belted coats and suit jackets and transformable laveuse (washerwoman) dresses with an apron effect that can be raised or lowered. Featured colors are "Maginot Line" blue, "Trench" brown, "Foreign Legion" red, "Aeroplane" gray, "Fusée" pink, and "Camouflage" taffetas.

November 15: The exhibition *Picasso: Forty Years of His Art* opens at the Museum of Modern Art in New York. Picasso's painting *Bird Cage and Playing Cards*, owned by Schiaparelli, is exhibited for the first time.

November 30: The Soviet Union attacks Finland.

1940

January: Schiaparelli's daughter, Gogo, joins a French ambulance brigade as a driver. She is nicknamed

"Maginot Mitzi" by her friends, a reference to the Maginot Line built between 1929 and 1940 to protect France from invasion along its eastern frontier.

January 26: Schiaparelli presents her collection for summer 1940, featuring slim, neat mermaid silhouettes molded by Formfit corsets; tiny hats over shirred silk caps; dresses with shirred hiplines; jet-embroidered boleros over low-cut evening gowns; Finnish-style hand-knitted cotton stockings worn with patent-leather Mary Jane shoes; Finnish-style embroidered belts; coats with knife pleats; buttons with gold sun motifs on leather or gold heads of laughing boys; and a dull black suit with a gold chain fastening. Print themes include slippers, penguins, and Colcombet's French regimental flag prints. The featured color is "Sleeping" blue. She also launches the perfume Sleeping.

March: Schiaparelli dresses Eve Curie, daughter and biographer of Nobel laureate Marie Curie, for her American lecture tour.

April 23: Her collection for fall 1940 includes short, straight skirts; white linen and lace choirboy jackets worn over slim evening gowns; white detachable and washable pocket flaps and linings; hand-knit silk stockings worn under straw bootees for beachwear; a white woolen evening coat embroidered with gold; "Lawrence of Arabia" beach headdresses; short-sleeved evening gowns with seed-pearl band collars; back-of-the-head hats with trimmings covering the forehead; hats with wavy-edged brims; high, looped ribbon turbans; stiffened shoulder bretelles (ornamental straps) and a puffed peplum on evening gowns with wider skirts; a bulky badger-fur topcoat; and a "Daily Ration" scarf.

May 10: Germany invades the Netherlands, Belgium, and Luxembourg.

June 10: Italy declares war on France and Great Britain.

June 14: German troops enter Paris.

June 27: General Charles de Gaulle becomes the leader of Free France.

July 11: Marshal Pétain establishes a German-controlled French state, with the capital at Vichy.

July 17: Schiaparelli arrives in New York aboard the *Yankee Clipper* to begin an American lecture tour titled "Clothes and the Woman."

September 10: In Dallas, Texas, she is presented with the Neiman Marcus Award for Distinguished Service to Fashion.

October 3: The Vichy government orders the first anti-Jewish statutes to be put into effect in occupied France.

October 8: In an interview in Harvard University's daily newspaper, *The Harvard Crimson*, Schiaparelli states that young women's adoption of the long, unfitted jacket usurps the traditional privilege of Ivy League men to wear their coats halfway down to their knees.

November 10: Lucien Lelong is named head of the fashion section of the Vichy government.

1941

January 4: Having decided to return to France despite

the war, Schiaparelli sails from Jersey City on the American export liner *Siboney*, traveling to Lisbon via Bermuda. She carries with her 13,000 vitamin capsules for delivery to the French minister in Lisbon on behalf of American-French War Relief, Inc. The vitamins are mistakenly confiscated by the British in Bermuda as suspicious but are eventually returned.

February: The occupying Germans impose a ration system in Paris, from which thirty-five designers are exempt.

February: Schiaparelli's collection for summer 1941 includes a dinner ensemble with the jacket embroidered with vegetables and fruit.

March: A small group of Surrealists, including André Breton, Marcel Duchamp, Max Ernst, Roberto Matta, and Yves Tanguy, leave France for the United States.

March 7: Gogo Schiaparelli marries Robert Lawrence Berenson, nephew of art historian Bernard Berenson, in New York.

May 25: Flying from Lisbon on the *Dixie Clipper*, Schiaparelli arrives in New York City, where she will live for the duration of the war.

June 4: She officiates at the First National Sewing contest at the Waldorf Astoria Hotel in New York.

June 22: Germany attacks the Soviet Union.

December 7: The Japanese bomb Pearl Harbor.

1942
With Marcel Duchamp and André Breton, Schiaparelli organizes the *First Papers of Surrealism* exhibition, which opens on October 14 in New York.

1943
July 25: In Italy, Mussolini is overthrown and arrested.

October 20: Parisians adopt black-and-yellow breast-pocket handkerchiefs to protest the German order that French Jews wear black-and-yellow stars.

1944
Daniel P. Wooley, regional chief of the U.S. Office of Price Administration, advocates standardized dress to keep prices under control. He invites Schiaparelli and actress Billie Burke to advise him on style.

April 21: France grants women the right to vote.

April 28: Couturier Paul Poiret dies in Paris.

May: In Paris, Jean-Paul Sartre's play *Huis Clos* (No Exit) is produced for the first time.

June 6: Allied troops land on the beaches at Normandy.

August 25: Paris is liberated by the Allies.

October 5: The house of Schiaparelli presents its collection for spring 1944 (designed by Irene Dana in Schiaparelli's absence). Included are "Redingote" cloaks with fur hoods; corduroy bicycle ensembles; and tricolor "liberation" ensembles with a blue moiré cloak overdress with red and white panels.

1945
The fashion magazine *Elle* is founded.

Pierre Cardin briefly joins the house of Schiaparelli as a design assistant.

March 15: The house of Schiaparelli presents its collection for winter 1945–46 (again designed by Irene Dana), featuring dresses and jackets with soft "flying" collars; coats with wide, square shoulders and flared skirts; short puffed sleeves; soft dresses that are full over the stomach and hips; and bright colors.

May 8: Germany surrenders, ending the war in Europe.

July: Schiaparelli returns to France.

August 14: Japan surrenders, ending the war in the Pacific.

September 13: Schiaparelli presents her first postwar collection, beginning where she had left off in 1940. Designed for winter 1945–46, the collection features square-shouldered short jackets; narrow skirts; "Talleyrand" suits (named after the French bishop famous for his diplomacy); top hats; Directoire-style dickeys; bonnets tied under the chin; and plaids.

October 24: With the ratification of its charter by twenty-nine nations, the United Nations is formed.

1946
February 21: Schiaparelli's collection for summer 1946 features influences from Indo-Chinese art, apparent in silhouettes, colors, and trimmings. There are long, straight coats with side slits and multicolored embroidery; amusing dress prints, including Les Vieux Beaux *(The Old Beauties); and a traveling wardrobe packed in a large leather bag and consisting of six chemise-style dresses, a reversible coat, and three folding hats.*

April 26: For fall 1946 the emphasis is on contrast, with rayon and linen embroidered jackets worn with plain gowns for late afternoon and evening; evening gowns with uneven hemlines; and pillbox and brimmed hats that match the suit blouses.

May: A traveling exhibition, *Théâtre de la mode*, with twenty-seven-inch-high mannequins and stage sets by Paris's leading fashion designers and artists, is presented in the United States to mark the rebirth of French haute couture after World War II.

July 5: The bikini bathing suit makes its début in a fashion show at the Piscine Molitor in Paris. It is named after Bikini Atoll, where the Americans had tested the atomic bomb just days before, because its creator, Louis Reard, hopes it will have the same explosive effect.

August 29: Schiaparelli's collection for winter 1946–47 features round, tailored "illusion" bustles with town jackets and coats; hip drapery pulled to the back on dresses; dropped, tucked shoulders on coats and suits; ample swing coats with low pouch pockets; scrolled hemlines on cocktail and evening dresses; and amusing buttons. Featured colors are golden-toned tweeds, mauves, greens, robin's-egg blues for plain wools, and dark shot satins.

She refurbishes the accessory shop of her salon.

October 13: By referendum, France ratifies the constitution of the Fourth Republic.

October 29: Schiaparelli arrives in New York on the S.S. *Ile de France*'s first commercial voyage in seven years.

November: Schiaparelli presents her collection for spring 1947, showing soft, dropped shoulders with tucks and nipped-in waists and a rounded bowler-shaped bustle at the back of skirts. The sensation of the collection is a pink-and-black jet-encrusted dinner ensemble.

December: An attack on French garrisons in Hanoi precipitates war in Indochina.

December 15: Christian Dior opens a couture salon in Paris.

1947
Hubert de Givenchy joins Schiaparelli and is placed in charge of the boutique.

January: Parfums Schiaparelli moves to a modern laboratory in a bombed-out former mansion in the Bois Colombe outside Paris.

February 5: Schiaparelli's collection for summer 1947 includes gaily colored ribbon trimmings; straight, tubular dinner gowns with gathers held in place by spiraling ribbon; and a fantasy pillbox hat in the form of a bird's nest made of twigs and leaves with nesting birds. Print themes include wood grain and a hostess apron printed with "5 percent reduction." She launches a new perfume, Le Roy Soleil, in a Baccarat bottle designed by Salvador Dalí.

February 12: In his first collection, couturier Christian Dior presents his "New Look," which features rounded shoulders, a cinched waist, and a very full skirt.

February 15: Marisa Berenson, Schiaparelli's first granddaughter, is born.

April: Schiaparelli makes a suit from American wool included in the first CARE package sent to France from the United States, and on April 29 Eleanor Roosevelt presents it to the six-year-old daughter of a hero of the French Resistance.

April 30: Cotton fabrics are promoted in Schiaparelli's collection for fall 1947, appearing in dresses with peg-top pleats standing away from the hips. There are also brightly colored waist-length capes worn with evening dresses; long handbags; stiff "camera-case" pockets on suits; and "transformation" ensembles with separates that can be worn in different ways, such as a skirt that can be worn as a cape. Print themes include blue postage stamps and Chinese motifs.

The first Cannes Film Festival is held.

August 6: Schiaparelli's collection for winter 1947–48 stresses color, fabrics, and cut instead of trimmings. There is a barrel line for jackets; influence once again from the Directoire period; double bustles for evening; longer lengths for cocktail and dinner dresses, including ankle length; and plaids.

August 14–15: India and Pakistan gain independence from Great Britain.

August 16: Police in Nice detain Schiaparelli and question her about gems she had reported stolen on August 6. They find some of the jewelry, which she had failed to report had been found, in her bag. They confiscate American currency ($1,485) and impose a fine for failing to declare the money.

October 1: Schiaparelli arrives in London to persuade British women to support the long skirt decreed by Paris, urging revolt against the government's edict, in an era of strict rationing, that it is an unnecessary luxury because it uses too much fabric.

November 3: She presents her collection for spring 1948, featuring slim lines broken by jutting drapes, some of them fur trimmed, and tailored suits with hip-length fitted jackets with pockets.

1948
African American writer James Baldwin moves to Paris, joining a group of black writers and artists that includes Richard Wright, Chester Himes, and Ollie Harrington.

February 4: Schiaparelli's collection for summer 1948 features an Amazone silhouette, characterized by balloon sleeves and a wasp waist. Included are natural shoulders with balloon fullness below; a back hem revealing petticoat flounces and pantalettes; narrow evening dresses with huge bow trains; light red stockings matching the newly launched lipstick, Stunning; and Perugia shoes with a dozen narrow straps over the instep.

For the first time, the Paris couture showings are televised, with the recording to be released in the United States after April 1.

April 14: Schiaparelli's second granddaughter, Berinthia (Berry) Berenson, is born.

April 29: Schiaparelli's collection for fall 1948 features varied sleeve treatments, including bottleneck shoulders with the width below, which are influenced by the centenary of the Second Empire. Other elements include a fold on the front edges of jackets to create a mantelet effect; winglike flares to the elbow; pencil-slim skirts; and short evening wraps.

August 4: In her collection for winter 1948–49 there are afternoon and evening dresses with cone-shaped hooped skirts; vividly colored satin evening gowns with back fullness; pleated "bat" sleeves on sack-shaped coats; detachable long puffed sleeves on evening dresses; distinctive seaming on impeccably cut suits; and a revival of her monkey fur bootees. The perfume Zut is launched.

November 3: For spring 1949 Schiaparelli offers slim lines broken by jutting drapes; necklines standing away from the bust; evening silhouettes that are slim to the knees and fan out around the feet; fur "tails" on evening coats; and fur yokes trimmed with draped fabric.

1949
Clothes rationing ends in Great Britain.

Simone de Beauvoir's *Le Dieuxième Sexe* (The Second Sex) is published.

February: Schiaparelli presents her collection for summer 1949, featuring a "Hurricane" silhouette; straw sunhats with holes in the brims for hands to pass through; straight, simple dresses with floating sashes; and leather belts with ring-shaped "luggage" handles at the sides. Print themes include blurred flowers, paisley, and tiny necktie motifs.

April 4: NATO (North Atlantic Treaty Organisation) is created.

May: In Schiaparelli's collection for fall 1949 the focus is on points. There are slim lines; natural shoulders; jagged décolletage; arc collars with points; short jackets with stiff points at front and back; and pointed peplums on skirts. Orange tones are featured.

July 28: Paris couture workers strike.

August 4: Schiaparelli presents her collection for winter 1949–50 despite the strikes. Models are unfinished, and the motto of the collection is "forgive us our needles and pins and please don't pull out those basting stitches." The focus is on a youthful look, with short skirts (including for evening); strapless décolletage for evening; and a "Forbidden Fruit" evening dress with the brassiere showing.

August: Negotiations take place between Schiaparelli and Donnybrook Fashion Ltd. to reproduce coats and suits to be sold at selected U.S. retailers, such as Lord & Taylor.

September 26: During a trip to the United States, Schiaparelli is featured on the cover of *Newsweek* magazine.

October 19: The People's Republic of China is formally established.

November: Schiaparelli's collection for spring 1950 features "Canasta" collarless coats; "Cookie Cutter" hats; "House of Cards" coats; peephole hats; draped berets; and a "Striptease" wedding dress. Featured colors are "Candybox" reds, greens, and blues.

c. 1950
Schiaparelli buys a house in Hammamet, Tunisia.

1950
February 2: In her collection for summer 1950, the emphasis is on modernity. There are full coats with short belled sleeves and back panels that can be draped like shawls; shoulder-high gloves and glovelike sleeves; accessories designed in recognition of the Holy Year, like the "Cardinal's cap"; bell-shaped straw hats; fringes and tassels; a wicker handbag shaped like a birdcage; oblique button fastenings replacing zippers; and balloon sleeves on cocktail blouses. Bold color combinations are featured, such as rich purple-red with deep blue.

February 28: The French Assembly in Paris decides to limit the sale of Coca-Cola.

May 4: Schiaparelli's fall 1950 collection features an evening dress with a dramatic "swan boat" hemline; beach clothes that include deep straw hats with see-through cellophane windows at the front and slacks that can be rolled up and buttoned to form shorts; and dresses with tunics draped up over hip pockets.

Short, belled sleeves and a slight flare continue on coats and jackets.

June 25: The Korean War begins.

August 1: Schiaparelli's collection for winter 1950–51 includes an ensemble called "The Front Line," which features a flat front with rounded or extended peplums. Other elements are a trim silhouette; knee-high slits in skirts; fur trimmings; pyramid-shaped coats; a slim formal gown with a stole looping into a train; a gold-embroidered white satin gown, street-length in front and dipping down at back; interesting buttons; opulent jewelry; small feather hats; and necklines that can be worn in two different ways.

November 14: For spring 1951 Schiaparelli shows skullcaps with fabric chignons; interpretations of the Spanish mantilla; oblique closings; and corselet belts. Part of the collection is previewed at a Hollywood fundraiser for the John Tracy Clinic. The Hollywood group stresses bright hues and daring contrasts; Paris additions to the group are in black and dark colors.

1951
Givenchy leaves Schiaparelli. Philippe Venet is named assistant designer of her salon.

February 7: Schiaparelli presents her collection for summer 1951, which includes hip-length tailored capes with large, flat pockets at the front and wide slits for arms worn over pencil-slim skirts; camouflage dresses with one color on the back and front and a second color on the sides; quilting; sun-ray pleating for panels and overskirts; oversize sleeves; buttons placed diagonally on coats; slim evening dresses with trailing stiffened back panels in a "horse's tail" silhouette; accordion-pleated blouses; sunglasses with black cellophane lashes; and "Cancan" crushed taffeta. There are striking color combinations like yellow with mauve.

April 5: In the United States, Julius and Ethel Rosenberg are convicted of conspiracy to commit espionage.

April 25: For fall 1951 Schiaparelli emphasizes the asymmetrical. Other features are cuts and seams suggesting an X formation; draped or adjustable necklines on simple dresses; flared coats; white handkerchief linen; boned collapsible hats; long handbags inspired by golf bags; giant openwork colored-stone earrings; and white broderie anglaise (a type of embroidery) on casual jackets.

June 12: The first collection of Schiaparelli Couture Lingerie is shown at the Waldorf Astoria Grand Ballroom in New York after premiering at Hess's Department Store in Allentown, Pennsylvania.

June 25: CBS presents the first color television broadcast, a one-hour special transmitted from New York to four other cities.

July 29: Schiaparelli's collection for winter 1951–52 exhibits an "Oriental" flavor, evident in Persian patterns and ornate costume jewelry. Also featured are the "SHAPE" silhouette; circular topcoats with slim dresses; harem hemlines on coats and dresses; wide ruffles on necklines; leather loop buttons; wide crushed-suede belts; and a tiered butterfly bow and back fullness on evening dresses.

Fall: She licenses fourteen different Paris-styled dolls to Effanbee Doll Company in New York.

November 5: Her collection for spring 1952 features a higher waistline; long, slim evening gowns with asymmetric drapes; an emphasis on bust and midriff; dresses with knife-pleated back fullness; and rigidly flared coats. Featured colors are "Shocking" pink, "Peony" violet-red, and "Hard" blue.

1952
January: Givenchy establishes his own couture house.

February 6: Schiaparelli presents her collection for summer 1952, showing slim coats and suits with yoke and lapel details; suit jackets with décolleté necklines revealing blouses; inverted heart-shaped necklines on day and evening dresses; loose fleece coats; slim evening gowns with huge twisted bustle drapes; umbrella-shaped beach hats; and a martingale half belt across the bosom of a topcoat and at the back of tulle evening dresses.

February 6: King George VI of England dies, and his daughter Elizabeth is proclaimed Queen Elizabeth II.

April 29: Schiaparelli emphasizes cotton in her collection for fall 1952. Cotton appears in terrycloth coats and dresses; printed, glazed chintz coats; and full-skirted evening dresses with hip-length tunics. The heart-shaped décolleté continues, and there are bib necklaces made of shells; belts holding cases for eyeglasses; and hats with flowerpot-shaped crowns.

August 1: For her winter 1952–53 collection, a grasshopper and katydid theme shows up in irregularly cut jacket edges and décolletés (continuing from the previous seasons); a sleek, smoothly rounded silhouette; hats inspired by the grasshopper outline; and "jut-out" collars and peplums. Featured colors are dark blackish gray and reds. The private showing is held at her home in the evening rather than at the salon during the day.

November 6: Schiaparelli's collection for spring 1953 includes after-ski costumes with leggings; fur-lined skirts; knee-length breeches; tiny fitted jackets with a narrow ruffle at the waist; and vivid colors.

She enters into an agreement with the American Optical Company to launch the first designer eyeglass collection.

1953
Philippe Venet leaves Schiaparelli to join Givenchy as a master tailor.

February 5: Schiaparelli presents her collection for summer 1953, featuring dramatic accessories; princess-cut jersey or lightweight wool day dresses; slightly flared skirts for day; stiff bell shapes for evening; shaggy wool coats; sports ensembles influenced by British Army uniforms; crescent-shaped décolleté; back fullness; original beachwear, including pedal pushers with five pockets down one leg, each holding a different colored handkerchief; ear hoops worn around the ear for evening; and a twisted link bracelet with tassels.

February 12: She announces that she has agreements with eleven American manufacturers to reproduce Schiaparelli-endorsed designs.

March 5: Stalin dies in Moscow of a cerebral hemorrhage.

April 22: Schiaparelli's collection for fall 1953 features silk fringed "angel hair" coats; sunglasses attached to cellophane pigtails; and flowered cotton party dresses.

Late April: She licenses a menswear line to Peerless Robes and Sportswear, an American manufacturer.

July 27: The Korean armistice takes effect.

July 30: Schiaparelli's collection for winter 1953–54 includes slim unbelted princess dresses worn with bulky finger-tip-length toppers; ladylike full-skirted ankle-length evening dresses; slim evening dresses with back fullness; derby hats; multi-strand crystal jewelry; a "saw-tooth" strapless bodice; and a short camel-hair coat with a scalloped front closing and a high wrapped collar.

October 3: She visits New York. During her stay, licensed "Schiaparelli Separates" are announced, designed by the American Pat Sandler. She also launches a new perfume, Success Fou, packaged in a gilt-veined ivy leaf designed by Raymond Peynet.

October 22: Her collection for spring 1954 is much reduced, consisting of only twenty-some models, including four multi-garment budget wardrobes.

December 8: She receives a U.S. patent for folding eyeglasses.

1954
Schiaparelli's biography, *Shocking Life*, is published in New York.

February 3: Schiaparelli presents what will turn out to be her last collection. She stresses supple lines and tightens her loose silhouettes at the waist with drawstrings. Features include bateau necklines and evening dresses with crossed bodices ending in draped sashes or drawstrings.

February 5: Chanel, who closed her salon during the war, returns to couture.

March 16: To meet the changing market for couture, Schiaparelli announces a plan to streamline production and focus on the private client.

July: France withdraws from Indochina.

November: The Algerian war for independence from France begins.

December 13: Schiaparelli's couture salon files for bankruptcy. Her perfume business continues.

1956
Elvis Presley's "Heartbreak Hotel" reaches number 1 on the charts in the United States and becomes his first international hit song.

1957
Christian Dior dies unexpectedly and his heir apparent, Yves Saint Laurent, leaves to open his own salon.

October 4: The Soviet Union successfully launches Sputnik I.

1959
The Barbie doll is introduced in New York City.

1962
Helen Gurley Brown's *Sex and the Single Girl* is published in New York.

1969
Schiaparelli donates more than seventy garments and accessories to the Philadelphia Museum of Art through the Fashion Group of Philadelphia.

1971
January 10: Chanel dies at the Ritz Hôtel in Paris at age eighty-seven.

1973
January: In *Roe v. Wade* the U.S. Supreme Court rules that women have the right to terminate a pregnancy.

November 13: Schiaparelli dies in her sleep at her home in Paris. She is buried in the village of Frucourt in Picardy, and masses are celebrated for her at the Église Saint-Philippe-du-Roule and at the church of Saint Thomas More in New York.

Sources Consulted

Introduction
Page 10
Elsa Schiaparelli, *Shocking Life* (New York: E. P. Dutton & Co., 1954), pp. 12–13, 18.

Pages 10–11
Man Ray, *Self Portrait* (1963; Boston: Little Brown and Co., 1988), p. 86.

Pour le Sport
Page 13
Thérèse and Louise Bonney, *A Shopping Guide to Paris* (New York: Robert M. McBride & Company, 1929), p. 51.
R. H., "On and Off the Avenue: Feminine Fashions," *New Yorker*, August 25, 1928, p. 48.
"Viola Paris Comes Back to Town," *Vogue*, December 15, 1927, p. 45.
Schiaparelli, *Shocking Life*, pp. 60–61.
Kathleen Cannell, "Paris Bouquet," unpublished typescript, 1953, Kathleen Cannell Papers, Harvard Theatre Collection, Houghton Library, Harvard University, Cambridge, Massachusetts.
"The Latest Word from Paris," *Women's Wear Daily*, November 21, 1927.
Janet Flanner, "Profiles: Comet," *New Yorker*, June 18, 1932, p. 19.
"Directions for Knitting the Chic Bowknot Sweater," *Ladies' Home Journal*, November 1928, p. 173.

Page 14
"Lorelei Lee Lingo Lingers—Lady's Line Lends Light Lilt," *Women's Wear Daily*, June 9, 1928.
"Import Models at R. H. Macy & Co. Typify Fashion Trend in Sportswear Offerings," *Women's Wear Daily*, September 28, 1927.
Elizabeth Hawes, *Fashion Is Spinach* (New York: Random House, 1938), pp. 87–88.
Les Echos, June 1929; as reported in B. J. Perkins, "French Weekly Attacks Macy's Ad on Copies," *Women's Wear Daily*, June 19, 1929 (with a reproduction of the original ad).

Pages 14–15
Women's Wear Daily, November 14, 1929; see also "Cheney Presents 'Staccato Prints' for 1929–30 Southern Beach Wear," *Women's Wear Daily*, September 11, 1929.

Page 15
Radclyffe Hall, *The Well of Loneliness* (Paris: Pegasus Press, 1928).

Page 16
Bonney and Bonney, *A Shopping Guide to Paris*, p. 87.

Page 20
Glenna Collett, *Ladies in the Rough* (New York and London: Alfred A. Knopf, 1928), pp. 27, 212.

Architect of Fashion
Page 33
Janet Flanner, "Profiles: Comet," *New Yorker*, June 18, 1932, p. 19.
Jean Désert sales registers, 1929, as cited in Peter Adam, *Eileen Gray: Architect, Designer* (New York: Harry N. Abrams, 1987), p. 241.
"The Studio" Yearbook: Decorative Arts 1931 (London: The Studio, 1931), p. 47.
Schiaparelli, *Shocking Life*, p. 67.
Paul T. Frankl, *New Dimensions: The Decorative Arts of Today in Words and Pictures* (New York: Brewer & Warren, 1928), p. 19.

"Schiaparelli," *Harper's Bazaar*, April 1932, p. 59.
Janet Flanner, "Profiles: Comet," p. 20.
"Black and White in Tweeds," British *Vogue*, January 22, 1930, p. 26.
Schiaparelli, *Shocking Life*, p. 255.

Page 34
"Vogue Points: About the New Suits," *Vogue*, October 15, 1931, p. 85.
"16 Couturiers Affiliate with Pattern Firm," *Women's Wear Daily*, April 8, 1929.
Elsa Schiaparelli, "Smartness Aloft," *Ladies' Home Journal*, March 1930, pp. 21, 69.
"Tweeds, Crepes, Velvety Woolens and Diagonals Strongly Endorsed for Winter," *Women's Wear Daily*, August 20, 1928.

Page 35
"Rayons: Schiaparelli Continues with Novelty Jerseys," *Women's Wear Daily*, October 27, 1932.
"Business & Finance: Haute Couture," *Time*, August 13, 1934, pp. 49–54, esp. p. 50.
"High Court of Justice," *The Times* (London), November 6–8, 23, 1935; "Foreign News," *Time*, November 18, 1935, p. 18.

Page 39
Caresse Crosby, *The Passionate Years* (New York: Dial Press, 1953), p. 277.
"Paris Prepares for Her Season," *Harper's Bazaar*, June 1930, p. 136.

Page 45
"Fashion Fads & Facts," *Harper's Bazaar*, July 1931, p. 27.

Page 52
"Inexpensive Prints and Schiaparelli Originals Features," *Women's Wear Daily*, November 30, 1931; "Saks 34 St. Presents 'Entire Collection' of Schiaparelli," *Women's Wear Daily*, December 1, 1931.
"The New Mode," British *Vogue*, September 16, 1931, p. 35.

Page 55
Schiaparelli, *Shocking Life*, p. 68.

Page 56
"Schiaparelli's Visit to Be Brief Tour of Observation," *Women's Wear Daily*, February 15, 1933.

Page 59
Schiaparelli, *Shocking Life*, p. 74.

Page 65
"A Searchlight over the Collections," *Harper's Bazaar*, October 1933, p. 134.

Page 66
"Paris Recognizes the Short Cape as a Rival of the Jacket," *Women's Wear Daily*, June 8, 1934.
"Fashions from Andalusia," *Harper's Bazaar*, June 1934, pp. 41–45.

Shadow of Napoleon
Page 71
Schiaparelli, *Shocking Life*, p. 85.
"A Designer Makes Her Home in Paris—in London," *Arts and Decoration*, May 1934, pp. 38–39; Jean-Michel Frank, "Decoration 1935," *Vogue*, April 3, 1935, p. 97; "Chez Schiaparelli: Decorator's Preview," *Vogue*, September 15, 1934, pp. 76–77; "On and Off the Avenue: Feminine Fashions," *New Yorker*,

March 2, 1935, p. 42.

Alison Settle, *Clothes Line* (London: Methuen and Co., 1937), p. 102.

Schiaparelli, *Shocking Life*, p. 86.

"New Vogue Will Be Forecast from Paris This Afternoon over WABC–Columbia Network," *Binghamton Sun* (N.Y.), February 4, 1935, and other press clippings in the archives of Schiaparelli France, Paris.

Tristan Tzara, in David Gascoyne, *A Short Survey of Surrealism* (London: Cobden-Sanderson, 1935), p. 107.

Pages 71–72

"Famous Frenchmen Sponsor 'Newsprint Silk,'" *Women's Wear Daily*, May 4, 1935.

Page 72

Meryle Secrest, *Kenneth Clark: A Biography* (New York: Fromm International, 1986), p. 123.

"Openings Today Reflect Hindu and Persian Influences," *Women's Wear Daily*, February 5, 1935.

"Orientale at Mrs. Fellowes'," *Harper's Bazaar*, August 1935, pp. 72–73, 126; "Odd Styles at Parisian Oriental Ball," *Hartford Times* (Conn.), July 9, 1935, press clipping in the archives of Schiaparelli France, Paris.

Schiaparelli, *Shocking Life*, p. 113.

Page 73

"Crowns, Cocks New Patterns at Schiaparelli," *Milwaukee Journal* (Wisc.), September 13, 1935; "Shorter Skirts; Padlocks and Francs for Buttons," *West Lancaster Evening Gazette* (Ohio), September 17, 1935, press clippings in the archives of Schiaparelli France, Paris.

"We Want to Dress Attractively," *New York Herald Tribune*, as reported in "'We Want Pretty Clothes' Is Cry of Soviet Youth," *Women's Wear Daily*, January 1, 1934.

"Soviet Girls Wait Months for Dress," *New York Times*, November 25, 1935.

Schiaparelli, *Shocking Life*, pp. 100–111; see also press clippings in the archives of Schiaparelli France, Paris.

Page 74

"Pour Habiller Ariane," *Je suis partout*, January 11, 1936, press clipping in the archives of Schiaparelli France, Paris.

Miguel Covarrubias, "Impossible Interview," *Vogue*, June 15, 1936, p. 43.

"Schiaparelli Makes Wardrobe for Amy Mollison on Cape Flight," *Women's Wear Daily*, c. 1936, press clipping in author's files; and Mary Fentress (U.P.), "Paris Styles," press clipping in the archives of Schiaparelli France, Paris.

Page 76

"Normandie, New Queen of the Seas, Starts on Maiden Voyage Laden with Rich Cargo of Fashions," *Women's Wear Daily*, May 29, 1935.

Hugo Vickers, *Cecil Beaton: The Authorized Biography* (London: Weidenfeld and Nicolson, 1985), pp. 207–8; see also writings on the back of the original Beaton sketch, Condé Nast Archives, New York.

Page 84

"Three Parisians Choose Same Cape Model," *Dixon Telegram* (Dixon, Ill.), July 20, 1935; see also press clippings in the archives of Schiaparelli France, Paris.

Kathleen Cannell, "A Fond Look Back," *Christian Science Monitor*, February 25, 1974.

Page 88

"Zippered Imports," *Business Week*, July 18, 1936,

pp. 30, 32; Robert Friedel, *Zipper: An Exploration in Novelty* (New York: W. W. Norton & Company, 1994), esp. pp. 160–61, 192–94.

Page 92

Press clippings in the archives of Schiaparelli France, Paris.

Miguel Covarrubias, "Impossible Interview," *Vogue*, June 15, 1936, p. 43.

Page 95

Cecil Beaton, *Photobiography* (Garden City, New York: Doubleday, 1951), p. 100.

"Macy's New Tailored Topper is a copy of Schiaparelli's Original 'Brown Derby'" [advertisement], *New York Sun*, February 28, 1936; "Five Dollar Bracket Played Up in End of Week Retail 'Ads,'" *Women's Wear Daily*, February 28, 1936; see also press clippings in the archives of Schiaparelli France, Paris.

Page 96

"Schiaparelli Arrives for 'Spree' in Shops and 5-and-10 Stores," *New York Times*, December 4, 1936.

Page 98

"High Paris Court Upholds Woman's Hat as a Work of Art," *Women's Wear Daily*, July 31, 1934.

After Dark

Page 101

B. J. Perkins, "Glimpses of Paris: Buyers Prepare to Quit a Changed Paris," *Women's Wear Daily*, February 13, 1931.

"Paris—1932," *Vogue*, February 1, 1932.

B. J. Perkins, "Renaissance of French Elegance Under Way, Restoring Paris to the Parisians," *Women's Wear Daily*, June 20, 1932.

"Paris—1932," *Vogue*, February 1, 1932, p. 30.

"Distinctions in Dress between Parisians and Americans Discussed in Radio Interview," *Women's Wear Daily*, November 8, 1934.

Schiaparelli, *Shocking Life*, p. 65.

Page 102

B. J. Perkins, "Renaissance of French Elegance Under Way, Restoring Paris to the Parisians," *Women's Wear Daily*, June 20, 1932.

"On and Off the Avenue: Feminine Fashions," *New Yorker*, September 1, 1934, p. 34.

B. J. Perkins, "Glimpses of Paris: Mary Nowitzky Granted Extension," *Women's Wear Daily*, February 8, 1932.

Janet Flanner, *Paris Was Yesterday, 1925–1939*, ed. Irving Drutman (New York: Viking Press, 1972), p. 94.

Page 103

Salvador Dalí, *The Secret Life of Salvador Dalí* (New York: Viking Press, 1942), p. 291.

Page 104

Vogue, October 1, 1937, p. 95.

Page 107

"The Slim Silhouette Gains in Today's Paris Openings: Schiaparelli Clothes, 'Brand New,' Are Brilliant and Optimistic," *Women's Wear Daily*, October 28, 1936.

Page 110

"Innovations in Staging Enliven Macy's 'Importants of Paris' Show," *Women's Wear Daily*, c. 1937, press clipping in author's files.

Page 111

"Schiaparelli Prints Reported Confined in U.S. to Two Firms," *Women's Wear Daily*, September 16, 1936; see also Drucker-Wolf advertisement in *Women's Wear Daily*, October 14, 1936.

Page 115

"The Truth about Stars' Figures," *Photoplay*, September 1941, p. 76.

Page 119

"Fashion Flashes from Paris," *Women's Wear Daily*, February 23, 1940.

Art into Fashion

Page 121

Franklin Rosemont, *André Breton and the First Principles of Surrealism* (London: Pluto Press, 1978), p. 125.

Dalí, *The Secret Life of Salvador Dalí*, p. 340.

Man Ray, *Self Portrait* (1963; Boston: Little Brown and Co., 1988), p. 86.

Page 122

Schiaparelli, *Shocking Life*, p. 116.

"Je veux qu'elle soit reine!" *Cahiers d'Art*, no. 14 (1939), pp. 138–39.

Roland Penrose, *Picasso: His Life and Work* (New York: Harper, 1959), pp. 283–84.

Page 123

Christiane Meyer-Thoss, *Meret Oppenheim Book of Ideas: Early Drawings and Sketches for Fashions, Jewelry, and Designs* (Bern, Switzerland: Gachnang & Springer, 1996).

Salvador Dalí, "New York as Seen by the Super-Realist Artist," *American Weekly*, articles running February through July 1935.

"The Camera Overseas: Schiaparelli Clothes the Bride of the Year," *Life*, May 17, 1937, pp. 64–65; "Paris Radio Sketches of Schiaparelli Costumes: Mrs. Simpson's Wardrobe," *Women's Wear Daily*, April 30, 1937; "Mrs. Simpson Selects Popular Schiaparelli Models for Her Spring Wardrobe," *Women's Wear Daily*, May 5, 1937.

Page 124

Lewis Kachur, *Displaying the Marvelous* (Cambridge, Mass., and London: The MIT Press, 2001), pp. 8, 36–67.

"New Ballet Décor," British *Vogue*, May 25, 1938, pp. 62–65.

Salvador Dalí, *The Conquest of the Irrational: With 35 Photographic Reproductions and an Hors-Texte in Colours*, trans. David Gascoyne (New York: Julien Levy, 1935), p. 15.

Page 125

Schiaparelli, *Shocking Life*, p. 91.

Coco Chanel, as reported in Edna Woolman Chase and Ilka Chase, *Always in Vogue* (Garden City, N.Y.: Doubleday, 1954), p. 228.

Cristóbal Balenciaga, as reported in Bettina Ballard, *In My Fashion* (London: Secker & Warburg, 1960), p. 69.

Anaïs Nin, *The Diary of Anaïs Nin*, vol. 2, *1934–39* (New York: Swallow Press, 1966–), entry for October 1935.

Schiaparelli, *Shocking Life*, p. 59.

Augustabernard, as reported in Settle, *Clothes Line*, p. 26.

Schiaparelli, *Shocking Life*, p. 59.

Page 127
Tristan Tzara, "D'un certain automatisme du goût,"
    Minotaure, nos. 3–4 (October–December 1933),
    pp. 81–84.

Page 128
Georges Hugnet, "Petite rêverie du grand veneur,"
    Minotaure, no. 5 (May 1934), p. 30.

Page 132
Beaton, *Photobiography*, p. 97.

Page 136
Eugene R. Gaddis, *Magician of the Modern: Chick Austin
    and the Transformation of the Arts in America* (New
    York: Alfred A. Knopf, 2000), p. 339.
"An Album of Color from the Paris Openings," *Harper's
    Bazaar*, September 15, 1937; "If the Shoe Fits, Put
    It On," *Women's Wear Daily*, September 1937,
    press clipping in author's files.

Page 143
René Magritte, "La Ligne de vie," in *L'Invention collective*,
    no. 2 (April 1940).

Page 147
René Magritte, "Les Mots et les images," *La Révolution
    surréaliste*, no. 12 (December 15, 1929), p. 33.

Page 149
Schiaparelli, *Shocking Life*, p. 166–68.

Metamorphosis
Page 151
Schiaparelli, *Shocking Life*, p. 10.
Ballard, *In My Fashion*, p. 71.
Schiaparelli, *Shocking Life*, p. 255.

Page 152
Schiaparelli, *Shocking Life*, p. 71.
"Movietone," *Harper's Bazaar*, February 1933, p. 65.
Miami Herald, February 27, 1936, press clipping in the
    archives of Schiaparelli France, Paris.
Azzedine Alaïa, personal communication, 2000.
Dalí, *The Secret Life of Salvador Dalí*, p. 340.
Schiaparelli, *Shocking Life*, p. 86.
Ballard, *In My Fashion*, p. 84.
Carmel Snow, with Mary Louise Aswell, *The World of
    Carmel Snow* (New York: McGraw-Hill, 1962), p. 86.
Marcel Vertès, as reported in Snow, *The World of Carmel
    Snow*, p. 86.
André Breton, *Nadja*, trans. Richard Howard (New York:
    Grove Press, 1960), p. 160.

Page 153
Dalí, *The Secret Life of Salvador Dalí*, p. 192.
Dorothy Cocks and Julia Coburn, "Do You Want to Look
    Pretty or—Do You Want to Look Smart?" *Ladies'
    Home Journal*, March 1933, p. 29.
Ballard, In My Fashion, p. 61; Snow, *The World of
    Carmel Snow*, p. 86.
Betsey Burke, "Take Your Personality with You When You
    Shop," *Independent Woman*, November 1954,
    p. 413.
Schiaparelli, *Shocking Life*, p. 125.
Settle, *Clothes Line*, p. 33.
"Schiaparelli Arrives for 'Spree' in Shops and 5-and-10
    Stores," *New York Times*, December 4, 1936.
Schiaparelli, *Shocking Life*, p. 10.

Page 156
"Fleurs et Papillons," Paris *Vogue*, July 1937, p. 23.

Page 158
"Mme. Schiaparelli Hostess at Opening of Perfume
    Salon," *Women's Wear Daily*, December 17, 1937;
    "Glimpses of Paris: Schiaparelli Perfume Company
    Organized," *Women's Wear Daily*, February 9, 1938;
    "Schiaparelli Perfume Firm for U.S. Formed,"
    Women's Wear Daily, press clipping in author's files.

Page 161
Ballard, *In My Fashion*, p. 71.
"Schiaparelli: 'Scanty' Lines, Rich Trims," *Women's Wear
    Daily*, August 5, 1937.
Snow, *The World of Carmel Snow*, p. 86.
Cecil Beaton, *The Glass of Fashion* (Garden City, N.Y.:
    Doubleday, 1954), p. 138.
Schiaparelli, *Shocking Life*, p. 255.
Daisy Fellowes, *Les Dimanches de la Comtesse de
    Narbonne* (Paris: Editions de France, 1935).

Page 162
"Dietrich Invades Paris," *Vogue*, November 1, 1936,
    p. 134; see also Schiaparelli bills in the Marlene
    Dietrich Collection, Filmmuseum Berlin.

Page 165
Beaton, *The Glass of Fashion*, p. 188.
Ballard, *In My Fashion*, p. 84.
Cecil Beaton, *Cecil Beaton's Scrapbook* (New York:
    Charles Scribner's Sons, 1937), p. 27.

Six Collections
Page 169
Kathleen Cannell, "Paris Bouquet," unpublished
    typescript, 1953, Kathleen Cannell Papers, Harvard
    Theatre Collection, Houghton Library, Cambridge,
    Massachusetts.
Ballard, *In My Fashion*, p. 71.
John Phillips, *John Phillips: Free Spirit in a Troubled World*
    (Zurich and New York: Scalo Publishers, 1996),
    p. 55.

Page 170
Schiaparelli, *Shocking Life*, p. 116.
"Schiaparelli Circus Buttons in Town," *Women's Wear
    Daily*, February 10, 1938.
"Circus Theme for Gay Window Displays at Bonwit Teller,"
    Women's Wear Daily, c. February 1938, press
    clipping in author's files.
"Fête at Versailles," *Vogue*, August 15, 1938, p. 89.

Page 175
Valerie Mendes, *Dressed in Black* (London: V & A
    Publications in association with Harry N. Abrams,
    1999), p. 40–41; see also John Lowe, *Edward
    James, Poet, Patron, Eccentric: A Surrealist Life*
    (London: Collins, 1991), p. 145.

Page 176
Schiaparelli, *Shocking Life*, pp. 39–40.

Page 180
B. J. Perkins, "Glimpses of Paris," *Women's Wear Daily*,
    May 12, 1938.
"Pagan Charm: A Formfit Creation, A Schiaparelli
    Inspiration" [advertisement], *Harper's Bazaar*,
    September 1, 1938, p. 139.
"Hail Curves Once Again," *Evening World* (Omaha, Nebr.),
    July 29, 1935 (Consolidated Press Clipping
    Bureaus, Chicago).
"Guests Invited to Come as Famous Paintings to Paris
    Costume Ball," *Women's Wear Daily*, July 25, 1935.
"Bonwit Teller Launches 'Field and Forest' Jewelry,"
    Women's Wear Daily, June 10, 1938.

Page 186
Schiaparelli, *Shocking Life*, pp. 25–26.
"In Terms of the Elements—Schiaparelli's Descriptions,"
    Women's Wear Daily, August 10, 1938.
Phillips, *John Phillips: Free Spirit in a Troubled World*, p. 56.

Page 194
"Pierrot, Harlequin and Pulcinella Key to Schiaparelli
    Showing," *Women's Wear Daily*, October 27, 1938.
"Fashion Flashes from Paris: 'They Are Wearing'—Bi-Color
    Shoes," *Women's Wear Daily*, December 23, 1938.
"Paris Mid-Season Openings," *Vogue*, December 1, 1938,
    pp. 82—83.
Joan Riviere, "Womanliness as a Masquerade,"
    International Journal of Psycho-Analysis, vol. 9,
    (1929), pp. 300–313.
"Fashion Flashes from Paris: Costume Ball Accents
    'Heads,'" *Women's Wear Daily*, December 16, 1938.

Page 200
"Out of the Paris Openings a New Breath of Life—The Air
    of Innocence," *Vogue*, March 1, 1939, p. 51.
"With Towering Ostrich and Burgeoning Bustle Schiaparelli
    Celebrates Eiffel Tower Birthday," *Women's Wear
    Daily*, July 7, 1939.
Ballard, *In My Fashion*, p. 140.

Page 203
"With Towering Ostrich and Burgeoning Bustle Schiaparelli
    Celebrates Eiffel Tower Birthday," *Women's Wear
    Daily*, July 7, 1939.

Page 208
"'The New Woman' a Sylph-like Figure," *Women's Wear
    Daily*, May 11, 1939.
Rowena Rutherford Farrar, *Grace Moore and Her Many
    Worlds* (New York and London: Cornwall Books,
    1982), pp. 259–60.
"Crinolines Go to Night Gala at Longchamps," *Women's
    Wear Daily*, July 13, 1939.

Page 211
See Lopez-Willshaw's jacket in the collection of the
    Musée de la Mode et du Textile, Paris,
    1966-38-2 AB

Page 215
"Gogo Schiaparelli Wardrobes New Exclusive Junior
    Promotion," *Women's Wear Daily*, December 18,
    1940.

Matter of Prestige
Page 221
B. J. Perkins, "Glimpses of Paris: Copyists Blamed for
    Schiaparelli Move," *Women's Wear Daily*, July 14,
    1939.
Schiaparelli, *Shocking Life*, p. 255.
Lowe, *Edward James, Poet, Patron, Eccentric: A Surrealist
    Life*, p. 145.
Flanner, *Paris Was Yesterday*, p. 220.
Ballard, *In My Fashion*, pp. 88–89; Schiaparelli, *Shocking
    Life*, pp. 127–28.
"Vogue's Voice on the Paris Openings," *Vogue*, September
    1, 1939, p. 43.
"War Adds Another Art to Shop Windows in Paris,"
    New York Times, December 10, 1939.

Page 222
"Asks U.S. Firms Tell Paris of Style Desires," *Women's
    Wear Daily*, September 19, 1939.
Bettina Wilson, "Our Lives in Wartime Paris," British
    Vogue, November 1939, p. 66.
Schiaparelli, *Shocking Life*, p. 132.

"Schiaparelli," *Officiel* (Paris), October–November 1939, p. 25.

"Paris Presents: Spring Collections Designed to Please Men," *Vogue*, March 15, 1940, p. 45.

Page 223

"'Dimanche—Tout est permis' Says Schiaparelli's Kerchief," *Women's Wear Daily*, May 31, 1940.

"Authorized Labels to Identify Schiaparelli Reproduction," *Women's Wear Daily*, August 14, 1940; "Announcement: The Personal Wardrobe of Madame Schiaparelli," *Women's Wear Daily*, August 21, 1940; "Schiaparelli Designs a Wardrobe Shown by Bonwit Teller," *Women's Wear Daily*, September 14, 1940; "Schiaparelli Opening Lecture Tour," *New York World-Telegram*, September 24, 1940; "Schiaparelli Designs a Wardrobe in the U.S.A.," *Vogue*, October 1, 1940, pp. 66–67, 137–38.

Page 223–24

"Schiaparelli Talk Creates a Mild Stir," *Women's Wear Daily*, September 25, 1940.

Page 224

"Shoe Designers Take Issue with Schiaparelli Talk," *Women's Wear Daily*, September 27, 1940.

"Neiman-Marcus Awards for Service to Fashion to Be Made on Sept. 9," *Women's Wear Daily*, August 19, 1940.

"Schiaparelli Sails with a Vitamin Kit," *New York Times*, January 5, 1941; "British Take Vitamins from Mme. Schiaparelli," *New York Times*, January 7, 1941.

"Mme. Schiaparelli Arrives on Clipper," *New York Times*, May 26, 1941.

Public Record Office, London, Ministry of Economic Warfare, Elsa Schiaparelli (FO 837/284).

Schiaparelli, *Shocking Life*, p. 178.

Pages 224–25

Public Record Office, London, Ministry of Economic Warfare, Elsa Schiaparelli (FO 837/284).

Page 225

Archives of Paris, file D31U³/2740.

M.D.C. Crawford, *The Ways of Fashion* (New York: G. P. Putnam's Sons, 1941), p. 23.

Page 226

Lucien Lelong, "Paris: Lelong Speaks for the Paris Couture," *Vogue*, November 15, 1944, p. 74.

"Schiaparelli Emphasizes Color in Fashions: Draped Print Dresses Feature Paris Show," *New York Times*, March 16, 1945.

Page 229

"Fashion Flashes from Paris: Parisian Designers Working on Air Raid Shelter Suits," *Women's Wear Daily*, September 29, 1939.

Page 235

"Schiaparelli—Via Clipper," *Vogue*, January 15, 1940, p. 73.

"Say Museum Work Offered to Schiaparelli," *Women's Wear Daily*, December 15, 1939.

Page 236

"Schiaparelli Designs a Wardrobe Shown by Bonwit Teller," *Women's Wear Daily*, September 14, 1940.

Page 237

"Simultaneous Corset Presentation—In Paris by Schiaparelli, in New York by Lord & Taylor," *Women's Wear Daily*, February 1, 1940.

Page 240

"Colcombet Silk Souvenirs Wanted," *Women's Wear Daily*, February 14, 1940; "Masterpieces in Printing," *Women's Wear Daily*, April 3, 1940.

Page 243

"The Birth of the Sloping Shoulder," *Harper's Bazaar*, March 1, 1941, p. 121.

Aline Bernstein, *Masterpieces of Women's Costume of the 18th and 19th Centuries* (New York: Crown Publishers, 1959).

Page 244

Bertram M. Gordon, ed., *Historical Dictionary of World War II France: The Occupation, Vichy, and the Resistance*, 1938–1946 (Westport, Conn.: Greenwood Press, 1998), p. 130.

Themes and Variations

Page 249

Schiaparelli, *Shocking Life*, pp. 163, 191.

Ballard, *In My Fashion*, pp. 62, 201.

Pages 249–50

Bettina Wilson, "Schiaparelli at Home in Paris," *Vogue*, November 1, 1945, pp. 166, 224–27.

Page 250

"Gowns Featured by Sloping Lines," *New York Times*, February 21, 1946.

Schiaparelli, *Shocking Life*, p. 92.

Page 251

Schiaparelli, *Shocking Life*, p. 251.

"Midseason Modes Displayed in Paris," *New York Times*, November 10, 1947.

Page 252

Schiaparelli, *Shocking Life*, pp. 217–18.

Virginia Pope, "Schiaparelli Uses Striking Features," *New York Times*, August 12, 1949.

"Schiaparelli Collection," *New York Times*, February 4, 1950.

"Schiaparelli the Shocker," *Newsweek*, September 26, 1949, p. 51.

Palais Galliera, Musée de la Mode et du Costume, *Robes de soir*, exh. cat. (Paris: Paris-Musées, 1990), p. 174.

Page 253

Valérie Guillaume, *Jacques Fath* (Paris: Editions Paris-Musées and Société nouvelle Adam Biro, 1993), p. 88, fig. 79.

"Schiaparelli Gowns to Be Flown to U.S. for Coast Showing," *Women's Wear Daily*, September 27, 1950; "Schiaparelli Show Full of New Ideas," *New York Times*, November 15, 1950.

"Paris: New Drama," *Vogue*, March 15, 1952, p. 71.

"Grasshopper Theme at Schiaparelli," *Women's Wear Daily*, August 1, 1952.

"Summary of Paris Midseason," *Women's Wear Daily*, November 19, 1953.

Page 254

"June 12 Debut Set for Line by Schiaparelli," *Women's Wear Daily*, April 26, 1951.

"From Sailcloth to Capeskin: Sportswear Separates," *Women's Wear Daily*, October 14, 1953.

Herbert Koshetz, "Schiaparelli Men's Wear Will Be Male Despite 'Couturier Design,'" *New York Times*, May 3, 1953.

Arthur Bachrach in Sidney Shalett, "It's the Craziest Business!" *Saturday Evening Post*, June 11, 1952, p. 73.

"Schiaparelli Shows Four Budget Wardrobes," *New York Times*, October 22, 1953, p. 36.

"Mme. Schiaparelli Plans to Meet Changing Market," *New York Times*, March 16, 1954; "Mme. Schiaparelli Denies Reports of Temporary Closing of Paris Shop," *New York Times,* March 20, 1954.

Pages 254–55

Schiaparelli, *Shocking Life*, p. 251, 8.

Page 257

"First Hat from Free Paris," *Vogue*, November 1, 1944, p. 118.

"Paris Sidelights on What Paris Reads, Wears, Does," *Vogue*, December 1, 1944, p. 95.

Page 267

"News from Schiaparelli," *Vogue*, February 15, 1947, p. 150.

Page 273

"Schiaparelli the Shocker," *Newsweek*, September 26, 1949, p. 51.

Virginia Pope, "Schiaparelli Uses Striking Features," *New York Times*, August 12, 1949.

Page 278

Palais Galliera, Musée de la Mode et du Costume, *Robes de soir*, exh. cat. (Paris: Paris-Musées, 1990), p. 174.

Page 281

"June 12 Debut Set for Line by Schiaparelli," *Women's Wear Daily*, April 26, 1951; "Mme. Schiaparelli Enters New Field: Designer's Initial New York Showing of Lingerie Is Seen at Lord & Taylor," *New York Times*, October 18, 1951; see also a photograph of Hess's lingerie showing in the archives of Schiaparelli France, Paris.

Page 286

Schiaparelli, *Shocking Life*, p. 231.

Page 288

"A Letter from Paris by Lady Muriel Beckwith" [Lux advertisement], *Vogue*, June 26, 1931, p. 27.

Emma Cabire, "Le Cinéma et la mode," *La Revue du cinéma*, September 1, 1931, pp. 21–34, esp. 24–25.

"Paris Answers Hollywood," *Women's Wear Daily*, November 2, 1933.

Marlene Dietrich to Elsa Schiaparelli, January 27, 1937, Marlene Dietrich Collection, Filmmuseum Berlin.

Evening Standard (London), December 24, 1936.

"Schiaparelli Designing for Film Stars," *Motion Picture*, December 1933, pp. 44–45, 74, 76.

Page 289

Edith Head and Jane Kesner Ardmore, *The Dress Doctor* (New York: Boston, Little, Brown, 1959), pp. 183–84.

Author's interview with Francine Galliard-Risler, fall 2002.

List of Illustrations

Page 2
Horst P. Horst (American, born Germany, 1906–1999). Model wearing a dinner ensemble from Schiaparelli's collection for spring 1947. Published in *Vogue*, February 15, 1947 © Condé Nast Publications Inc.

Page 12
Thérèse Bonney (American, 1897–1977). Schiaparelli wearing a sweater with knitted-in bow and yoke from her January 1928 collection and a hat by Suzanne Talbot. The New York Public Library. Astor, Lenox and Tilden Foundations. Miriam and Ira D. Wallach Division of Art, Prints and Photographs © Bancroft Library, University of California, Berkeley

Page 13
Wm. H. Davidow Sons Co. Fashion sketch of Schiaparelli's sweater with hip kerchief, model no. 115 from her January 1928 collection. The Fashion Institute of Technology, New York. Special Collections, Davidow Archives, box A

Page 16
(top) Thérèse Bonney (American, 1897–1977). *Schiaparelli Interior No. 3*, c. 1928. The New York Public Library. Astor, Lenox and Tilden Foundations. Miriam and Ira D. Wallach Division of Art, Prints and Photographs © Bancroft Library, University of California, Berkeley

(center) Thérèse Bonney. *Schiaparelli Interior No. 2*, c. 1928. The New York Public Library. Astor, Lenox and Tilden Foundations. Miriam and Ira D. Wallach Division of Art, Prints and Photographs © Bancroft Library, University of California, Berkeley

(bottom) Thérèse Bonney. *Schiaparelli Interior No. 1*, c. 1928. The New York Public Library. Astor, Lenox and Tilden Foundations. Miriam and Ira D. Wallach Division of Art, Prints and Photographs © Bancroft Library, University of California, Berkeley

Page 17
(top) Thérèse Bonney. Schiaparelli's modernist sweater no. 19, January 1928 collection. Musée de la Mode et du Textile, Paris. Collection UCAD © Bancroft Library, University of California, Berkeley

(bottom) Thérèse Bonney. Schiaparelli's modernist sweater no. 15, January 1928 collection. Musée de la Mode et du Textile, Paris. Collection UCAD © Bancroft Library, University of California, Berkeley

Pages 18–19
Elsa Schiaparelli. Hand-knit pullover sweater with bowknot, November 1927. Black and white wool. Philadelphia Museum of Art. Gift of Mme Elsa Schiaparelli, 1969-232-54

Page 20
Photographer unknown. Display window of Gimbel Brothers department store, New York. Published in *Women's Wear Magazine*, vol. 1, 1928. The New York Public Library. Astor, Lenox and Tilden Foundations. Science, Industry & Business Library

Page 21
Photographer unknown. Tennis professional Glenna Collett posing with a golf trophy, 1929 © Underwood & Underwood/CORBIS

Pages 22–23
Elsa Schiaparelli. Hand-knit pullover sweater with sailor collar, summer 1928. Black, white, and red wool. Philadelphia Museum of Art. Gift of Vera White, 1952-9-1

Page 24
Studio V. Henry, 13 rue Forest, Paris. Schiaparelli's bathing suit with boat motif, summer 1928. Musée de la Mode et du Textile, Paris. Collection UCAD

Page 25
Elsa Schiaparelli. Hand-knit bathing-suit top with fish motif, summer 1928. White, green, black, and yellow wool. Philadelphia Museum of Art. Gift of Mr. and Mrs. Edward L. Jones, Jr., 1996-15-23

Page 26
George Hoyningen-Huene (American, born Russia, 1900–1968). Model Bettina Jones wearing Schiaparelli's bathing suit, shorts, and bathing socks (No. 1) from her January 1928 collection. Published in *Vogue*, July 1, 1928, p. 42 © Condé Nast Publications Inc.

Page 27
U.S. patent issued to Elsa Schiaparelli for a bathing suit with brassiere, filed December 20, 1932. U.S. Patent Office, Washington, D.C., no. 1,891,610

Page 28
Man Ray (American, 1890–1976). Elsa Schiaparelli in beach pajamas, 1930. Courtesy of Telimage, Paris © 2003 Man Ray Trust/Artists Rights Society (ARS), New York/ADAGP, Paris

Page 29
(left) Thérèse Bonney (American, 1897–1977). Schiaparelli's beach pajamas with patches, no. 13, c. 1928. Musée de la Mode et du Textile, Paris. Collection UCAD © Bancroft Library, University of California, Berkeley

(right) Thérèse Bonney. Schiaparelli's beach pajama suit, no. 12, c. 1928. Musée de la Mode et du Textile, Paris. Collection UCAD © Bancroft Library, University of California, Berkeley

Page 30
Photographer unknown. "Elsa Schiaparelli in Hyde Park, London, wearing her 'trousered skirt' illustrating her current fashion message: 'Trousers For Women!'" May 19, 1931 © Hulton Archive/Getty Images

Page 31
(left) Photographer unknown. "Spanish tennis player Lili de Alvarez shows off her divided skirt at the North London Tennis Tournament in Highbury, London," April 1931 © Hulton Archive/Getty Images

(right) Wm. H. Davidow Sons Co. fashion sketch of Schiaparelli's wraparound dress for summer 1930. The Fashion Institute of Technology, New York. Special Collections, Davidow Archives, box A5

Page 32
Jean Dunand (French, born Switzerland, 1877–1947). Elsa Schiaparelli wearing model no. 102 from her collection for fall 1933. Lacquer. Reproduced from Sotheby's catalogue, *Arts Décoratifs du XXe siècle*, April 23, 1989, no. 712 © 2003 Artists Rights Society (ARS), New York/ADAGP, Paris

Page 33
House of Schiaparelli. Fashion sketch of evening dress with "wings" at hips and back, for spring 1934. Musée de la Mode et du Textile, Paris. Collection UFAC, no. 312

Pages 36–37
Dining room of Schiaparelli's apartment on the boulevard Saint-Germain. Reproduced from *Studio Yearbook*, 1931, p. 47. Courtesy of Syracuse University Library, New York

Page 38
Man Ray (American, 1890–1976). Elsa Schiaparelli wearing a black evening dress with white wraparound jacket from her fall 1930 collection. Reproduced from Palmer White, *Elsa Schiaparelli* (in Japanese), ed. and trans. Yasuo Kuboki (Tokyo: Parco Co., 1994), p. 95 © 2003 Man Ray Trust/Artists Rights Society (ARS), New York/ADAGP, Paris

Page 39
Edward Steichen (American, born Luxembourg, 1879–1973). Countess Edith di Zoppola wearing dinner pajamas from Schiaparelli's summer 1931 collection. Published in *Vogue*, June 1, 1931, p. 65 © Condé Nast Publications Inc.

Page 40
Elsa Schiaparelli. Afternoon dress, winter 1930–31. Black wool and silk. Philadelphia Museum of Art. Gift of Vera White, 1957-9-3a

Page 41
Elsa Schiaparelli. Coat, winter 1930–31. Black wool. Philadelphia Museum of Art. Gift of Vera White, 1957-9-3b

Page 42
Man Ray (American, 1890–1976). Marie-Laure, Vicomtesse de Noailles wearing model no. 861 from Schiaparelli's summer 1931 collection. Courtesy of Telimage, Paris © 2003 Man Ray Trust/Artists Rights Society (ARS), New York/ADAGP, Paris

Page 43
Man Ray. Elsa Schiaparelli wearing an evening dress painted by Jean Dunand, from her fall 1931 collection. Courtesy of Telimage, Paris © 2003 Man Ray Trust/ Artists Rights Society (ARS), New York/ADAGP, Paris

Page 44
Man Ray. Elsa Schiaparelli wearing the Dunand-painted evening dress and a feather cape from her fall 1931 collection. Courtesy of Telimage, Paris © 2003 Man Ray Trust/Artists Rights Society (ARS), New York/ ADAGP, Paris

Page 45
Photographer unknown. Anna Pavlova as "The Dying Swan" © Roger-Viollet/Hulton-Getty

Pages 46–47
George Hoyningen-Huene (American, born Russia, 1900–1968). Elsa Schiaparelli wearing a white dress with a white coq-feather boa from her collection for summer 1932. Published in *Vogue*, September 1, 1932, p. 64 © Condé Nast Publications Inc.

Page 48
Elsa Schiaparelli. Evening dress (front view), winter 1931–32. Black rayon crêpe. Philadelphia Museum of Art. Gift of Anne Sayen in memory of Mrs. Lucy B. Harvey, 1993-39-1

Page 49
Elsa Schiaparelli. Evening dress (back view), winter 1931–32. Black rayon crêpe. Philadelphia Museum of Art. Gift of Anne Sayen in memory of Mrs. Lucy B. Harvey, 1993-39-1

Page 50
Edward Steichen (American, born Luxembourg, 1879–1973). Model wearing a long dress with velvet long-sleeved jacket from Schiaparelli's winter 1931 collection. Published in *Vogue*, November 1, 1931, p. 40 © Condé Nast Publications Inc.

Page 51
(left) Photographer unknown. Elsa Schiaparelli, winter 1931 © Associated Press/Wide World Photos, New York

(right) Elsa Schiaparelli. Evening dress, summer 1932. Coral and dark red silk. Drexel University, Philadelphia. The Drexel Historic Costume Collection. Gift of Mrs. Rodolphe Meyer de Schauensee, 55-33-12

Page 52
George Hoyningen-Huene (American, born Russia, 1900–1968). Model wearing Schiaparelli's ensemble no. 1045 from her spring 1932 collection. Published in *Vogue*, February 1, 1932, p. 50 © Condé Nast Publications Inc.

Page 53
Elsa Schiaparelli. Jacket, winter 1931–32. Brown wool with seal collar. Philadelphia Museum of Art. Gift of Vera White, 1961-91-1

Page 54
Madame Yevonde (French, 1893–1975). Cathleen Mann wearing a suit from Schiaparelli's collection for spring 1932. Vivex print. National Portrait Gallery, London © Yevonde Portrait Archive

Page 55
George Hoyningen-Huene (American, born Russia, 1900–1968). Ina Claire wearing a Schiaparelli ensemble and "Mad Cap," 1932. Reproduced from Horst P. Horst, *Salute to the Thirties* (New York: Viking Press, 1971), p. 161

Page 56
(left) Photographer unknown. Model wearing an ensemble from Schiaparelli's collection for summer 1933 © Roger-Viollet/Hulton Getty

(right) Photographer unknown. Elsa Schiaparelli arriving in the United States on the *Conte di Savoia* wearing an ensemble from her February collection for summer 1933 © Bettmann/CORBIS

Page 57
Edward Steichen (American, born Luxembourg, 1879–1973). Ruth Covell wearing model no. 445 from Schiaparelli's winter 1932–33 collection. Published in *Vogue*, October 15, 1932, p. 35 © Condé Nast Publications Inc.

Page 58
(top) Still from the film *Je te confie ma femme*, 1933. Bibliothèque du Film, Paris, PK 60815

(bottom) Arletty and Julien Carette in the film *Je te confie ma femme*, 1933. Bibliothèque du Film, Paris, PK 60814

Page 59
(top, left) Mary Petty (American, 1899–1976). "Why should Madam be afraid? Schiaparelli isn't." Published in *The New Yorker*, January 21, 1939, p. 41. Courtesy of *The New Yorker*, Condé Nast Publications Inc.

(top, right) House of Schiaparelli. Fashion sketch of cape with pleated shoulders for spring 1933. Musée de la Mode et du Textile, Paris. Collection UFAC, 169

(bottom, right) House of Schiaparelli. Fashion sketch of coat with pointed shoulders for spring 1933. Musée de la Mode et du Textile, Paris. Collection UFAC, 349

Page 60
Elsa Schiaparelli. Evening dress and jacket ensemble, winter 1934. Rayon crêpe. Collection of Marc Walsh

Page 61
La Femme idéale, with Arlette Marchal, 1933. Reproduced from the cover of *Le Film complet du Samedi*, August 18, 1934. Courtesy of Dilys Blum

Page 62
Buffotot. The bedroom of Elsa Schiaparelli's apartment on the rue Barbet-de-Jouy, designed by Jean-Michel Frank. Published in *Vogue*, September 15, 1934, p. 76 © Condé Nast Publications Inc.

Page 63
Buffotot. The living room of Elsa Schiaparelli's apartment on the rue Barbet-de-Jouy, designed by Jean-Michel Frank. Published in *Vogue*, September 15, 1934, p. 77 © Condé Nast Publications Inc.

Page 64
Photographer unknown. Model wearing Schiaparelli's *robe d'interieur* for spring 1934 © Roger-Viollet/Hulton Getty

Page 65
George Hoyningen-Huene (American, born Russia, 1900–1968). Elsa Schiaparelli wearing a dinner suit and cape from her winter 1933–34 collection. Published in *Vogue*, November 15, 1933, p. 47 © Condé Nast Publications Inc.

Page 66
(left) Photographer unknown. Model wearing an evening dress from Schiaparelli's collection for fall 1934 © Roger-Viollet/Hulton Getty

(right) House of Schiaparelli. Fashion sketch of "Spanish" ensemble with starched linen collar for fall 1934. Musée de la Mode et du Textile, Paris. Collection UFAC, 4031

Page 67
Dora Maar (French, 1907–1997). *Untitled* (fashion photograph), c. 1934. Musée National d'Art Moderne, Centre Georges Pompidou, Paris. Courtesy of Art Resource, New York © CNAC/MNAM/Dist. Réunion des Musées Nationaux/Art Resource, New York. Photograph by Jacques Faujour

Page 68
George Hoyningen-Huene (American, born Russia, 1900–1968). Madame Vittorio Crespi wearing a satin dress with "glass" (Rhodophane) apron from Schiaparelli's October 1934 collection for spring 1935. Published in *Vogue*, January 15, 1935, p. 54 © Condé Nast Publications Inc.

Page 69
Photographer unknown. Models wearing coats from Schiaparelli's collection for winter 1934–35 © Roger-Viollet/Hulton Getty

Page 70
François Kollar (French, 1904–1979). Schiaparelli seated at the window of her salon at 21 Place Vendôme. Published in *Good Housekeeping*, June 1938, p. 113.

Courtesy of Patrimoine Photographique, Paris
© Ministère de la Culture-France

Page 71
John Phillips (American, born Algeria, 1914–1996). The exterior of Schiaparelli's salon at 21 Place Vendôme, 1937 © John Phillips/Time Life Pictures/Getty Images

Page 75
Photographer unknown. English aviator Amy Mollison (née Johnson) wearing a Schiaparelli suit and a blouse printed with newspaper clippings, probably May 1936 © Hulton Archive/Getty Images

Page 76
Colcombet for Elsa Schiaparelli. Dress fabric printed with a collage of Schiaparelli's press clippings, 1935. Printed cotton, 39 x 23 inches (99 x 58.4 cm). Allentown Art Museum, Allentown, Pennsylvania. Gift of Kate Fowler Merle-Smith, 1978 (1978.26.352)

Page 77
Cecil Beaton (English, 1904–1980). *Fun at the Openings*, pencil, ink, and gouache. Published in *Vogue*, April 1, 1935, p. 67 © Condé Nast Publications Inc.

Page 78
Elsa Schiaparelli. Sari dress, summer 1935. Rayon, metallic thread, and glass beads. Collection of Marc Walsh

Page 79
(left) Cecil Beaton (English, 1904–1980). Princess Karam of Kapurthala. Published in *Vogue*, July 1, 1935, p. 53 © Condé Nast Publications Inc.

(right) Man Ray (American, 1890–1976). *Nusch au Miroir*, 1935. Published in *Harper's Bazaar*, March 1935, p. 53. Courtesy of Telimage, Paris © 2003 Man Ray Trust/Artists Rights Society (ARS), New York/ADAGP, Paris

Page 80
Roger Schall (French, 1904–1989). Elsa Schiaparelli wearing a "sari" wrap from her collection for summer 1935. Published in *Vogue*, June 15, 1935, p. 31 © Condé Nast Publications Inc.

Page 81
Bergdorf Goodman fashion sketch showing Schiaparelli's "sari" wrap for summer 1935. The Metropolitan Museum of Art, New York. The Costume Institute

Page 82
Horst P. Horst (American, born Germany, 1906–1999). Daisy Fellowes wearing a Schiaparelli design at the Oriental Ball. Published in *Vogue*, August 1, 1935, p. 31 © Condé Nast Publications Inc.

Page 83
Horst P. Horst. Elsa Schiaparelli dressed as a Venetian page at the Oriental Ball. Published in *Vogue*, August 1, 1935, p. 34 © Condé Nast Publications Inc.

Page 84
House of Schiaparelli. Fashion sketch of the silk "Venetian" evening cape and gown from the collection for fall 1935. Musée de la Mode et du Textile, Paris. Collection UFAC, 698

Page 85
François Kollar (French, 1904–1979). Model wearing the "Italian primitive" dress and head veil from

Schiaparelli's collection for fall 1935. Courtesy of Patrimoine Photographique, Paris © Ministère de la Culture-France

Page 86
Ilse Bing (French, 1899–1998). *Study for "Salut de Schiaparelli" (Lily Parfume)*, Paris, 1934. Gelatin silver print, 11⅛ x 8¾ inches (28.2 x 22.3 cm). National Gallery of Art, Washington, D.C. Gift of Ilsa Bing Wolff, Board of Trustees, 2001.147.42 © The Estate of Ilse Bing, courtesy of the Edwynn Houk Gallery, New York. Photograph © 2003 Board of Trustees, National Gallery of Art, Washington, D.C.

Page 87
(left) Lusha Nelson (American, 1900–1938). Schiaparelli's Salut perfume with cork box by Jean-Michel Frank. Published in *Vogue*, September 15, 1934, p. 90 © Condé Nast Publications Inc.

(right) Elsa Schiaparelli. Evening dress, fall 1935. Black and white rayon. Museum at the Fashion Institute of Technology, New York. Gift of Yeffe Kimball Slatin, 71.263.1

Page 88
Elsa Schiaparelli. Evening dress, winter 1935–36. Blue, black, and white silk taffeta. Drexel University, Philadelphia. The Drexel Historic Costume Collection. Gift of Mrs. Rodolphe Meyer de Schauensee, 55-33-1a

Page 89
Frances Drake and Sir Guy Standing in the film *I'd Give My Life*, 1936. British Film Institute, London © Paramount Pictures, Los Angeles

Page 90
Elsa Schiaparelli. Evening dress, winter 1935–36. Purple, rose, and navy silk. Drexel University, Philadelphia. The Drexel Historic Costume Collection. Gift of Mrs. Rodolphe Meyer de Schauensee, 55-33-5

Page 91
(left) Betty Stockfeld and Maurice Chevalier in the film *Le Vagabond bien-aimé* (or *The Beloved Vagabond*), 1936. British Film Institute, London © Canal + Image, U.K., Pinewood Studios

(right) Man Ray (American, 1890–1976). *Three Times Same Model*, c. 1935. Courtesy of Telimage, Paris © 2003 Man Ray Trust/Artists Rights Society (ARS), New York/ADAGP, Paris

Page 92
(left) House of Schiaparelli. Fashion sketch of "parachute" dinner ensemble for summer 1936. Musée de la Mode et du Textile, Paris. Collection UFAC, 1083

(center) Photographer unknown. Woman wearing Schiaparelli ensemble designed for the Russian working woman, 1935. National Museum of Photography, Film & Television, Bradford, England. Science & Society Picture Library, Daily Herald Archive, 6942

(right) John Phillips (American, born Algeria, 1914–1996). The head *vendeuse* of Schiaparelli's hat salon, 1937 © John Phillips/Time Life Pictures/Getty Images

Page 93
Miguel Covarrubias (Mexican, 1904–1957). *Impossible Interview*, 1936. Courtesy of the Library of Congress, Washington, D.C. Prints, Drawings & Photographs Division, LC-USZ62-1234. Published in *Vogue*, June 15,

1936, p. 43 © Condé Nast Publications Inc. Reprinted with permission of Maria Elena Rico Covarrubias

Page 94
Cecil Beaton (English, 1904–1980). Model wearing a shirttail topcoat from Schiaparelli's collection for spring 1936. Published in *Vogue*, January 15, 1936, p. 66 © Condé Nast Publications Inc.

Page 95
Man Ray (American, 1890–1976). Model wearing suit and hat from Schiaparelli's collection for spring 1936, c. 1936. Courtesy of Telimage, Paris © 2003 Man Ray Trust/Artists Rights Society (ARS), New York/ADAGP, Paris

Page 96
Photographer unknown. Elsa Schiaparelli on board the S.S. *Europa*, December 4, 1936 © Bettmann/CORBIS

Page 97
Elsa Schiaparelli. Suit, winter 1936–37. Purple wool, dark brown velvet, and brown leather. Museum at the Fashion Institute of Technology, New York. Gift of Mrs. Stewart McDonald, 78.125.1

Page 98
Photographer unknown. Schiaparelli's tricorne hat known as "His Honor," for winter 1937–38, July 1937 © Roger-Viollet/Hulton Getty

Page 99
Photographer unknown. Schiaparelli's uptilted beret for winter 1937–38, July 1937 © Roger-Viollet/Hulton Getty

Page 100
George Hoyningen-Huene (American, born Russia, 1900–1968). Bettina Jones wearing Schiaparelli's first evening dress. Published in *Vogue*, March 1, 1930, p. 79 © Condé Nast Publications Inc.

Page 101
Elsa Schiaparelli. Evening coat (detail), winter 1935–36. Red wool with gold snail-shaped buttons. Philadelphia Museum of Art. Gift of Mme Elsa Schiaparelli, 1969-232-4

Page 104
(left) Elsa Schiaparelli. Evening coat, winter 1935–36. Red wool with gold buttons. Philadelphia Museum of Art. Gift of Mme Elsa Schiaparelli, 1969-232-4

(right) House of Schiaparelli. Fashion sketch of "Persian Prince" tunic-length jacket for winter 1937–38. Musée de la Mode et du Textile, Paris. Collection UFAC, D 73.21.1460

Page 105
Elsa Schiaparelli. Evening jacket, winter 1937–38. Purple wool with gold metallic strip embroidery and metal buttons. Philadelphia Museum of Art. Gift of Mme Elsa Schiaparelli, 1969-232-9

Page 106
Elsa Schiaparelli. Evening cape, spring 1937. Dark navy wool and red silk embroidered with gilt metal thread. Philadelphia Museum of Art. Gift of Mme Elsa Schiaparelli, 1969-232-5

Page 107
(left) Man Ray (American, 1890–1976). Bettina Jones in Schiaparelli evening cape with gold and orange braid, c. 1937. Courtesy of Telimage, Paris © Man Ray Trust/Artists Rights Society (ARS), New York/ADAGP, Paris

(right) Elsa Schiaparelli. Evening coat, winter 1936–37.

Black and sapphire-blue silk taffeta with blue cellophane sequins. Philadelphia Museum of Art. Gift of Mme Elsa Schiaparelli, 1969-232-2

Page 108
House of Schiaparelli. Fashion sketch of cape for spring 1937. Musée de la Mode et du Textile, Paris. Collection UFAC, D 73.21.1327

Page 109
Elsa Schiaparelli. Evening cape (detail), spring 1937. Black wool with pink silk taffeta embroidered with metal thread, glass buttons. Philadelphia Museum of Art. Gift of Mme Elsa Schiaparelli, 1969-232-1

Page 110
Photographer unknown. Model wearing waltz-length evening dress from Schiaparelli's collection for summer 1937, March 1937 © Roger Viollet/Hulton Getty

Page 111
Drucker-Wolf and William Wilhelm Co. for Schiaparelli. Dress fabric (Schiaparelli's "Paris Exposition"), 1937. Multi-colored printed silk crêpe, 16⅞ x 19½ inches (42.9 x 49.5 cm). Allentown Art Museum, Allentown, Pennsylvania. Gift of Kate Fowler Merle-Smith, 1978 (1978.026.379)

Page 112
Alfred Otto Wolfgang Schulze (Wols) (German, 1913–1951). The *Pavillon de l'Elégance* at the 1937 *Exposition internationale des arts et techniques dans la vie moderne*, Paris. Reproduced from *Le Pavillon de l'élégance à l'Exposition internationale des arts et techniques, Paris 1937* (Paris: Arts et Métiers Graphiques, 1938), p. 10

Page 113
André Durst (French, 1907–1949). Two models wearing "Paris Exposition" dinner ensembles from Schiaparelli's collection for fall 1937. Published in *Vogue*, June 1, 1937, p. 51 © Condé Nast Publications Inc.

Page 114
Photographer unknown. Window display for Shocking perfume at 21 Place Vendôme, c. 1937. Archives of Schiaparelli France, Paris

Page 115
Mae West in the film *Every Day's a Holiday*, 1937. Courtesy of Dilys Blum. Film © 1937 Paramount Pictures. Courtesy of Universal Studios Licensing LLLP. Mae West™ Represented by The Roger Richman Agency, Inc., www.therichmanagency.com

Page 116
John Phillips (American, born Algeria, 1914–1996). An artist from one of the fashion magazines sketching a Schiaparelli model for fall 1937 © John Phillips/Time Life Pictures/Getty Images

Page 117
Mae West in the film *Every Day's a Holiday*, 1937 © Bettmann/CORBIS. Film © 1937 Paramount Pictures. Courtesy of Universal Studios Licensing LLLP. Mae West™ Represented by The Roger Richman Agency, Inc., www.therichmanagency.com

Page 118
Photographer unknown. "Brassiere" evening dress with ballerina-style laced shoes from Schiaparelli's collection for winter 1937–38 © Roger-Viollet/Hulton Getty

Page 119
Man Ray (American, 1890–1976). Actress Jany Holt wearing Schiaparelli's evening dress, from Jean Cocteau's play *Les Monstres sacrés*, 1940. Published in *Harper's Bazaar*, April 1, 1940, p. 74. The Metropolitan Museum of Art, New York. The Costume Institute, LY55BA-1 © Man Ray Trust/Artists Rights Society (ARS), New York/ADAGP, Paris

Page 120
Pablo Picasso (Spanish, 1881–1973). *Portrait of Nusch Eluard*, 1937. Oil on canvas, 36¼ x 25⅝ inches (92 x 65 cm). Musée Picasso, Paris. Courtesy of Art Resource, New York © Réunion des Musées Nationaux/Art Resource, New York. Photograph by Gerard Blot

Page 121
Jean Schlumberger for Elsa Schiaparelli. Cherub lapel clips, winter 1937–38. Gilt copper alloy, 1⅝ x 1⅜ inches (4 x 3.5 cm). Collection of Leslie Chin

Page 126
Man Ray (American, 1890–1976). *Schiaparelli's Head on a Plaster Torso*, c. 1933. Reproduced from *Minotaure* magazine, nos. 3–4 (October–December 1933), p. 4. Courtesy of the Philadelphia Museum of Art Library © Man Ray Trust/Artists Rights Society (ARS), New York/ADAGP, Paris

Page 127
(top, left) Man Ray. Hat from Schiaparelli's collection for winter 1933–34. Reproduced from *Minotaure* magazine, nos. 3–4 (October–December 1933), p. 81. Courtesy of the Philadelphia Museum of Art Library © Man Ray Trust/Artists Rights Society (ARS), New York/ADAGP, Paris

(top, right) Man Ray. Hats from Schiaparelli's collection for winter 1933–34. Reproduced from *Minotaure* magazine, nos. 3–4 (October–December 1933), p. 83. Courtesy of the Philadelphia Museum of Art Library © Man Ray Trust/Artists Rights Society (ARS), New York/ADAGP, Paris

(bottom) House of Schiaparelli. Fashion sketch of hats for winter 1933–34. Musée de la Mode et du Textile, Paris. Collection UFAC, 225

Page 128
(left) Jean Schlumberger for Elsa Schiaparelli. Lapel clip in the form of a hand, 1936–37. Gilt copper alloy, enamel, and cut glass, 1¾ x ¾ inches (4.5 x 2 cm). Collection of Leslie Chin

(right) Man Ray (American, 1890–1976). Hands. Reproduced from *Minotaure* magazine, no. 5 (May 1934), p. 30. Courtesy of the Philadelphia Museum of Art Library © Man Ray Trust/Artists Rights Society (ARS), New York/ADAGP, Paris

Page 129
Man Ray. *Portrait of Dora Maar*, 1936. Black-and-white print of original solarized gelatin silver print. Courtesy of Telimage, Paris © 2003 Man Ray Trust/Artists Rights Society (ARS), New York/ADAGP, Paris

Page 130
Elsa Schiaparelli. Gloves, winter 1936–37. Black suede with red snakeskin simulating painted fingernails. Philadelphia Museum of Art. Gift of Mme Elsa Schiaparelli, 1969-232-55e, d

Page 131
(left) Man Ray (American, 1890–1976). *Hands Painted by Picasso*, 1935. Courtesy of Telimage, Paris © 2003 Man Ray Trust/Artists Rights Society (ARS), New York/ADAGP, Paris

(top, right) Man Ray. *Hommage à Nusch*, 1937. Reproduced from *Les Mains libres: Dessins illustrés par les poèmes de Paul Eluard* (Paris: Editions Jeanne Bucher, 1937), p. 179. Courtesy of the Philadelphia Museum of Art Library. Presented to the library by Louise and Walter Arensberg © Man Ray Trust/Artists Rights Society (ARS), New York/ADAGP, Paris

(bottom, right) Elsa Schiaparelli. Clip shaped like a hand, c. 1937–38. Gilt copper alloy and enamel, 3⅜ x 1⅝ inches (8.5 x 4 cm). Collection of Marc Walsh

Page 132
(left) Bergdorf Goodman fashion sketch of Schiaparelli's model no. 435 (drawer suit) and no. 418 (gloves with snakeskin nails), 1936. The Metropolitan Museum of Art, New York. The Costume Institute, LY4051-2

(center) Salvador Dalí (Spanish, 1904–1989). Sketch for clothing design, c. 1936. Archives of Schiaparelli France, Paris © 2003 Salvador Dalí, Gala-Salvador Dalí Foundation/Artists Rights Society (ARS), New York

(right) Salvador Dalí. Cover for *Minotaure* magazine, 1936. Reproduced from *Minotaure*, no. 8 (June 15, 1936). Courtesy of the Philadelphia Museum of Art Library © 2003 Salvador Dalí, Gala-Salvador Dalí Foundation/Artists Rights Society (ARS), New York

Page 133
Cecil Beaton (English, 1904–1980). Models wearing Schiaparelli's wool suits with Salvador Dalí–inspired bureau-like pockets. Published in *Vogue*, September 15, 1936, p. 70 © Condé Nast Publications Inc.

Page 134
Elsa Schiaparelli. Evening dress with lobster print (collaboration with Salvador Dalí), summer/fall 1937. White and red silk organza. Philadelphia Museum of Art. Gift of Mme Elsa Schiaparelli, 1969-232-52

Page 135
(left) Salvador Dalí (Spanish, 1904–1989). *Lobster Telephone*, 1936. Painted plaster and mixed media, 7⅛ x 13 x 7⅛ inches (18 x 33 x 18 cm). Tate Gallery, London. Courtesy of Art Resource, New York © 2003 Salvador Dalí, Gala-Salvador Dalí Foundation/Artists Rights Society (ARS), New York. Photograph © Tate Gallery, London/Art Resource, New York

(right) Cecil Beaton (English, 1904–1980). Wallis Simpson wearing Schiaparelli's lobster-print evening dress. Published in *Vogue*, June 1, 1937, p. 54 © Condé Nast Publications Inc.

Page 136
(left) Man Ray (American, 1890–1976). Dalí mannequin wearing Schiaparelli's ski helmet at the *Exposition internationale du Surréalisme*, Paris, 1938. Courtesy of Telimage, Paris © Man Ray Trust/Artists Rights Society (ARS), New York/ADAGP, Paris

(right) House of Schiaparelli. Fashion sketch of lip suit with shoe hat, winter 1937–38. Musée de la Mode et du Textile, Paris. Collection UFAC, 1412

Page 137
Elsa Schiaparelli. Shoe hat (collaboration with Salvador Dalí), winter 1937–38. Black wool felt. The Metropolitan Museum of Art, New York. Gift of Rose Messing, 1974 (1974.139). Photograph © 2002 The Metropolitan Museum of Art

Page 138
Elsa Schiaparelli. Evening dress and head scarf with tear design (collaboration with Salvador Dalí), summer 1938. Light blue, magenta, and black silk crêpe. Philadelphia Museum of Art. Gift of Mme Elsa Schiaparelli, 1969-232-45a, b

Page 139
(top) Salvador Dalí (Spanish, 1904–1989). *Printemps necrophilique* (*Necrophiliac Springtime*), 1936. Oil on canvas, 21⅝ x 25⅝ inches (55 x 65 cm). Private collection. Courtesy of Christie's Images, New York (TCA101298526+01) © 2003 Salvador Dalí, Gala-Salvador Dalí Foundation/Artists Rights Society (ARS), New York

(bottom) Salvador Dalí. *Three Young Surrealist Women Holding in Their Arms the Skins of an Orchestra*, 1936. Oil on canvas, 21¼ x 25⅝ inches (54 x 65.1 cm). The Salvador Dalí Museum, Saint Petersburg, Florida © 2003 Salvador Dalí, Gala-Salvador Dalí Foundation/Artists Rights Society (ARS), New York

Page 140
Elsa Schiaparelli. Evening coat (collaboration with Jean Cocteau), fall 1937. Blue (now faded) silk jersey with gold metal and red silk embroidery and pink silk appliquéd flowers. Philadelphia Museum of Art. Gift of Mme Elsa Schiaparelli, 1969-232-7

Page 141
Elsa Schiaparelli. Evening jacket (collaboration with Jean Cocteau), fall 1937. Embroidered gray linen, gilt metal thread, bugle beads, and paillettes. Philadelphia Museum of Art. Gift of Mme Elsa Schiaparelli, 1969-232-22

Page 142
Meret Oppenheim (German-Swiss, 1913–1985). *Le Déjeuner en fourrure* (Breakfast in Fur), 1936. Fur-covered cup, saucer, and spoon. Cup diameter, 4⅜ inches (10.9 cm); saucer diameter, 9⅜ inches (23.7 cm); spoon length, 8 inches (20.2 cm); overall height 2⅞ inches (7.3 cm). The Museum of Modern Art, New York. Purchase © 2003 Artists Rights Society (ARS), New York/ProLitteris, Zurich

Page 143
Elsa Schiaparelli. Boots, summer 1938. Black suede, black monkey fur. Philadelphia Museum of Art. Gift of Mme Elsa Schiaparelli, 1969-232-55a, b

Page 144
Madame Yevonde (French, 1893–1975). *Still Life with Head of Nefertiti*, 1938. Dye transfer print. The British Council, London © Yevonde Portrait Archive

Page 145
Horst P. Horst (American, born Germany, 1906–1999) and Salvador Dalí (Spanish, 1904–1989). Study for *The Dream of Venus*, 1939. Gelatin silver print with black gouache, 10 x 8 inches (25.3 x 20.2 cm). The Baltimore Museum of Art, Baltimore, Maryland. Purchase with exchange funds from the Edward Joseph Gallagher III Memorial Collection; and partial gift of George H. Dalsheimer, Baltimore, 1988.286. Reprinted courtesy of the Horst Estate

Page 146
Roger Schall (French, 1904–1989). Elsa Schiaparelli's installation for the New York World's Fair, designed by Marcel Vertès. Published in *Vogue*, May 15, 1939, p. 62 © Condé Nast Publications Inc.

Page 147
(top) Parfums Schiaparelli. Snuff, men's perfume, 1940. Bottle: glass, metal, silk thread; box: paper- and foil-covered box, cellophane. Collection of Leslie Chin

(bottom) René Magritte (Belgian, 1898–1967). *The Treachery of Images* (*This is Not a Pipe*), c. 1928–29. Oil on canvas, 25 7/16 x 37 1/16 inches (64.61 x 94.13 cm). Los Angeles County Museum of Art. Purchased with funds provided by the Mr. and Mrs. William Preston Harrison Collection, 78.7 © 2003 C. Herscovici, Brussels/Artists Rights Society (ARS), New York. Photograph © 2003 Museum Associates/LACMA

Pages 148–49
Marcel Duchamp (French, 1887–1968). *Sixteen Miles of String*, installation for the exhibition *First Papers of Surrealism*, October 14–November 7, 1942, photographed by John D. Schiff. Philadelphia Museum of Art. Marcel Duchamp Archive. Gift of Jacqueline, Peter, and Paul Matisse in memory of their mother, Alexina Duchamp © 2003 Artists Rights Society (ARS), New York/ADAGP, Paris/Succession Marcel Duchamp

Page 150
Horst P. Horst (American, born Germany, 1906–1999). Woman wearing a jacket with butterfly buttons from Schiaparelli's collection for summer 1937. Published in *Vogue*, March 15, 1937, p. 90 © Condé Nast Publications Inc.

Page 151
Pablo Picasso (Spanish, 1881–1973). *Bird Cage and Playing Cards*, 1933. Oil on canvas. Reproduced from Elsa Schiaparelli, *Shocking Life* (New York: E. P. Dutton & Co., 1954), p. 2. Courtesy of Dilys Blum © 2003 Estate of Pablo Picasso/Artists Rights Society (ARS), New York

Page 154
Elsa Schiaparelli. Waltz-length evening dress, summer 1937. Ivory organdy with multi-colored butterfly print. Philadelphia Museum of Art. Gift of Mme Elsa Schiaparelli, 1969-232-49

Page 155
(left) Photographer unknown. Model wearing a waltz-length evening dress printed with butterflies, from Schiaparelli's collection for summer 1937 © Roger-Viollet/Hulton Getty

(right) Man Ray (American, 1890–1976). *Butterflies*, 1930–35. Three-color carbon transfer print, 9¼ x 11¼ inches (23.4 x 28.5 cm). The J. Paul Getty Museum, Los Angeles, 84.XP.446.18 © Man Ray Trust/Artists Rights Society (ARS), New York/ADAGP, Paris

Page 156
Bergdorf Goodman fashion sketch of Schiaparelli's butterfly evening dress with "cage" coat, summer 1937. The Metropolitan Museum of Art, New York. The Costume Institute, B04679-1

Page 157
Horst P. Horst (American, born Germany, 1906–1999). Princess Jean Poniatowski in a Schiaparelli hat with mesh veil. Published in *Vogue*, June 15, 1939, p. 23 © Condé Nast Publications Inc.

Page 158
Hans Wild (British, 1914–1969). Saleswoman in Schiaparelli's perfume boutique, September 1947 © Hans Wild/Time Life Pictures/Getty Images

Page 159
(left) Wendy Hiller as Eliza Doolittle and Scott Sunderland as Colonel George Pickering in the film *Pygmalion*, 1938. MGM/Kobal Collection, 1938

(right) Wendy Hiller as Eliza Doolittle in the film *Pygmalion*, 1938. MGM/Kobal Collection, 1938

Page 160
Horst P. Horst (American, born Germany, 1906–1999). Elsa Schiaparelli wearing an ensemble from her winter 1937–38 collection. Courtesy of the Staley-Wise Gallery, New York. Published in *Vogue*, September 1, 1937, p. 97 © Condé Nast Publications Inc.

Page 161
Photographer unknown. Mrs. Reginald (Daisy) Fellowes attending a wedding in London, December 7, 1934 © Bettmann/CORBIS

Page 162
Cecil Beaton (English, 1904–1980). Marlene Dietrich wearing a fur ensemble from Schiaparelli's collection for winter 1936–37. Published in British *Vogue*, October 28, 1936, p. 62 © *Vogue*/The Condé Nast Publications Ltd.

Page 163
Elsa Schiaparelli. Evening jacket, winter 1936–37. Black wool with gold and metal embroidery and gold paillettes. Philadelphia Museum of Art. Gift of Mme Elsa Schiaparelli, 1969-232-12

Page 164
Horst P. Horst (American, born Germany, 1906–1999). Mrs. Ronald Balcom (Millicent Rogers) wearing a dinner ensemble from Schiaparelli's collection for winter 1938–39. Published in *Vogue*, January 1, 1939, p. 39 © Condé Nast Publications Inc.

Page 165
Cecil Beaton (English, 1904–1980). The Duchess of Windsor wearing an ensemble from Schiaparelli's summer 1937 collection. Published in *Vogue*, June 1, 1937, p. 56 © Condé Nast Publications Inc.

Page 166
Herbert Gehr (American, 1910–1983). Gala and Salvador Dalí and Jane and Kenneth Clark at the opening night party for the Museum of Modern Art, New York, 1939 © Herbert Gehr/Time Life Pictures/Getty Images

Page 167
Elsa Schiaparelli. Evening jacket, winter 1937–38. Silk velvet with silk and metallic thread embroidery, sequins, rhinestones, and metal buttons. Philadelphia Museum of Art. Gift of Mme Elsa Schiaparelli, 1969-232-19

Page 168
John Phillips (American, born Algeria, 1914–1996). The mannequin Christiane waiting until Roberte finishes showing her model to a group of clients and their *vendeuses*, 1937 © John Phillips/Time Life Pictures/Getty Images

Page 169
John Phillips. Elsa Schiaparelli studying the charts

of her new collection, 1937 © John Phillips/Time Life Pictures/Getty Images

Page 171
Photographer unknown. Helena Rubenstein wearing an evening jacket from Schiaparelli's collection for summer 1938 © Roger-Viollet/Hulton Getty

Page 172
Photographer unknown. Elsa Schiaparelli holding a lobster-print fabric from spring 1937, with a model wearing a gown from her collection for summer 1938 © Roger-Viollet/Hulton Getty

Page 173
(left) House of Schiaparelli. Fashion sketch of evening dress and veil for summer 1938. Musée de la Mode et du Textile, Paris. Collection UFAC, D 73.21.1838

(right) Elsa Schiaparelli. Evening dress and veil, summer 1938. Turquoise silk printed with a circus pattern. Philadelphia Museum of Art. Gift of Mme Elsa Schiaparelli, 1969-232-39a, b

Page 174
Elsa Schiaparelli. Dinner dress, summer 1938. Shocking pink silk chiffon printed with a circus pattern. Philadelphia Museum of Art. Gift of Mme Elsa Schiaparelli, 1969-232-38

Page 175
(top) House of Schiaparelli. Fashion sketch of "skeleton" evening dress for summer 1938. Musée de la Mode et du Textile, Paris. Collection UFAC, D 73.21.1874

(bottom, left) Arletty in the play *Cavalier Seul*, February 1938 © Roger-Viollet/Hulton Getty

(bottom, right) Arletty in the play *Cavalier Seul*, February 1938 © Roger-Viollet/Hulton Getty

Pages 176–77
(left) House of Schiaparelli. Fashion sketch of harem skirt and jacket with prancing circus horses for summer 1938. Musée de la Mode et du Textile, Paris. Collection UFAC, D 73.21.1825

(center) Elsa Schiaparelli. Evening dress with tiered sleeves, summer 1938. Midnight-blue Amoroso crêpe. Philadelphia Museum of Art. Gift of Mme Elsa Schiaparelli, 1969-232-51

(right) House of Schiaparelli. Fashion sketch of evening dress with tiered sleeves for summer 1938. Musée de la Mode et du Textile, Paris. Collection UFAC, D 73.21.1867

Page 178
Elsa Schiaparelli. Wedding veil, summer 1938. White net embroidered with blue bugle beads. Philadelphia Museum of Art. Gift of Mme Elsa Schiaparelli, 1969-232-26

Page 179
House of Schiaparelli. Fashion sketch for wedding gown and veil embroidered with blue bugle beads for summer 1938. Musée de la Mode et du Textile, Paris. Collection UFAC, D 73.21.1828

Page 181
Signed "Meerson." Vicomtesse Benoist d'Azy as the "Birth of Venus" at Comte Etienne de Beaumont's Famous Paintings Ball, summer 1935. Courtesy of Anne Benoist d'Azy, France

Page 182
Elsa Schiaparelli. Evening dress (detail), fall 1938. Black silk crêpe with plastic and silk embroidery. Philadelphia Museum of Art. Gift of Mme Elsa Schiaparelli, 1969-232-40

Page 183
Elsa Schiaparelli. Evening dress, fall 1938. Black silk crêpe with plastic and silk embroidery. Philadelphia Museum of Art. Gift of Mme Elsa Schiaparelli, 1969-232-40

Page 184
Elsa Schiaparelli. "Insect" necklace, fall 1938. Rhodoid (cellulose acetate) with painted metallic insects, 8¼ x 7½ inches (21.0 x 19.1 cm). Brooklyn Museum of Art, New York. Gift of Paul and Arturo Peralat-Ramos, 55.26.247

Page 185
(top) Horst P. Horst (American, born Germany, 1906–1999). Model wearing doll-sized hat from Schiaparelli's collection for fall 1938. Published in *Harper's Bazaar*, July 1938, p. 25. The Metropolitan Museum of Art, New York. The Costume Institute, LY 42.1.146.

(bottom, left) House of Schiaparelli. Fashion sketch of wood-print evening ensemble, fall 1938. Musée de la Mode et du Textile, Paris. Collection UFAC, D 73.21.1839

(bottom, center) Paul Delvaux (Belgian, 1897–1994). *The Break of Day* (*L'Aurore*), July 1937. Oil on canvas, 47¼ x 59¼ inches (120 x 150.5 cm). The Solomon R. Guggenheim Foundation, New York. Peggy Guggenheim Collection, Venice, 1976.2553.103 © 2003 Artists Rights Society (ARS), New York/SABAM, Brussels. Photograph by Carmelo Guadagno © The Solomon R. Guggenheim Foundation

(bottom, right) House of Schiaparelli. Fashion sketch of leaf cape worn with gamboling faun gown, fall 1938. Musée de la Mode et du Textile, Paris. Collection UFAC, D 73.21.2359

Page 187
John Phillips (American, born Algeria, 1914–1996). Elsa Schiaparelli wearing a jacket of her new pink color known as "Shocking," 1937 © John Phillips/Time Life Pictures/Getty Images

Page 188
Photographer unknown. Model wearing "celestial" evening gown with fringed cape from Schiaparelli's collection for summer 1935 © Roger-Viollet/Hulton Getty

Page 189
Elsa Schiaparelli. Evening jacket (detail), winter 1938–39. Blue silk velvet, metallic thread, glass beads, and rhinestones, embroidered by Maison Lesage. Brooklyn Museum of Art, New York. Gift of Mrs. Anthony V. Lynch, 71.67

Page 190
Elsa Schiaparelli. Evening jacket (detail), winter 1938–39. Black silk velvet embroidered with gold metal-wrapped thread and mirrors. The Metropolitan Museum of Art, New York. Gift of Mrs. Pauline Potter, 1950

(CI.50.34.2). Photograph © 1995 The Metropolitan Museum of Art

Page 191
(left) Cecil Beaton (English, 1904–1980). Elsie de Wolfe (Lady Mendl) wearing a cape with a design inspired by the Neptune Fountain at Versailles from Schiaparelli's winter 1938–39 collection © Sotheby's Picture Library, London

(right) Elsa Schiaparelli. Evening cape, winter 1938–39. Black silk velvet embroidered with gold sequins. The Metropolitan Museum of Art, New York. Bequest of Lady Mendl, 1951 (CI.51.83) Photograph © 1995 The Metropolitan Museum of Art

Page 192
Elsa Schiaparelli. Evening coat, winter 1938–39. Black wool with pink silk, gold embroidery, paillettes, and porcelain flowers. Philadelphia Museum of Art. Gift of Mme Elsa Schiaparelli, 1969-232-6

Page 193
Elsa Schiaparelli. Evening coat (detail), winter 1938–39. Black wool with pink silk, gold embroidery, paillettes, and porcelain flowers. Philadelphia Museum of Art. Gift of Mme Elsa Schiaparelli, 1969-232-6

Page 195
Erwin Blumenfeld (American, born Germany, 1897–1969). Models wearing coats from Schiaparelli's collection for spring 1939. Published in *Vogue*, December 1, 1938, p. 82 © Condé Nast Publications Inc.

Page 196
Elsa Schiaparelli. Evening coat, spring 1939. Blue, black, red, yellow, and white wool felt with silk embroidery. Philadelphia Museum of Art. Gift of Mme Elsa Schiaparelli, 1969-232-3

Page 197
(top, left) House of Schiaparelli. Fashion sketch of evening coat for spring 1939. Musée de la Mode et du Textile, Paris. Collection UFAC, D 73.21.2130

(bottom, left) Marcel Vertès (Hungarian, 1895–1961). Advertisement for Sleeping perfume. Reproduced from Palmer White, *Elsa Schiaparelli* (in Japanese), ed. and trans. Yasuo Kuboki (Tokyo: Parco Co., 1994), p. 220. Published in Paris *Vogue*, April 1, 1940, p. 10

(right) Man Ray (American, 1890–1976). *Le Beau Temps*, 1939. Oil on canvas, 6 feet, 10¾ x 6 feet, 6¾ inches (2.1 x 2 m). Philadelphia Museum of Art. Promised gift of Sidney Kimmel © Man Ray Trust/Artists Rights Society (ARS), New York/ADAGP, Paris

Page 198
(top, left) Elsa Schiaparelli. Evening jacket, spring 1939. Black wool with black velvet appliqué. Philadelphia Museum of Art. Gift of Mme Elsa Schiaparelli, 1969-232-13

(top, right) House of Schiaparelli. Fashion sketch of patchwork jacket with embroidered sleeve, for spring 1939. Musée de la Mode et du Textile, Paris. Collection UFAC, D 73.21.2143

(bottom, left) House of Schiaparelli. Fashion sketch of patchwork jacket with zipper front for spring 1939. Musée de la Mode et du Textile, Paris. Collection UFAC, D 73.21.2145

Page 199
Elsa Schiaparelli. Evening jacket, spring 1939. Red velvet with pink, yellow, and violet silk embroidery. Philadelphia Museum of Art. Gift of Mme Elsa Schiaparelli, 1969-232-18

Page 201
François Kollar (French, 1904–1979). Three young women in bustled evening dresses from Schiaparelli's collection for summer 1939. Courtesy of Patrimoine Photographique, Paris © Ministère de la Culture-France, Paris

Page 202
Elsa Schiaparelli. Two evening dresses, summer 1939. Multicolored silk satin and faille stripe (left). White silk satin with multicolored "Mae West" figures (right). Philadelphia Museum of Art. Gift of Mme Elsa Schiaparelli, 1969-232-29a, b; 1969-232-27a, b

Page 203
(left) House of Schiaparelli. Fashion sketch of bustled evening dress printed with Mae West–like figures walking poodles, for summer 1939. Musée de la Mode et du Textile, Paris. Collection UFAC, D 73.21.2238

(right) Elsa Schiaparelli. Evening dress, summer 1939. Pink and black silk satin. Philadelphia Museum of Art. Gift of Mme Elsa Schiaparelli, 1969-232-48a, b

Page 204
Elsa Schiaparelli. Evening dress, summer 1939. Pink, black, blue, and white silk. Philadelphia Museum of Art. Gift of Mme Elsa Schiaparelli, 1969-232-47a

Page 205
Elsa Schiaparelli. Evening dress, summer 1939. Orange crêpe embroidered with metallic thread, pearls, and seed beads. Philadelphia Museum of Art. Gift of Mme Elsa Schiaparelli, 1969-232-33

Pages 206–7
Elsa Schiaparelli. Gloves, summer 1939. Green doeskin and gold kid. Philadelphia Museum of Art. Gift of Mme Elsa Schiaparelli, 1969-232-69a, b

Page 209
Louise Dahl-Wolfe (American, 1895–1989). Model wearing Schiaparelli's tunic dress posed between two Brancusi sculptures at the Museum of Modern Art, New York, 1938. University of Arizona, Tucson. Center for Creative Photography, 93:073:008 © 1989 Center for Creative Photography, Arizona Board of Regents

Page 210
Elsa Schiaparelli. Evening jacket, fall 1939. Black silk chiffon embroidered with gilt metallic thread. Philadelphia Museum of Art. Gift of Mme Elsa Schiaparelli, 1969-232-16

Page 211
Elsa Schiaparelli. Evening jacket, fall 1939. Purple silk chiffon embroidered with silk and metallic thread, pearl beadwork, silver buttons. Philadelphia Museum of Art. Gift of Mme Elsa Schiaparelli, 1969-232-23

Pages 212–13
Elsa Schiaparelli. Evening dress (detail), fall 1939. Purple silk crêpe embroidered with metallic and silk thread, silk lining. Philadelphia Museum of Art. Gift of Mme Elsa Schiaparelli, 1969-232-34

Page 214
Elsa Schiaparelli. Evening dress, fall 1939. Purple silk crêpe embroidered with metallic and silk thread, silk lining. Philadelphia Museum of Art. Gift of Mme Elsa Schiaparelli, 1969-232-34

Page 215
(top) William Vandivert (American, 1912–1990). Lady Mendl's party, 1939 © William Vandivert/Time Life Pictures/Getty Images

(bottom) House of Schiaparelli. Fashion sketch of music-note evening dress for fall 1939. Musée de la Mode et du Textile, Paris. Collection UFAC, 2363

Page 216
William Vandivert (American, 1912–1990). Lady Mendl's party, 1939 © William Vandivert/Time Life Pictures/Getty Images

Page 217
Elsa Schiaparelli. Evening coat, fall 1939. White silk faille with gold embroidery. Philadelphia Museum of Art. Gift of Mme Elsa Schiaparelli, 1969-232-8

Page 218
Elsa Schiaparelli. Evening dress (detail), summer 1939. Lavender crêpe embroidered with sequins, pearls, and metallic thread. Philadelphia Museum of Art. Gift of Mme Elsa Schiaparelli, 1969-232-46

Page 219
Elsa Schiaparelli. Evening dress, summer 1939. Lavender crêpe embroidered with sequins, pearls, and metallic thread. Philadelphia Museum of Art. Gift of Mme Elsa Schiaparelli, 1969-232-46

Page 220
George Hoyningen-Huene (American, born Russia, 1900–1968). Model wearing evening jacket from Schiaparelli's collection for winter 1939–40. Published in Harper's Bazaar, September 15, 1939. The Metropolitan Museum of Art, New York. The Costume Institute, HARPER-4

Page 221
House of Schiaparelli. Fashion sketch of hats, c. 1942. Musée de la Mode et du Textile, Paris. Collection UFAC, D 73.21.3264

Page 227
(left) Jean Moral (French, 1906–1999). Model wearing Schiaparelli's "washerwoman" dress for winter 1939–40, continuing into spring 1940. Published in Harper's Bazaar, September 15, 1939, p. 103. The Metropolitan Museum of Art, New York. The Costume Institute, HARPER-3 © Jean Moral, A.P.H. Christian Bouqueret, Paris

Page 228
François Kollar (French, 1904–1979). Model wearing Schiaparelli's air-raid-shelter suit from 1939 © Hulton-Deutsch Collection/CORBIS

Page 229
House of Schiaparelli. Fashion sketch of air-raid-shelter suit, 1939. Musée de la Mode et du Textile, Paris. Collection UFAC, D 73.21.2391

Page 230
Lee Miller (American, 1907–1977). Elsa Schiaparelli and William L. Gower bowling at the Palace Hôtel, Saint-Moritz. Published in Vogue, January 1, 1948, p. 167.

Courtesy of the Condé Nast Archive, New York © Lee Miller Archives, Chiddingly, England

Page 231
(top) Elsa Schiaparelli. Bootees, winter 1939–40. Leopard skin. Philadelphia Museum of Art. Gift of Mme Elsa Schiaparelli, 1969-232-56a, b

(bottom) House of Schiaparelli. Fashion sketch of leopard-skin ensemble for winter 1939–40. Musée de la Mode et du Textile, Paris. Collection UFAC, D 73.21.2440

Page 232
(top) Elsa Schiaparelli. Bootees, winter 1939–40. Pink, green, and white silk satin and leather with mother-of-pearl buttons. Philadelphia Museum of Art. Gift of Mme Elsa Schiaparelli, 1969-232-57a, b

(bottom) House of Schiaparelli. Fashion sketch of striped harem-skirted evening dress for winter 1939–40. Musée de la Mode et du Textile, Paris. Collection UFAC, D 73.21.2538

Page 233
Elsa Schiaparelli. Bootees, winter 1939–40. Multicolored leather and pearl buttons. Philadelphia Museum of Art. Gift of Mme Elsa Schiaparelli, 1969-232-58a, b

Page 234
Elsa Schiaparelli. Evening jacket, spring 1940. Black rayon embroidered with gilt metallic thread. Philadelphia Museum of Art. Gift of Mme Elsa Schiaparelli, 1969-232-71a

Page 235
François Kollar (French, 1904–1979). Model wearing dinner ensemble from Schiaparelli's collection for spring 1940. Published in Harper's Bazaar, December 1939, p. 99. The Metropolitan Museum of Art, New York. The Costume Institute, HARPER-1

Page 236
(top, left) House of Schiaparelli. Fashion sketch of "great coat," 1940. Musée de la Mode et du Textile, Paris. Collection UFAC, D 73.21.2383

(top, center) House of Schiaparelli. Fashion sketch of suit with scarf hat, 1940. Musée de la Mode et du Textile, Paris. Collection UFAC, D 73.21.2379

(top, right) House of Schiaparelli. Fashion sketch of suit with Scotch cap, Musée de la Mode et du Textile, Paris. Collection UFAC, D 73.21.2380

(bottom) U.S. Patent issued to Elsa Schiaparelli, filed October 15, 1940. U.S. Patent Office, Washington, D.C., Des. 123,136

Page 237
(left) Elsa Schiaparelli. Evening dress, summer 1940. Black ribbed silk with jet beads and taffeta lining. Philadelphia Museum of Art. Gift of Mme Elsa Schiaparelli, 1969-232-36

(right) House of Schiaparelli. Fashion sketch of evening ensemble for summer 1940. Musée de la Mode et du Textile, Paris. Collection UFAC, D 73.21.2610

Page 238
Elsa Schiaparelli. Afternoon jacket, summer 1940. Beige linen and velvet with silk and metal embroidery,

enameled buttons. Philadelphia Museum of Art. Gift of Mme Elsa Schiaparelli, 1969-232-21

Page 239
House of Schiaparelli. Fashion sketch of afternoon ensemble for summer 1940. Musée de la Mode et du Textile, Paris. Collection UFAC, D 73.21.2740

Page 240
(left) Elsa Schiaparelli. Evening dress, summer 1940. Silk printed with flag of the Royal des Vaisseaux. Philadelphia Museum of Art. Gift of Mme Elsa Schiaparelli, 1969-232-44

(right) House of Schiaparelli. Fashion sketch of evening dress decorated with flag of the regiment Royal des Vaisseaux, for summer 1940. Musée de la Mode et du Textile, Paris. Collection UFAC, D 73.21.2630

Page 241
Man Ray (American, 1890–1976). Model wearing evening dress printed with flags of the Scottish Ogilvy Regiment, from Schiaparelli's collection for summer 1940. Published in *Harper's Bazaar*, March 1, 1940, p. 62. The Metropolitan Museum of Art, New York. The Costume Institute, LY4320-3 © Man Ray Trust/ Artists Rights Society (ARS), New York/ADAGP, Paris

Page 242
François Kollar (French, 1904–1979). Model wearing dinner ensemble with embroidered Finnish wedding belt from Schiaparelli's collection for summer 1940. Published in *Harper's Bazaar*, March 1, 1940, p. 66. The Metropolitan Museum of Art, New York. The Costume Institute, LY4320-2

Page 243
(left) Jean Moral (French, 1906–1999). Model in front of Schiaparelli's salon, wearing suit and Finnish hand-knit linen stockings from her collection for summer 1940. Published in *Harper's Bazaar*, April 1940, p. 95. The Metropolitan Museum of Art, New York. The Costume Institute, LY4320-1 © Jean Moral, A.P.H. Christian Bouqueret, Paris

(right) Photographer unknown. Model wearing Schiaparelli's loose-fitting coat with sloping shoulders, March 1941. Courtesy of Deutsche Presse-Agentur GmbH, Hamburg

Page 244
House of Schiaparelli. Fashion sketch for dinner ensemble from February 1941 for summer. Musée de la Mode et du Textile, Paris. Collection UFAC, D 73.21.2714

Page 245
Elsa Schiaparelli. Afternoon jacket, summer 1941. Black rayon with multicolored embroidery. Philadelphia Museum of Art. Gift of Mme Elsa Schiaparelli, 1969-232-17

Page 246–47
Italian poster for the film *L'Amante di Borneo*, starring Arletty, 1942. Private collection

Page 248
Hans Wild (British, 1914–1969). Elsa Schiaparelli at home at 22 rue de Berri, May 1947 © Hans Wild/Time Life Pictures/Getty Images

Page 249
House of Schiaparelli. Fashion sketch of beret and dress made of fabric decorated with flags, October 1944.

Musée de la Mode et du Textile, Paris. Collection UFAC, D 73.21.3743

Page 256
Cecil Beaton (English, 1904–1980). Elsa Schiaparelli wearing a striped silk hat for fall 1944. Published in *Vogue*, November 1, 1944, p. 118 © Condé Nast Publications Inc.

Page 257
(left) Lee Miller (American, 1907–1977). Model wearing fur culotte designed by Irene Dana for Schiaparelli, for winter 1944–45. Published in *Vogue*, November 15, 1944, p. 76. Courtesy of the Condé Nast Archive, New York © Lee Miller Archives, Chiddingly, England

(right) Photographer unknown. Marlene Dietrich looking at soldiers' legs, November 30, 1944 © Bettmann/CORBIS

Page 258
(top) Irene Dana for Schiaparelli. Jacket, March 1945. Black rayon crêpe with gilt and multicolored silk embroidery. Philadelphia Museum of Art. Gift of Mme Elsa Schiaparelli, 1969-232-20

(bottom) House of Schiaparelli. Fashion sketch of jacket for March 1945. Musée de la Mode et du Textile, Paris. Collection UFAC, D 73.21.3680

Page 259
(top) Irene Dana for Schiaparelli. Hat, March 1945. Black satin and pink, yellow, and purple feathers. Philadelphia Museum of Art. Gift of Mme Elsa Schiaparelli, 1969-232-62

(bottom, center) House of Schiaparelli. Fashion sketch of polka-dot hat for March 1945. Musée de la Mode et du Textile, Paris. Collection UFAC, D 73.21.3656

Page 260
Bergdorf Goodman fashion sketch of Schiaparelli ensemble for fall 1934. The Metropolitan Museum of Art, New York. The Costume Institute, LY4051

Page 261
François Kollar (French, 1904–1979). *Création Schiaparelli*, probably September 1945. Courtesy of Patrimoine Photographique, Paris © Ministère de la Culture-France

Page 262
Elsa Schiaparelli. Dinner dress, summer 1946. White rayon with multicolored printing. Philadelphia Museum of Art. Gift of Elsa Schiaparelli, 1969-232-28

Page 263
Photographer unknown. Model wearing bustle dress from Schiaparelli's collection for winter 1946–47 © Roger-Viollet/Hulton Getty

Page 264
Hans Wild (British, 1914–1969). Schiaparelli's perfume Le Roy Soleil, September 1947 © Hans Wild/Time Life Pictures/Getty Images

Page 265
Horst P. Horst (American, born Germany, 1906–1999). Model wearing a dinner ensemble from Schiaparelli's collection for spring 1947. Reproduced from Martin Kasmaier, *Horst: Sixty Years of Photography*, ed. Richard J. Horst and Lothar Schirmer (New York: Universe, 1996), p. 61. (Outtake) *Vogue*, February 15, 1947 © Condé Nast Publications Inc.

Page 266
Elsa Schiaparelli. Dinner jacket (detail), spring 1947. Black crêpe and pink silk taffeta with paillette and seed-pearl embroidery and jet buttons. Philadelphia Museum of Art. Gift of Mme Elsa Schiaparelli, 1969-232-24

Page 267
Elsa Schiaparelli. Dinner jacket, spring 1947. Black crêpe and pink silk taffeta with paillette and seed-pearl embroidery and jet buttons. Philadelphia Museum of Art. Gift of Mme Elsa Schiaparelli, 1969-232-24

Page 268
(left) Elsa Schiaparelli. Evening dress and jacket, spring 1948. Silk satin (jacket and bodice) and rayon damask (skirt). Philadelphia Museum of Art. Gift of Mme Elsa Schiaparelli, 1969-232-30a, b

(right) House of Schiaparelli. Fashion sketch of evening ensemble for winter 1947–48. Musée de la Mode et du Textile, Paris. Collection UFAC, D 73.21.4132

Page 269
Horst P. Horst (American, born Germany, 1906–1999). Model wearing a gown from Schiaparelli's collection for winter 1947–48, posed in front of a painting by Henri de Toulouse-Lautrec. Published in British *Vogue*, December 1947, p. 321 © *Vogue*/The Condé Nast Publications Ltd.

Page 270
Elsa Schiaparelli. Hat, spring 1948. Felt, feathers, mink, and net. Philadelphia Museum of Art. Gift of Mme Elsa Schiaparelli, 1969-232-60

Page 271
(top) Elsa Schiaparelli. Sweater, spring 1948. Black wool jersey and monkey fur. Philadelphia Museum of Art. Gift of Mme Elsa Schiaparelli, 1969-232-55c

(bottom) House of Schiaparelli. Fashion sketch of monkey-fur evening ensemble for spring 1948. Musée de la Mode et du Textile, Paris. Collection UFAC, D 73.21.4171

Page 272
Elsa Schiaparelli. Evening dress, summer 1949. Black and white warp-printed silk satin. Philadelphia Museum of Art. Gift of Mrs. Morris H. Merritt, 1965-210-1

Page 273
Nina Leen (Russian, c. 1914–1995). Model Shari Herbert wearing Schiaparelli's "brassiere" gown from August 1949. Published in *Time* magazine, October 10, 1949 © Nina Leen/Time Life Pictures/Getty Images

Page 274
(left) Photographer unknown. Woman wearing a Schiaparelli dress with a square motif, November 26, 1949 © Bettmann/CORBIS

(right) Photographer unknown. Model wearing a Schiaparelli hat with triangular openings for the eyes, November 1949 for winter 1950. Archives of Schiaparelli France, Paris

Page 275
Photographer unknown. Woman modeling peephole hat from Schiaparelli's collection, November 12, 1949 © Bettmann/CORBIS

Page 276
Irving Penn (American, born 1917). *Schiaparelli Suit (Bettina)*, Paris, 1950. Published in *Vogue*, September 1, 1950, p. 139 © 1950 (renewed 1978) by Condé Nast Publications Inc.

Page 277
(left) Cecil Beaton (English, 1904–1980). The Duchess of Windsor wearing a suit from Schiaparelli's 1950 collection © Sotheby's Picture Library, London

(right) Genevieve Naylor (American 1915–1989). Modeling a coat from Schiaparelli's February collection for summer 1950 © Genevieve Naylor/CORBIS

Page 278
Robert Doisneau (French, 1912–1994). Jean Babilée and Nathalie Philippart at a ball at the Hôtel Lambert, Paris, June 1950. Archives of Schiaparelli France, Paris

Page 279
Horst P. Horst (American, born Germany, 1906–1999). "Chinese-lantern" dress from Schiaparelli's collection for summer 1951. Published in *Vogue*, April 15, 1951, p. 110 © Condé Nast Publications Inc.

Page 280
François Kollar (French, 1904–1979). Model wearing an evening dress from Schiaparelli's "SHAPE" collection for winter 1951–52. Courtesy of Patrimoine Photographique, Paris © Ministerè de la Culture-France

Page 281
Sharland. Model wearing a mink-trimmed peignoir from Schiaparelli's first lingerie collection, 1951 © Sharland/Time Life Pictures/Getty Images

Page 282
(left) Baron. Actress Zsa Zsa Gabor in the film *Moulin Rouge*, 1952 © Hulton-Deutsch Collection/CORBIS

(right) Bob Wendlinger (American, born 1922). Fashion designer Elsa Schiaparelli conversing with the Gabor sisters at a party, September 23, 1952 © Bettmann/CORBIS

Page 283
Henry Clarke (American, 1918–1996). Model wearing an evening dress with a Venus de Milo drapery of paper from Schiaparelli's February 1952 collection. Published in *Vogue*, March 15, 1952, p. 71 © Condé Nast Publications Inc.

Page 284
Elsa Schiaparelli. Evening coat and dress, fall 1953. White coat with rayon fringe shading from white to pink. Philadelphia Museum of Art. Gift of Mme Elsa Schiaparelli, 1969-232-10; 1969-232-11

Page 285
Photographer unknown. Model and two Air France stewardesses in front of a collage by Marcel Vertès in Schiaparelli's salon, 1953. Archives of Schiaparelli France, Paris

Page 286
(left) Gordon Parks (American, born 1912). "Silly sunglasses featuring long blue eyelashes and small lenses were dreamed up by designer Schiaparelli," February 1951 © Gordon Parks/Time Life Pictures/Getty Images

(center) U.S. patent issued to Elsa Schiaparelli, filed October 28, 1952. U.S. Patent Office, Washington, D.C., Des. 171,056

(right) Andy Warhol (American, 1928–1987). *Untitled (Two Vespas)*, c. 1956. Courtesy of Sotheby's, New York © 2003 The Andy Warhol Foundation for the Visual Arts/Artists Rights Society (ARS), New York

Page 287
Photographer unknown. Model posing in front of the display window of Schiaparelli's salon, featuring the 1954 Vespa 150, c. 1954. Archives of Schiaparelli France, Paris

Page 290
Nova Pilbeam in the film *Little Friend*, 1934. Gaumont/Kobal Collection, 1934

Page 291
Maria Casarès, Pierre Brasseur, and Marie Olivier in a scene from the play *Le Diable et le bon Dieu*, 1951 © Roger-Viollet/Hulton Getty

Page 292
Photographer unknown. Elsa Schiaparelli at the theater, c. 1950 © Roger-Viollet/Hulton Getty

Page 294
John Phillips (American, born Algeria, 1914–1996). Mrs. Hortense MacDonald, Schiaparelli's publicity director, 1937 © John Phillips/Time Life Pictures/Getty Images

Page 296
John Phillips. Schiaparelli's head tailor, René, 1937 © John Phillips/Time Life Pictures/Getty Images

Page 298
John Phillips. Schiaparelli's financial administrator, Louis Meunier, 1937 © John Phillips/Time Life Pictures/Getty Images

Selected Bibliography

Allilaire, Jean. *Les Industries de l'habillement et du travail des étoffes*. Paris: Société d'Editions françaises et internationales, 1947.

Allio, Loïc. *Boutons*. Paris: Editions du Seuil, 2001.

Ballard, Bettina. *In My Fashion*. New York: D. McKay Co., 1960.

Beaton, Cecil. *The Glass of Fashion*. London: Weidenfeld and Nicolson, 1954.

Benaïm, Laurence. *Marie Laure de Noailles: La Vicomtesse du bizarre*. Paris: Bernard Grasset, 2001.

Bonney, Thérèse, and Louise Bonney. *A Shopping Guide to Paris*. New York: Robert M. McBride & Company, 1929.

Chadwick, Whitney. *Women Artists and the Surrealist Movement*. New York: Thames and Hudson, 1985.

Charles-Roux, Edmonde. *Chanel*. Trans. Nancy Amphoux. London: The Harvill Press, 1995.

_____. *Chanel and Her World*. London, Paris, and Lausanne: The Vendôme Press, 1979.

Chase, Edna Woolman. *Always in Vogue*. Garden City, N.Y.: Doubleday, 1954.

Crawford, M.D.C. *The Ways of Fashion*. New York: G. P. Putnam's Sons, 1941.

Dalí, Salvador. *The Secret Life of Salvador Dalí*. Trans. Haakon M. Chevalier. New York: Dial Press, 1942.

Deschamps, G. *La Crise dans les industries du vêtement et de la mode à Paris pendant la période de 1930 à 1937*. Paris: Librairie technique et économique, 1937.

Ewing, William A. *The Photographic Art of Hoyningen-Huene*. London: Thames and Hudson, 1986.

Flanner, Janet. *Paris Was Yesterday, 1925–1939*. Ed. Irving Drutman. New York: Viking Press, 1972.

Gibson, Robin, and Pam Roberts. *Madame Yevonde: Colour, Fantasy, and Myth*. London: National Portrait Gallery Publications, 1990.

Gordon, Bertram M., ed. *Historical Dictionary of World War II France: The Occupation, Vichy, and the Resistance, 1938–1946*. Westport, Conn.: Greenwood Press, 1998.

Hawes, Elizabeth. *Fashion Is Spinach*. New York: Random House, 1938.

Horst, Horst P. *Salute to the Thirties*. New York: Studio Press, 1971.

Josephy, Helen, and Mary Margaret McBride. *Paris Is a Woman's Town*. New York: Coward-McCann, 1929.

Kachur, Lewis. *Displaying the Marvelous: Marcel Duchamp, Salvador Dalí, and Surrealist Exhibition Installations*. Cambridge, Mass., and London: The MIT Press, 2003.

Kolosek, Lisa Schlansker. *The Invention of Chic: Thérèse Bonney and Paris Moderne*. New York: Thames and Hudson, 2002.

Lawford, Valentine. *Horst: His Work and His World*. New York: Alfred A. Knopf, 1984.

Liaut, Jean-Noël. *Hubert de Givenchy: Entre vies et légendes*. Paris: Bernard Grasset, 2000.

Man Ray. *Self Portrait*. Boston and Toronto: Little, Brown and Company, 1963.

Martin, Richard. *Fashion and Surrealism*. New York: Rizzoli, 1987.

Meyer-Thoss, Christiane. *Meret Oppenheim Book of Ideas: Early Drawings and Sketches for Fashions, Jewelry, and Designs*. Trans. Catherine Schelbert. Bern, Switzerland: Gachnang & Springer, 1996.

Musée de la Mode et du Costume, Palais Galliera. *Hommage à Elsa Schiaparelli*. Exh. cat. Paris: Ville de Paris, Musée de la Mode et du Costume, 1984.

———. *Paris couture années trente*. Exh. cat. Paris: Le Musée, Le Palais, 1987.

———. *Paul Poiret et Nicole Groult: Maîtres de la mode art déco*. Exh. cat. Paris: Editions Paris Musées, 1986.

Musée Historique des Tissus, Lyon. *Les Folles Années de la soie*. Exh. cat. Lyon, France: Musée Historique des Tissus, 1975.

Musées de Marseilles. *Dora Maar: Bataille, Picasso et les surréalists*. Marseille, France: Musées de Marseilles, 2002.

Picken, Mary Brooks, and Dora Loues Miller. *Dressmakers of France: The Who, How and Why of the French Couture*. New York: Harper & Brothers, 1956.

Schiaparelli, Elsa. *Shocking Life*. New York: E. P. Dutton & Co., 1954.

Settle, Alison. *Clothes Line*. London: Methuen and Company, 1937.

Simon, Philippe. *La Haute Couture*. Monographie d'une industrie de luxe. Paris: Les Presses Universitaires de France, 1931.

Snow, Carmel, and Mary Louise Aswell. *The World of Carmel Snow*. New York, Toronto, and London: McGraw-Hill, 1962.

Triolet, Elsa. *Colliers de Paris*. Ed. Susanne Nadolny. Berlin: Edition Ebersbach, 1999.

Veillon, Dominique. *Fashion under the Occupation*. Trans. Miriam Kochan. Oxford and New York: Berg, 2002.

Weber, Eugen. *The Hollow Years: France in the 1930s*. New York and London: W. W. Norton & Company, 1994.

White, Palmer. *Elsa Schiaparelli: Empress of Paris Fashion*. London: Aurum Press, 1986.

_____. *Haute Couture Embroidery: The Art of Lesage*. Paris: The Vendôme Press, 1988.

Acknowledgments

This book and the exhibition would not have been possible without the enthusiasm and encouragement of many individuals. I wish first to thank Marisa Berenson for her gracious continuation of the trust her grandmother placed in the Philadelphia Museum of Art almost thirty-four years ago. Count Guido Sassoli de Bianchi, President of Schiaparelli France, has been more than accommodating in providing us with essential information from his archives as well as generously loaning original works of art from Schiaparelli's salon on the Place Vendôme.

I owe a debt of gratitude to the Schiaparelli Honorary Committee, co-chaired by Leonore Annenberg, Marisa Berenson, and Oscar de la Renta, who have worked to ensure that Schiaparelli will be remembered as a tour de force in the history of fashion and art. I warmly thank the members of the committee: Azzedine Alaïa, Richard Avedon, Geoffrey Beene, David Bowie and Iman, Marchesa Cacciapuoti di Giugliano, Hélène David-Weill, Tom Ford, Diane von Furstenberg, John Galliano, Hubert de Givenchy, Agnes Gund, Mrs. Samuel M. V. Hamilton, Carolina Herrera, Caroline Kimmel, Michael Kors, Marguerite Brooks Lenfest, Suzy Menkes, Nicole Miller, Ruth Perelman, Ariel de Ravenel, Count Guido Sassoli de Bianchi, Vera Wang, and Anna Wintour.

Generous contributions to the exhibition came from Carefree, The Annenberg Foundation, The Pew Charitable Trusts, the Robert Montgomery Scott Endowment for Exhibitions, and the National Endowment for the Arts. NBC 10 WCAU and the Greater Philadelphia Tourism Marketing Corporation provided important promotional backing, and, in addition, NBC 10 WCAU ran an informative half-hour television special on the exhibition. As always, the support of the members of The Women's Committee of the Philadelphia Museum of Art and of the Costume and Textiles Committee of the Board of Trustees has been invaluable. I greatly appreciate the kind attention, encouragement, and significant contributions they have made to this and many other projects through the years. We extend a special thank you to Ann Dee Rome, chair of The Women's Committee's gala, who put together a spectacular opening night for the exhibition. The gracious members of Schiaparelli's List, through their financial support, have done much to guarantee that the exhibition would happen. We are particularly grateful to Barbara B. Aronson, Maude de Schauensee, Sandy Elgin, Maxine and Howard H. Lewis, Lisa Roberts, and Joan and Bernie Spain, who set splendid examples in their leadership gifts.

Exhibitions cannot take place without the generosity of institutions and individuals willing to part with treasured objects for a period of time, and I have the pleasure of expressing my sincere gratitude to the exhibition's lenders: David Brigham, Ruta Saliklis, and Sofia Bakis at the Allentown Art Museum, Pennsylvania; Arnold Lehman, Patricia Mears, Ken Moser, and Ruth Janson at the Brooklyn Museum of Art, New York; Bella Veksler at Drexel University, Philadelphia; Valerie Steele, Ellen Shanley, Fred Dennis, Deborah Norden, Carmen Saavedra, and Irving Solero and at the Fashion Institute of Technology Museum, New York; Barbara Schröter and Werner Sudendorf at the Marlene Dietrich Collection, Filmmuseum Berlin; Marilyn DeLong and Nancy J. Cyr at The Goldstein Museum of Design, University of Minnesota, Saint Paul; Akiko Takahashi Fukai at The Kyoto Costume Institute, Japan; Jeremy Adamson and Tambra Johnson at the Library of Congress, Washington, D.C.; Philippe de Montebello, Harold Koda, Andrew Bolton, Stéphane Houy-Towner, Lisa Faibish, Chris Paulocik, and Melinda Webber Kerstein at The Metropolitan Museum of Art, New York, Costume Institute; Catherine Join-Diéterle and Fabienne Falluel at the Musée Galliera, Musée de la Mode de la Ville de Paris; Wilhelm Hornbostel and Ursula Strate at the Museum für Kunst und Gewerbe Hamburg; Rosemary Harden at the Museum of Costume, Assembly Rooms, Bath, England; Susan Henshaw Jones and Phyllis Magidson at the Museum of the City of New York; Philip Rylands at the Peggy Guggenheim Collection, Venice; William Thorsell and Alexandra Palmer at the Royal Ontario Museum, Toronto; Charles Henri Hine, William Jeffet, and Joan R. Kropf at The Salvador Dalí Museum, Saint Petersburg, Florida; Hélène David-Weill, Béatrice Salmon, Pamela Golbin, Olivier Saillard, and Marie-Hélène Poix at the Union Centrale des Arts Décoratifs, Musée de la Mode et du Textile, Paris; and private lenders Azzadine Alaïa, Anne Benoist d'Azy, Leslie Chin, Gene London of London Studios, Andrea Pfister, Schiaparelli Archives in Paris, Sandy Schreier, the Sidney Kimmel Foundation, Lucien Treillard, and Mark Walsh.

To the many museums, archives, photographers, collectors, and individuals who have so generously shared their collections and expertise with us to help realize this book, we are indeed in your debt. I wish to thank in particular the following people and institutions: Sue Mendives at AFP; Dick Whitney at the American Optical Museum, Southbridge, Massachusetts; Michael Hermann at The Andy Warhol Foundation for the Visual Arts, New York; Margery King at The Andy Warhol Museum, Pittsburgh, Pennsylvania; Christiane

Filloles at the Archives of Paris; Cristin O'Keefe Aptowicz and Janet Hicks at the Artists Rights Society, New York; Gerhard Gruitrooy and Humberto DeLuigi at Art Resource, New York; Carolyn McMahon at the Associated Press Photo Archive, New York; Beth Ryan and Jenny Flemming at The Baltimore Museum of Art; Charles Faulhaber and Susan Snyder at The Bancroft Library, University of California, Berkeley; Peter Pagan at the BBC, London; Benham Gallery, Seattle, Washington; Cécile Blanc at the Bibliothèque du Film, Paris; Monique Moulène at the Bibliothèque Nationale de France, Paris; Cécile Bréhant; David Reeve at The British Film Institute, London; Tamsin Godfrey at the British Council, London; John Herron at Canal + Image UK Ltd.; Denise Gosé and Dianne Nilsen, Rights and Reproductions, at the Center for Creative Photography, University of Arizona, Tucson; Annyck Graton at the Centre Georges Pompidou, Paris; Christie's, New York; Jemal Creary and Alyssa Sachar at Corbis, New York; Maria Elena Rico Covarrubias; Peter Stroh at Deutsche Presse Agentur, Hamburg; Carrie Moorehead at the Edwynn Houk Gallery (for the Estate of Ilse Bing), New York; Félix Fanes; Deana Farnetti-Cera; Joshua Waller, Maris Heller, and John Corins at the library of the Fashion Institute of Technology, New York; Montse Aguer at the Fundació Gala-Salvador Dalí, Figueres, Spain; Valérie Zars at Getty Images, New York; Grinberg Film Libraries, Chatsworth, California; Filippo Tattoni-Marcozzi at Hamiltons Gallery, London; Fredric Wilson and Kathleen Coleman at the Harvard Theatre Collection, Houghton Library, Cambridge, Massachusetts; Gert Elfering and Veronica Scharf-Garcia at the Horst Estate, Miami; Jacklyn Burns at the J. Paul Getty Museum, Los Angeles; Lauretta Dives at The Kobal Collection, New York; Library of Congress, Washington, D.C.; Cheryle T. Robertson, Sharon Takeda, Dale Gluckman, Sandy Rosenbaum, and Shaula Coyl at the Los Angeles County Museum of Art; Lawrence N. Hole at the Madame Yevonde Archive, England; Laura R. Moakley and Eric Browner at the Man Ray Trust, Jericho, New York; Félix Marcilhac; MGM, Los Angeles; Sylvie Richoux at the Musée de la Mode, Marseille, France; James Kilvington at the National Portrait Gallery, London; Tom Lisanti, Devon Cummings, Melanie Yolles, and the staff of the manuscripts division at the New York Public Library; Jessica Berman-Bogdan at Pathé Archives–France, Saint-Ouen; Christophe Mauberret at Patrimoine Photographique, Paris; Paramount Pictures, Los Angeles; Monique Comminges and Delphine Desveaux at Roger-Viollet, Paris; Toni Booth and Venita Paul at the Science and Society Picture Library, National Museum of Science & Industry, London; Kim Bush at the Solomon R. Guggenheim Museum, New York; Sotheby's New York and Sue Daly at Sotheby's London; Etheleen Staley at the Staley-Wise Gallery, New York; Pierre-Yves Butzbach at Telimage, Paris; Hilary Johnston and Tom Gilbert at Time Life Pictures, New York; the U.S. Patent Office, Alexandria, Virginia; Linda Parry, Sonnet Stanfill, and Jonathan Gray at the Victoria and Albert Museum, London; Hamish Bowles at *Vogue* magazine, New York; Bob Wendlinger, photographer; and Diane Paradiso at the WPA Film Library, Orlando Park, Illinois. I am especially grateful to the wonderful people at Condé Nast Archives, who granted me access and allowed me to reproduce so much of their fabulous collection. In particular, I thank Anthony Petrillose, Charles Scheips, Michael Stier, Ena Wojciechowski, and Cornelia Woods in New York, and Lisa Hodgkins and Romney Park in London. I would particularly like to thank Suzanne Sutton for her help in arranging appointments and navigating the French libraries and archives, and Caroline Rennolds Milbank for sharing information with me. I was fortunate in having the opportunity to meet with Dorothea Towles Church, one of Schiaparelli's ex-models, and with theater designer Francine Galliard-Risler, who graciously shared with me their reminiscences of postwar Paris and provided insight into Schiaparelli's personality.

There are many people at the Philadelphia Museum of Art without whom this book and the exhibition never would have happened. I first wish to thank Anne d'Harnoncourt, our director, for her enthusiastic support and encouragement from the onset of this project, and Danielle Rice, Associate Director for Program, who went out of her way to help in a multitude of ways. I would also like to thank Gail Harrity, Chief Operating Officer, and Gerry Lenfest, Chairman of the Museum's Board of Trustees, for their support.

The contributions of the staff and interns in the Department of Costume and Textiles have been invaluable throughout the course of this project. I owe a special thank you to H. Kristina Haugland, Mayumi Yoshizawa, Kristin Pereira, and Suzanne Carnes. Monica Brown, with her inimitable knack for styling, was responsible for dressing the mannequins for the exhibition and in preparation for photography. Deborah Lippincott was extremely helpful organizing loans and graciously acted as a liason with the lending institutions and individuals. Thanks also go to our loyal volunteers, including Nancy Bergman, Barbara Darlin, Valerie Kontes-Baron, and Dean Ockert, for their commitment and unending enthusiasm. The conservation

Acknowledgments

team of Costume and Textiles—Sara Reiter, Howard Sutcliffe, Lisa Stockebrand, Julie Randolph, and Amy Gallagher—worked tirelessly to preserve the integrity of Schiaprelli's workmanship. Adding important expertise to this team were Nancy Ash, Gwynne Barney, Anne Marie Hughes, Adam Jenkins, Sally Malenka, Melissa Meighan, Joe Mikuliak, Beth Price, Behrooz Salimnejad, Michael Stone, and Kenneth Sutherland in the Museum's Department of Conservation.

Much of this book depended on the sensitivity and skills of the Museum's photographers, Graydon Wood and Lynn Rosenthal. I am especially grateful to Lynn Rosenthal, who handled most of the in-house photography, for her creativity and understanding of my vision. Conna Clark, Stacy Bomento, and Jason Wierzbicki in the ever-busy Rights and Reproductions Department provided ongoing support and expertise. As always, I could count on Suzanne Wells and Bethany Morris of Special Exhibitions for vital information, diligence, and good humor. The expertise and professionalism of our registrars—Irene Taurins, Nancy Baxter, Elie-Anne Chevrier, Clarissa Carnell, Sara Loughman, and Michelle Povilaitis—is much appreciated. I would also like to acknowledge the valiant efforts of Betty Marmon, Warwick Wheeler, Mimi Stein, Kelly O'Brien, and Kerry Church in Development. Charles Croce, Norman Keyes, and Emily Raabe of Marketing and Public Relations did much to generate excitement for the exhibition and the book. Lyn Elliott and Hasan Shaheed were responsible for creating the wonderful website that accompanied the exhibition. Thanks go to Matthew Pimm, Robin Brown, Maia Wind, Gretchen Dykstra, and Donna Brandolisio in Editorial and Graphic Design for their hard work. I would also like to express my appreciation to Jeanine Kline in Facilities and Operations and to Michael MacFeat and Martha Masiello in Installations and Packing.

In Education, I thank Marla Shoemaker, Elizabeth Anderson, Emilie Parker, and Lynda O'Leary for the great programs they created. Essential contributions were made, too, by the library staff at the museum, Mary Wassermann, Lilah Mittelstaedt, Jesse Trbovich, Sara Hayden, and Cecilia Howard, and by our archivist, Susan Anderson. Jack Schlechter, our talented Installations Designer, and his equally talented staff, Ann-Barbara Kessler and Andrew Slavinskas, as usual produced a wonderful exhibition space. Stephen Keever and Bonnie MacAllister handled all of the audio-visual accompaniments to the exhibition. I thank my colleagues in Prints, Drawings and Photographs, curator Katherine Ware, curatorial fellow William Breazeale, and preparator Gary Hiatt, for their helpfulness and patience. Ann Temkin and Michael Taylor in Modern and Contemporary Art, and Donna Corbin in European Decorative Arts, also graciously shared their knowledge. *Merci beaucoup*, as well, to those among the museum staff who helped me with translations: Pierre Terjanian, Elie-Anne Chevrier, and Jennifer Vanim. Additional research was kindly completed by Jane E. Boyd and Guigone Rolland. A special salute to Dean Walker and John Ittmann, charter members of the "breakfast club" where I received much encouragement and advise.

Once again, the museum's Publishing Department has produced an outstanding book. The success of this project would not have been possible without their enthusiastic support. I am immensely grateful to Sherry Babbitt for her insight, advice, and planning; to Kathleen Krattenmaker for her partnership (great minds think alike!), her patience, attention to detail, and professionalism; to Richard Bonk for his management and production skills; and to the generous and able publications volunteers, Roz Jay and Ellen Glassie. Yale University Press, our co-publisher, was wonderful to work with, and we extend a special thank you to Patricia Fidler and Michelle Komie for their collegiality.

When I learned that Takaaki Matsumoto had been chosen to design this book I was thrilled, knowing what spectacular work he had done in the past. I am even more delighted now, for he has exceeded all my expectations. I thank him for his brilliant design and offer thanks as well to his skilled assistants, Amy Wilkins and Thanh Tran.

Finally, I would like to thank my two research assistants, Elizabeth Bryan and Deborah E. Kraak. Deborah assisted with the early stages of research, combing through microfilms of magazines from Schiaparelli's lifetime for information on the designer. Elizabeth Bryan handled multiple tasks, including compiling the final research for the stylistic chronology and ordering and tracking the many images contained in this book. Her dedication, hard work, and organizational skills have been invaluable in bringing both the book and the exhibition to fruition. To all those listed here, and countless others who have assisted in the realization of this book and the exhibition, or simply offered a shoulder to lean on, I extend my heartfelt thanks.